THE MEDIUM
AND THE LIGHT

THE MEDIUM AND THE LIGHT

Reflections on Religion

MARSHALL McLUHAN

Edited by Eric McLuhan and Jacek Szklarek

WIPF & STOCK · Eugene, Oregon

Wipf and Stock Publishers
199 W 8th Ave, Suite 3
Eugene, OR 97401

The Medium and the Light
Reflections on Religion and Media
By McLuhan, Marshall
Copyright©1999 by McLuhan Estate
ISBN 13: 978-1-60608-992-7
Publication date 3/1/2010
Previously published by Stoddart, 1999

Contents

Part III   Vatican II, Liturgy, and the Media

Part IV   Tomorrow's Church

Preface

This book presents various reflections of Marshall McLuhan concerning religion. Some he wrote for public consumption, such as an article in *The Critic* or *The Listener*, or the introduction to a book. Some were written as letters to family, friends, or colleagues, or delivered as speeches. A few were published as interviews. Four of the pieces included here have never before been seen in English. Included also is his first published essay, "G. K. Chesterton: A Practical Mystic." It appeared in 1936, when he was but twenty-five.

Rather than offering these pieces in chronological order, we have grouped them around four main themes. The first deals with the period surrounding McLuhan's conversion and consists of the article by Chesterton and his letters to his mother and his wife. The second carries a more general theme, that of the Church's understanding — or ignorance — of media. The third group revolves around the theme of Vatican II (the Second Vatican Council), which promulgated such sweeping alterations in liturgy, a basic medium for the faithful. The last group, entitled "Tomorrow's Church," looks to the probable consequences for it of the new media.

Unless otherwise noted at the beginning of selections in this book, the footnotes are those of the editors.

The four "Conversations with Pierre Babin" were originally recorded in English between 1974 and 1977, and were then translated into

French by H. du Halgouët, a French Oblate father doing community work in Toronto at the time. The book they appeared in, *Autre homme, autre chrétien à l'âge electronique*, was printed only in French, so these pieces appear here in English for the first time. Unfortunately, the original tapes, manuscripts, and transcripts were lost over the years. They were retranslated from French into English by Wayne Constantineau for publication here.

Introduction

by Eric McLuhan

No man's stature is increased by the accumulation of myths, and nothing is detracted from genuine historical greatness by the consideration of a man's purely human side.
— Heinrich Fichtenau on Charlemagne[1]

Perhaps the person most surprised by Marshall McLuhan's conversion to Catholicism was Marshall himself.

He told me the story of his conversion several times over the years that we worked together. It had, in his mind, two phases. The first consisted of how the Church and its claims repeatedly intruded on his attention while he was trying to focus on other, scholarly, matters — so often and so powerfully that he eventually felt forced to "deal" with them. The second consisted of the events that precipitated his actual conversion and acceptance into the Church.

The first phase took many years and includes the time in the mid-to-late thirties that he spent in research for his Ph.D. at Cambridge University. As that document formed the basis of not only his intellectual approach to the Church but also much else in later studies in communication, I will go into a bit of detail.

Marshall McLuhan was raised in a loose sort of Protestantism. That

---

1 Heinrich Fichtenau, *The Carolingian Empire* (Toronto: University of Toronto Press, in association with the Medieval Academy of America, 1978, 1982, 1986), page 25.

is, the family, living in Edmonton, Alberta, was liberal as to which denomination — Baptist, Methodist, etc. — they followed. They, like many independent-thinking Protestants, didn't really "belong" to one or another, but would attend on a weekend whatever church or meeting place could provide the best or most interesting preaching, the best "mover." I cannot help mentioning here what seems to me a curious coincidence: how rhetoric and public speaking run through my father's life as a sort of ground-theme or bass-line over which the rest is played. His mother, Elsie, was on the stage as a one-woman show of readings and interpretations. His father was an insurance salesman — and renowned as a good talker and raconteur. My father's brother, Maurice, also become a speaker: a minister and preacher, and, later, a teacher. And the woman my father married, my mother, trained as an actress, studied and taught dramatics and public speaking, and directed plays. He himself became renowned for his skill as a speaker. He wrote his doctoral thesis on the history of the trivium (rhetoric, dialectic, and grammar), and he made rhetoric his particular study: Practical Criticism, which is based in rhetoric, formed the secret under-pinning of his entire approach to media and literature.

My father had decided to write his dissertation about an obscure but vigorous Elizabethan pamphleteer Thomas Nashe (1567–1601). Researching that spirited satirist clearly meant digging into the back-ground of the quarrels he engaged in. One thing led to another; before long my father decided that he would have to write more than the brief note he had planned to explain the differences between Nashe and his principal antagonist, Gabriel Harvey. The two men, it turned out, were merely the latest combatants in a struggle that had been going on, by then, for over 1500 years and which for hundreds of years more showed no signs of abating. (In many ways, it can be seen still raging beneath the major arguments in Western intellectual and polit-ical and religious circles today, but that's another story.) By the time he was finished, the brief background note had turned into the first three-quarters of one of the most learned theses that Cambridge had ever seen. He dug back through our intellectual traditions, beginning with their foundations in the educational systems and techniques bequeathed us by Greece and then Rome, and pursued them on through the Middle Ages, the period of Scholasticism, the Reformation, the Enlightenment, and ending with some remarks about James Joyce in the twentieth century. The time covered began with Cicero in

Augustan Rome and ran to Nashe in Elizabethan England; the matter concerned the debates and rivalries — surprisingly consistent — that distinguished various intellectual camps and even such great universities as Paris, Oxford, and Cambridge. All this was necessary to put Nashe and his activities "in context": without it, much of Nashe's activity seemed, even to Elizabethan experts, quite inexplicable; with it, perfectly rational.

Needless to say, Nashe soon took a back seat to the panorama that unfolded, one which my father was evidently the first for centuries to uncover and discuss. For many hundreds of the years covered in his investigations, the antagonists were clergy. And their debates concerned not simply this or that idea or doctrine but rather the very tools of intellectual endeavour, the nature and seriousness of philosophy and literature, and the techniques of interpretation and their spheres of application. It was on these terms that McLuhan encountered Catholicism, terms that concerned the nature of human understanding and the entire practice of learning and tradition of interpretation right across the whole of the arts and the sciences. Today, these are considered recondite "academic" debates, arguments of little practical significance. But for well over a thousand years they were the very foundation of schooling and society, the cornerstone of all politics and policy. And if they were vital to understanding Nashe, they also underlay the differences between the Church and the Protestant reformers. Nashe represented the age-old claims of grammar (allied with rhetoric) for dominance in the trivium — which meant dominance of both the intellectual world and the political one; Harvey, the rival claims of the dialectical reformers in literary and theological matters. There was at this time little or no distinction between literature, theology, and politics. To get a sense of the depth and ferocity of the debate, call to mind the rivalry today between conservatives and reformers, or capitalists and socialists, and magnify the differences four- or five-fold.

To accomplish this background meant that he had to embark on a study program of encyclopedic dimensions.[2] He decided that he had to master and then draw the outlines of the trivium, which had for many centuries been the traditional Western system for organizing intellectual activity. The trivium compressed all knowledge into three

---

2 He had arrived at Cambridge with both a B.A. and an M.A. from the University of Manitoba; he proceeded to acquire at Cambridge another B.A. and M.A. before moving on to the Ph.D.

streams: rhetoric (communication), dialectic (philosophy and logic), and grammar (literature, both sacred and profane, including modes of interpretation). Grammar included written texts of all sorts, as well as the world and the known universe, which were considered as a book to be read and interpreted, the famous "Book of Nature."

Incredible as it may seem, the job had never before been done. Certainly, there were — and are — plenty of histories of philosophy, for example, and histories of literature as well as accounts of rhetoric. But when each of these is viewed not singly but as one of a set of Siamese triplets, the perspective changes enormously as does the entire significance of every development in their histories. His reading, then, covered the widest imaginable area and, because the Catholic clergy was intimately involved in most of it, he became familiar not only with what they had said on a wide array of matters but also with why they had taken this or that position.

The reading included the standard classics: the principal philosophers, such as the pre-Socratics, Plato, and Aristotle, and representatives of the main philosophical schools; the rhetoricians; the major literary and poetical texts; and the principal schools of textual exegesis of everything from Homer to the Bible. Interpreters of the Bible included Origen and Philo of Alexandria, who set the pattern for centuries of later practitioners. He read the Apostolic Fathers, of course, as well as their interpreters and commentators, and the entire of the ante-Nicene Fathers. (I recently found his own battered 24-volume, second-hand set of *Ante-Nicene Fathers*, each volume obviously read, and many annotated and cross-referenced, some of them heavily. It is the same with the five-volume set of the sermons of Lancelot Andrewes, also used in the thesis.) He was quite able to read Latin and Greek as well as the standard languages of scholarship, French and German. In short he had, from early in his literary studies, also surveyed the entire spectrum of Catholic doctrine and philosophy — an overview such as few Catholic theologians possessed.[3]

Consequently, when he came to consider the essential truth or otherwise of Catholicism or to discuss its merits he did so with a profound and encyclopedic knowledge that far surpassed that of the average convert, to say nothing of that of the "cradle Catholic" or even of the average priest or theologian. Ironically enough, his learned

---

3 See Appendix 1 of this book for a sample from the introduction to the thesis (1943, unpublished).

approach to the Faith was simply a side-effect of his studies: he had not set out to investigate Catholicism. Rather, while mapping out the intellectual background of the Nashe–Harvey disputes he picked up an extensive grounding in Catholic theology and the hidden underpinnings of the Reformation. When it came time, therefore, to investigate the Church and its claims, he already knew where to look for evidence or proof, how to look (that is, how to allow for partisanship and bias), and what to look for.

Let me insist right away that my father was not a theologian. Nor did he undertake formal theological studies in preparation for any of the pieces included in this collection, although he would naturally have boned up a bit on this or that topic before writing. For the most part, his Catholic education was the ordinary one of the convert — as amplified by his own study. Out of curiosity he did read St. Thomas's *Summa Theologica*, for example (in Latin as well as in English), and the *Summa Contra Gentiles*, among other things. And he had trained in philosophy as part of his study at Cambridge for the doctorate in English. He had taken the trouble to acquaint himself with a lot of the basic material as a part of his study of the trivium.

My father frequently attributed his conversion to the influence of two writers, St. Thomas Aquinas and G. K. Chesterton, particularly the latter's *What's Wrong with the World* and *Orthodoxy* — in much the same way that C. S. Lewis credited his own conversion to reading GKC's *The Everlasting Man*. Not surprisingly, then, McLuhan's first published academic article was on Chesterton, and we reproduce it here as our first chapter. Although it does not concern itself with theological disputation, we include it because of his fondness for Chesterton's way of thinking, and because of the place that Chesterton (also a convert to Catholicism) holds in the story of his conversion. His introduction to Chesterton's writing and thought had occurred much earlier, during his days as a student at the University of Manitoba. He had been fascinated with Chesterton's wit and style and acuity of perception and had even tried imitating his style on occasion. (Imitation was the traditional way to learn to write, one that he often advocated.) As J. G. Keogh wrote in the December 1996 Ottawa *Chesterton Newsletter*:

> From Cambridge McLuhan carefully mailed home to family and friends all his copies of *G.K.'s Weekly*. Even before coming to England, he had been fascinated by Chesterton. René Cera's wife

once showed me a clipping from the student newspaper during McLuhan's days at the University of Manitoba in the early thirties, saying, "Shhh! Don't let Marshall know I've shown you this", the subject being G. K. Chesterton.

Chesterton's familiar way with paradox showed my father how to operate on the border between idea and metaphor, between concept and percept. During the great depression, he and a fellow student from Manitoba, Tom Easterbrook, worked their way across to England on a cattle-boat to attend Cambridge together. (Tom, a lifelong friend, studied economics at Cambridge and went on to head the Department of Economics at University of Toronto.) One day, at Cambridge, Tom handed my father a copy of GKC's *What's Wrong With the World*, saying, "Here, Mac; I think you'll like this. I hated it."

At every turn, while he was investigating the background for his study of Thomas Nashe, he would encounter the Church — what Chesterton called (another book title) *The Thing*. It was everywhere. At one point, he later told me (and he was never very specific just when that point occurred), he decided that *the thing* had to be sorted out or he couldn't rest. Either it was true, or it wasn't. Either the entire matter was true, all of it, *exactly* as the Church claimed, or it was the biggest hoax ever perpetrated on a gullible mankind. With that choice clearly delineated, he set out to find which was the case. What came next was not more study, but testing.

The matter had to be tested — on its own terms: that is, by prayer. He told me that the principal prayer that he used was not some long or complex formula, but simply, "Lord, please, send me a sign." He reported that, almost immediately, not one but a deluge of signs arrived. And they continued to arrive unabated for a long time. As to just what the signs consisted in and what happened next, well, some things must remain private. The reader may deduce the rest from the fact of his conversion. But for many years the matter did not go past the stage of intellectual assent.

Practical Criticism demands that the reader perform texts and so find the voice that utters them. In turn, finding the speaker's tone and feeling leads directly to analysing the audience and the effect produced. A great deal of stress is thus placed, for the critic, on training of sensibility and of multisensory critical awareness. The experience of performing a poem or passage supplies the basis of understanding and of analysis, and is never subordinated to the ideas it contains. Consequently the stress is on *percepts* more than on *concepts*. He often reminded me that Catholics cannot pick and choose doctrines as can Protestants. Catholics have an authority to help with both teaching and interpretation, a *translatio studii*. You accept Catholicism all as a piece or nothing at all. Appositely enough, faith, the Church had always taught, is a way of knowing. Faith, as the Epistle to the Hebrews (New Testament) points out, is "the substance of things hoped for, the evidence of things unseen."

This distinction between concept and percept, ideas and sheer awareness, became crucial to revealing much in media study and in meditating upon the Church and related matters. McLuhan wrote to Jim Taylor, then editor of *The United Church Observer*, that he did "not think of God as a concept, but as an immediate and ever-present fact — an occasion for continuous dialogue."[4] He stated that he was

> . . . a Thomist for whom the sensory order [i.e., the world] resonates with the Divine Logos. I don't think concepts have any relevance in religion. Analogy is not a concept. It is resonance. It is inclusive. It is the cognitive process itself. That is the analogy of the Divine Logos. I think of Jasper, Bergson, and Buber as very inferior conceptualist types, quite out of touch with the immediate analogical awareness that begins in the senses and is derailed by concepts or ideas.[5]

To a Catholic, faith is not simply an act of the mind, that is, a matter of ideology or thought (*concepts*) or belief or trust, although it is usually mistaken for these things. Faith is a mode of *per*ception, a sense like sight or hearing or touch and as real and actual as these, but a spiritual rather than a bodily sense. (The Protestants, he found in his research, had decided to regard faith in terms of ideas and concepts. Their decision meant that they had, in terms of the trivium, hitched their fortunes to dialectic, and abandoned the old alliance of rhetoric and grammar to which the Church still resolutely adhered.) Faith, we Catholics are taught, is a gift of the Holy Ghost, available for the asking — in prayer. As a *way of knowing*, faith operates in the realm of percepts, not that of concepts. It is a mode of spiritual awareness and knowing, as acute and as real as vision, touch, smell, hearing. No

---

4 *Letters of Marshall McLuhan*, page 362.
5 *Letters of Marshall McLuhan*, pages 368-69.

healthy sense needs constant questioning and reexamination: if you can see or hear, well enough; you don't have to keep asking yourself, "Can I see? Can I hear?" You know beyond question whether you can hear or not, and it has nothing to do with theory or concepts. This attitude the outsider reads as arrogance or delusion, or both. Hence the paradox of assent (which appears to the outsider as blind subservience), on the one hand, and the Church's intense intellectualism, on the other. Hence, too, that other paradox that the Church is infinitely larger on the inside that it appears from the outside.

To become a Catholic has been for centuries equated with committing intellectual suicide — a reputation largely engendered by the freethinking-Protestant antipathy to catechisms and authority. But the catechism, as McLuhan had found, gave shorthand answers to incredibly complex questions. In his research he had viewed the prolonged process of development of doctrine and the centuries-long process of testing and defining doctrines. He had studied for himself and written extensively in the thesis about the *translatio studii* — the tradition of learned commentary on texts both sacred and profane, what the Church called "Tradition" (and literary study calls "the tradition"). Using the Tradition means engaging in a complex conversation: distinctions of past and present are suspended and everyone is your contemporary. Less than a century earlier, John Henry Cardinal Newman had written his own celebrated *Essay on Development of Christian Doctrine*, which discussed the exact manner in which new doctrine was tested by Tradition. And T. S. Eliot, something of a hero in Cambridge literary circles, had just recently written, in obvious imitation of Newman's *Essay*, his own statement, "Tradition and the Individual Talent."[6]

∞

If the first phase occupied a number of years of intense erudition and scrutiny, the second phase took far less. Here is his own account, many years (1970) after the fact:

> I had no religious belief at the time I began to study Catholicism. I was brought up in the Baptist, Methodist and Anglican churches. We went to all of them. But I didn't believe anything. I did set to find

---

6 See Appendix 2 of this book for editors' note on Newman, Eliot, and tradition.

out, and literally to research the matter, and I discovered fairly soon that a thing has to be tested on its terms. You can't test anything in science or in any part of the world except on its own terms or you will get the wrong answers.

The church has a very basic requirement or set of terms, namely that you get down on your knees and ask for the truth. I was told by one of my friends, "You don't believe in [Our Lord] therefore you can only pray to God the Father; you cannot pray to the Trinity." I prayed to God the Father for two or three years, simply saying "Show me." I didn't want proof of anything. I didn't know what I was going to be shown because I didn't believe in anything.

I was shown very suddenly. It didn't happen in any expected way. It came instantly as immediate evidence, and without any question of its being a divine intervention. There was no trauma or personal need. I never had any need for religion, any personal or emotional crisis. I simply wanted to know what was true and I was told . . . Wham! I became a Catholic the next day.

What was that day like?

[I]t's not easy to describe. I was with a group of people who said as I spoke, "Why aren't you a Catholic?" I couldn't think of one reason. I was beat. I became a Catholic at once, because I knew that was the divine work.

I had converted myself by working at the whole question. I didn't have any point of view, any problems; I had no difficulties. I've never had any difficulties. By the way, faith is not a matter of concepts: it's percepts, a matter of immediate reality.

He was baptized and confirmed on the same day: 25 March 1937, Holy Thursday. In his journals for the rest of his life he never failed to mark the anniversary, but always on Holy Thursday before Easter, whatever the calendar date.

∞

In introducing this collection of his observations about religion, I think it proper to note that Marshall McLuhan was not reticent, exactly, about his Catholicism, but neither was he given to discussing it lightly. He was not what might be called a "public Catholic" or a "professional Catholic." He never considered writing a book about his faith. At one point, though, as we were working with a group of themes for what later became *Laws of Media*,[7] some church controversies or difficulties, probably in newspaper articles, crossed our bows. The result was the chapter outline for a book on Christianity in the Electronic Age (Chapter 18, below). He carefully kept his private and public lives quite separate. For example, he very rarely ventured his private opinion about any matter, such as media, that he was called upon to discuss publicly and professionally. A trained — and immensely learned — critic and observer, he was quite able to detach professional observation from personal feeling.

To illustrate: once, a student in one of his literature classes asked him, did he experience any *feelings* when reading a poem? They had just spent an hour or more in exhaustive analysis and critical examination of some verses. He was evidently quite surprised at the question and replied that of course he experienced feelings. He seemed to feel that the answer was obvious. The student (himself a poet) then asked, why then did he never mention, let alone discuss, these feelings in class? Didn't it occur to him that perhaps other students needed some inducement or encouragement in the matter, some guidance as to how to respond more fully to poetry? My father replied, in effect, that such matters were naturally private and not a proper subject of public or critical discourse.[8]

Such an attitude is difficult to imagine today, when feelings of every stripe are virtually required of everyone, and of public figures in particular. People who can compartmentalize their beings so strictly seem to us to be cold, inhuman, unfeeling. Yet there are many people among us still who belong to that former age and set of habits, and who regard the matter of privacy not only as absolutely normal but also as absolutely necessary to both sanity and civilization. In fact, such control of the emotive faculties is a normal consequence of alphabetic literacy and is part of the private individualism that it breeds; our contemporary surprise or dismay at it gives some indication of the degree

---

7 University of Toronto Press, 1988.

8 On the other hand, he could be quite candid and once (in 1969) remarked to a group of graduate students, "I have never failed to thrill at the words in the Mass "Mirabiliter condidisti mirabilius reformasti" — man, who had been amazingly and wonderfully made before the fall, was even more wonderfully remade at the Incarnation. The theology on this subject is mostly lacking: there isn't any."

of our own estrangement from literacy and privacy. Possessed of a firm sense of private identity, he conducted his classes with the courtliness of a gentleman of an earlier era, a manner he may have picked up at Cambridge. Although outspoken about the present he was always formal and gentlemanly in his classes; in contrast to today's classroom practice, he never used first-name chumminess with his students.

He once wrote to the anthropologist Edward T. Hall, whose work he admired and often used, that, in addition to privacy, there was a technical reason for not bringing religious matters into his discussions of media and their effects: "I deliberately keep Christianity out of all these discussion lest perception be diverted from structural processes by doctrinal sectarian passions. My own attitude to Christianity is, itself, awareness of process."[9]

I have occasionally, in the years since his death, heard my father's methods and insights dismissed as "applied Catholicism," the contention being that he was simply a tool of the Catholic Church. Or that his media work is just ages-old Catholic doctrine in new clothes and that he is merely spouting some Catholic party line. (The people who make such assertions clearly must not be Catholics: the Catholics were themselves as irritated by his insights as everyone else and never detected the slightest relation to doctrine in his observations.) At a recent (1997) conference at York University in Toronto at which Neil Postman and Arthur Kroker were featured speakers, the new conventional line was revealed: it runs, "McLuhan's work is basically age-old Christian Humanism in modern dress." (One might as well charge that Northrop Frye was simply a tool of the Masons, or that his literary theories were merely age-old Masonic philosophy dressed up and regurgitated as literary criticism.) There's evidence aplenty in the chapters that follow to discourage or disprove any such imputation. But it is true that he used to drive ossified conservatives and the slow-witted to distraction. Himself neither a raving liberal nor a tight-lipped conservative, he was rather a learned man on a constant quest for understanding.

In an interview with Gerald Stearn, he refuted the suggestion that his work on media derives from Catholicism or Catholic doctrine:

> There have been many more religious men than I who have not made even the most faltering steps in this direction. Once I began to

---

9 *Letters of Marshall McLuhan*, page 384.

move in this direction, I began to see that it had profound religious meaning. I do not think it my job to point this out. For example, the Christian concept of the mystical body — all men as members of the body of Christ — this becomes technologically a fact under electronic conditions. However, I would not try to theologize on the basis of my understanding of technology. I don't have a background in scholastic thought, never having been raised in any Catholic institiution. Indeed, I have been bitterly reproached by my Catholic confrères for my lack of scholastic terminology and concepts. [10]

On occasion he would remark to a Catholic colleague that his own approach to media was similar to St. Thomas's methods of understanding, for example — as a means of engaging the colleague. This was not to say that his work derived from Thomas's but that they were in parallel. He found insight in the most disparate places and never hesitated to co-opt it whenever it could be useful. St. Thomas was particularly useful because he had addressed many of the same problems. Aquinas pointed out that all being was by analogy with the font of being, God. My father's idea of media as extensions was that they were analogues to our limbs and organs. Thomas made much use in his work of Formal Causality; my father's idea of a medium as an environment of services as disservices is exactly that of Formal Causality — which may be why so many people have trouble with it. As he wrote to Fr. John Culkin (see letter, page 76, below),

> [Fritz Wilhelmsen] is interested in working on St. Thomas's theory of communication, and I have pointed out to him that Aquinas designates his audience, the people he wants to influence and alter, in the Objections of each article. Then I realized that the audience is, in all matters of art and expression, the formal cause, e.g., fallen man is the formal cause of the Incarnation, and Plato's public is the formal cause of his philosophy. Formal cause is concerned with effects and with structural form, and not with value judgments. My own approach to the media has been entirely from formal cause. Since formal causes are hidden and environmental, they exert their structural pressure by interval and interface with whatever is in their environmental territory. Formal cause[s are] always hidden, whereas

---

10 *McLuhan: Hot and Cool: A Primer for the Understanding of & a Critical Symposium with a Rebuttal by McLuhan*, ed. Gerald Emanuel Stearn (New York: Dial, 1967), page 267.

the things upon which they act are visible. The TV generation has been shaped not by TV programs, but by the pervasive and penetrating character of the TV image, or service, itself.

At the same time, he saw a direct relation of another kind between media study and study of the Church and the scriptures. He wrote to one correspondent, "The Church is so entirely a matter of communication that like fish that know nothing of water, Christians have no adequate awareness of communication. Perhaps the world has been given to us as an anti-environment to make us aware of the word."[11]

Rather constantly, over the years, before breakfast he used to read a few verses from the New Testament each morning in English and then in two or three other languages. This provided a double benefit: that of beginning the day with something to meditate upon, and that of refreshing — or learning, on occasion — a language. (Like many scholars, he knew two or three other languages fairly well — Latin, French, and German, for example — and could read roughly in several more.) His morning reading of the NT used, among others, Greek, Latin, German, Italian, Portuguese, Spanish, French. Often, the "meditating" produced insights into both areas, media and the meaning of a passage. For example, he wrote Bill Kuhns:

> It is the same as the difference indicated in Luke 8:18: "Heed *how* you hear." The entire text depends on understanding that. Those who get the word of God as a wonderful idea or concept soon lose it. Those who get it as a percept, a direct thing, interfacing and resonating, are those who represent the "good ground." The sower and the seed image is a direct anticipation of the gestalt figure-ground relationship. All those who are having difficulty with their Catholic faith today tend to be the victims of a post-Renaissance conceptualized theology and catechism.[12]

---

11 Letter to Kristin L. Popik (28 May 1971), in the National Archives of Canada collection.

12 Letter (5 January 1970) in the National Archives of Canada collection. In a letter to Allen Maruyama, he amplifies, " . . . 'The user is the content' — always — so that the hearer who has ears to hear is able to respond to the revealed word because of the content of his own being. There is a good deal of this sort of observation in the Acts, chapters 16-17. The message is the effect on the general society, whereas the meaning is the effect on the individual, but don't say that I think 'the medium has no content'! All media are mythical in the strict sense of being artificial fictions, and forms designed to enhance or speed human transactions. (Letter to Allen Maruyama, 11 January 1972, National Archives of Canada collection.)

That figure-ground relationship was central to his approach to the study of media. The approach, based in formal causality, that is, in observing the form of the media and discussing them as forms and as having formal power over their users, derived variously from the ancients, from the Tradition, from Eliot's remarks about con-formity, from the new Structuralism, from Practical Criticism, from audience study, etc. He wrote, "The study of effects has lately driven me to the study of causality, where I have been forced to observe that most of the effects of any innovation occur before the actual innovation itself. In a word, a vortex of effects tends, in time, to become the innovation. It is because human affairs have been pushed into pure process by electronic technology that effects can precede causes."[13] One observation directly owing to working with figure/ground dynamics and their relation to formal causality came about when we read one morning in the papers another article discussing the controversy over the Anglican church's intention to ordain women. After some discussion, he quickly dashed off this little note for future reference:

> This is just a note about the ordination of women, which concerns "formal causality," i.e., structural form which is inseparable from "putting on" one's public. The writer's or the performer's public is the formal cause of his art or entertainment or his philosophy. The *figure/ground* relation between the artist and his making is an interplay, a kind of intercourse. This interplay is at its peak in all performance before the public and is characteristic of role-playing in general. There is, as it were, a sexual relation between performer and public, which relates specifically to the priest or minister. The congregation is necessarily feminine to the masculine role of the priest. (This is characteristic also in medicine, of the surgeon who is only exceptionally a woman.) It is, therefore, this inherent sexual aspect of the priesthood that makes the ordination of women impractical and unacceptable to a congregation in their feminine role.
>
> Perhaps there has been insufficient thought given to the nature of role-playing in its metaphysical or formal causality. This is a propos the local headlines about Anglican synod OK-ing the ordination of women.[14]

---

13 Letter to Muriel Bradbrook (5 November 1971), National Archives of Canada collection.
14 On Centre for Culture and Technology stationery, dated June 20, 1975. Never used.

This notion of formal cause and its relation to ground crops up in several of the chapters, below.

He frequently turned his attention to examining the relation between the Church and media:

> It is not brains or intelligence that is needed to cope with the problems which Plato and Aristotle and all of their successors to the present have failed to confront. What is needed is a readiness to undervalue the world altogether. This is only possible for a Christian . . . All technologies and all cultures, ancient and modern, are part of our immediate expanse. There is hope in this diversity since it creates vast new possibilities of detachment and amusement at human gullibility and self-deception. There is no harm in reminding ourselves from time to time that the "Prince of this World" is a great P. R. man, a great salesman of new hardware and software, a great electric engineer, and a great master of the media. It is his master stroke to be not only environmental but invisible, for the environmental is invincibly persuasive when ignored.[15]

He was continually amazed at the reluctance, often the downright refusal, of people to pay attention to the effects of media, and at their hostility to him for what he revealed. They included those, clergy and lay, who enthusiastically embrace the latest technologies without regard for their effects. Such people are blindly eager to make the Mass or the sacraments, or the congregation the content of each new gadget or technology that comes along — in the interest of "bringing the Church up to date" and "making the Church relevant." They are quite innocent of the power of these forms to transform their users — innocent but not guiltless. They share the Protestant attitude, "if God gave them to us they must be good." McLuhan incessantly studied and occasionally wrote about these new forms and their impact on the Church. One article (Chapter 13, below) showed, in particular, that the use of microphones on the altar would destroy the psychology of the Latin rite: it would signal the replacement of sacral prayer with pedagogic conversation. Events have proven him right.

He saw a parallel between Christians and non-Christians in their common reluctance to look at the media themselves. As he wrote to Alan Maruyama,

---

15 *Letters of Marshall McLuhan*, pages 386-87.

You seem to have forgotten your own contribution here! After we had discussed phonetically literate man as the only private individual in human history, you mentioned that the reluctance [of this type] of Western man to consider the effects of his own technologies upon his psyche and society was his simple resistance to any invasion of privacy. Let us recall how violently people resisted and resented Jung and Freud when they invaded our privacy. I see no reason, however, to suppose that the Christian is more inclined to study these matters that the non-Christian."[16]

Again,

I continue to be baffled by the panic and anger people feel when the effects of any technology or pursuit are revealed to them. It is almost like the anger of a householder whose dinner is interrupted by a neighbour telling him his house is on fire. This irritation about dealing with the effects of anything whatever, seems to be a specialty of Western man.[17]

Further conversation aided in finding at least one source for the resistance:

Bob Logan [a colleague at the University of Toronto] mentioned that many people resent me because I have made so many discoveries and from the point of view of subliminal life this may well be a clue. People feel angry when something they had "known" all along surfaces. It happened with Freud. The point is, we create our subconscious ourselves and resent anybody fooling around with it. When I study media *effects*, I am really studying the subliminal life of a whole population, since they go to great pains to hide these effects from themselves.[18]

Constantly frustrated by encounters with bureaucratic intransigence, he turned to studying the difficulty facing print-based bureaucracies immersed in electricity.

You can see how this [difficulty] afflicts the vast predominance of nineteenth-century mentalities that constitute the bureaucracies

---

16 Letter to Allen Maruyama (11 January 1972), National Archives of Canada collection.
17 Letter to Pete Buckner (19 June 1974), National Archives of Canada collection.
18 Letter to Barbara Rowes (15 April 1976), National Archives of Canada collection.

of the Catholic church. In the electric or resonant age of tactility, they are hung up. They don't understand "drop out" as the necessary mode of dialogue and interface but merely the scrapping of their entire world, and of any conceivable world . . . Aquinas has been translated into visual terms from the first and never more than by Gilson. Naturally, I am distressed at the total unawareness of the rationale of electro-technics among the Catholic hierarchy. There was no one at the Council of Trent who understood the psychic and social effects of Gutenberg. The Church is no better off now, humanly speaking.[19]

Much significance has been attributed to the appointment of my father to the Vatican's Social Communications Committee. I regret to say that the significance has been grossly inflated. The appointment was made, true. But it meant little other than receiving in the mail from time to time a notice of a meeting (always to be held in Rome) or some such. My father tried several times to strike up a correspondence with someone, anyone, on the committee. He was anxious to be of some service and to help them with the study and understanding of media. His efforts attracted, unfortunately, no response, which was a source of great disappointment.

Equally, a great deal of significance has been attached to his habit of attending daily mass. Another exaggeration, I fear. First, recall that St. Basil's church was and is at the centre of the campus of St. Michael's College at the University of Toronto. For those who have their offices and classes there, it is almost impossible to get from office to classroom without having to go around — or at least quite near to — the church. My father's office at "house 96" lies less than a hundred yards away from the church, and his later Centre for Culture and Technology not twice that distance. To get from either to the little dining room at Brennan Hall staffed by the College also requires walking around the church. What more natural than to drop in for a noon mass in passing, as it were? The mass was always well-attended in those days, by faculty and students alike. Nothing exceptional about it, really, but daily mass makes a wonderful way to punctuate the academic day, to keep in touch with priorities, and to meditate on the morning's readings or put some current problem into perspective.

He had a number of unusual theological ideas, among them the

---

19 Letter to the Rev. Walter Ong, S.J. (18 December 1969), National Archives of Canada collection.

observation that, given the structure of the Church, if there were only two Catholics left in the world, one of them would have to be Pope. Unusual, perhaps, but theologically accurate: it throws a peculiar light on the papacy and its relation to the rest of the faithful. He also warned (in "Catholic Humanism and Modern Letters," Chapter 17, below) that

> Perhaps the besetting Catholic danger is to live with the truth until one is not concerned to look at it. We know it so well that we "couldn't care less."

He pondered the popular slogan "God is dead" when it was current, and observed in his journal, "Suddenly really got the 'God is dead' message. They mean that the Incarnation was His death because He became visible. Now in the non-visual time, the visual alienates them" (25 July 1967). And he wrote his friend Marshall Fishwick that, "Apropos Pop Theology, the God who is dead, of course, is the Newtonian God, the visual image of a visually-organized cosmos. With the dethronement of the visual sense by the audile-tactile media of radio and TV, religion, or the relating to the divine, can no longer have a primarily visual bias. The present irrelevance of our political and educational establishments stems from the same situation. God, of course, is not involved in any of this."[20] He also pointed out that "If the Catholic schools of the future choose to program themselves electronically they could create a symmetry between the secular environment of information and the environment of grace."[21]

My father had no aversion to discussing unusual or outré ideas. He and I once discussed the notion of there being life on other planets. Somehow the conversation came around to what the Church might have to say about such an idea. He pointed out (this is not discussed in the chapters below) that while it is accepted that Adam in the Garden clearly possessed all knowledge, quite possibly he conveyed a very great deal of it to his children. It is entirely possible, therefore, that they, one or more of them, relocated to some other part of the universe for a while, to see how we might get along and work out our problems.

And a colleague, Joe Keogh, wrote in the Ottawa, Ontario *G. K. Chesterton Newsletter* of a curious exchange between my father and

20 Letter of 5 January 1973, National Archives of Canada collection.
21 "Spectrum of Catholic Attitudes," 1969.

Toronto's (then) Archbishop Pocock. The good Bishop, it is said, once asked that given John's famous prologue to the fourth gospel, did this not indicate that Christ Himself is the archetypal example of the medium as message? He readily assented.

Here, from a letter, is another example of how media study can illuminate a theological matter in an unusual manner:

> Another characteristic of man's humanity is his freedom in community, which the Christian community provides. Christian freedom is found in the corporate freedom in the mystical body of Christ, the Church. The electric age has so involved man with his whole world that he has no individual freedom left. He only has a corporate freedom in the tribal context. The hope of man is that he can be changed sacramentally so that he will eventually come to an awareness of himself in his community and discover individual freedom in the community.[22]

Instead of dropping the matter there, he went deeper, writing to many friends and colleagues.

> [Eric] Havelock was the person who explored the fact that the private individual person was in fact an artefact, or development, from the technology of the phonetic alphabet. I think that this is a very great and urgent theological matter at the present time. If the private individual, as we know him in the Western world, is indeed an artefact rather than an inevitable aspect of the human condition, then we have to regard the Greco-Roman tradition and Western literacy in quite a special light . . . I am myself completely baffled by the relation of the Greco-Roman tradition to the Church at the present time. Basically, it seems to me an inescapable fact that the Incarnation and the Passion occurred in the Greco-Roman context. Since God does nothing in vain and nothing idly, or insignificantly, His providence in setting the Church centrally in the Greco-Roman context has an enormous significance which has merely been taken for granted up to now. At the present time, when the entire Western establishment is dissolving very rapidly under the impact of electric technology and when tribal man is resuming his dominance over the world, the question of the relevance of the Graeco-Roman thing

---

22 Letter to Allen Maruyama (31 December 1971), National Archives of Canada collection.

becomes a central concern . . . If the private person is an artefact, then it becomes criminal to perpetuate him technologically in the electronic age.[23]

∞

It now seems clear, from the remarks in this book about media and about Vatican Councils I and II, that there will *have* to be a Vatican Council III in the very near future. The purpose of this third Council will, like that of Vatican Council II, also be pastoral and will be to respond to the current assault on our society by the computer. It will have to deal with shedding the bureaucratic and administrative apparatus that the Church accumulated in response to the alphabet and to print. Something more like the Eastern Church may be in the offing: there will still be a magisterium and a doctrinal authority and a Pope, but no longer a Rome, that is, no longer a centralized bureaucracy. Asked about this aspect of the Church, McLuhan replied to the interviewer (in 1970),

> In its merely bureaucratic, administrative, and institutional side, I think, it is going to undergo the same pattern of change as the rest of our institutions. In terms of, say, a computer technology, we are heading for cottage economies, where the most important industrial activities can be carried on in any little individual shack anywhere on the globe. That is, the most important designs and the most important activities can be programmed by individuals in the most remote areas. In that sense, Christianity — in a centralized, administrative, bureaucratic form — is certainly irrelevant. (See below, page 85)

My father had made a date to give a talk, at the outset of the fall term, 1979, on the topic of "Discarnate Man and the Incarnate Church," to a class at St. Michael's College, or somewhere similar nearby in Toronto. Just before he was due to give the talk he had the stroke that took away his power of speech. That topic, however, plays a large role in the essays that follow. The reader might be interested in piecing together, from remarks in the chapters below, the probable text of that talk — The Talk He Never Gave.

---

23 Letter to Alexis de Beauregard (11 May 1972), National Archives of Canada collection.

PART
1

Conversion

1

G. K. Chesterton:
A Practical Mystic

When it is seen that there are two principal sides to everything, a practical and a mystical, both exciting yet fruitful, then the meaning and effect of Mr. Chesterton can become clear, even to those who delight to repeat that he stands on his head. This tireless vigilance in examining current fashion and fatalism, which has characterized him for more than thirty years, clearly depends upon his loyalty to a great vision: "His creed of wonder was Christian by this absolute test, that he felt it continually slipping from himself as much as from others." Therefore the prosaic is invariably the false appearance of things to fatigued intellect and jaded spirit. This is the basis of Mr. Chesterton's inspiriting opposition to the spread of officialdom and bureaucracy. The cynical social legislation of today, undertaken in supposed accord with unyielding economic circumstance, is often light-headed because it is not light-hearted. And Mr. Chesterton is a revolutionary, not because he finds everything equally detestable, but because he fears lest certain infinitely valuable things, such as the family and personal liberty, should vanish. That Beauty transformed the Beast only because she loved it while it was yet a beast, is timelessly significant.

It is necessary to define the sense in which Mr. Chesterton is a mystic, before the relation of this to the practical side can be judged. He once wrote: "Real mystics don't hide mysteries, they reveal them.

∞ First published in The Dalhousie Review, January 1936, pages 455-64.

They set a thing up in broad daylight, and when you've seen it, it is still a mystery. But the mystagogues hide a thing in darkness and in secrecy; and when you find it, it's a platitude." The mysteries revealed by Mr. Chesterton are the daily miracles of sense and consciousness. His ecstasy and gratitude are for what has been given to all men. He rejoices at the "green hair" on the hills, or "the smell of Sunday morning," and

> Those rolling mirrors made alive in me,
> Terrible crystal more incredible
> Than all the things they see.

Here it is possible only to speak of the sacramental sense of the life of earth and sea and sky, of tillage and growth, and of food and wine, which informs his work. For to him existence has a value utterly inexpressible, and absolutely superior to any arguments for optimism or pessimism. What truce could such a great lover of life make with agnostic humanitarianism and world-weary eugenists? To those "who have snarled through the ages" he hurls this reply:

> Know that in this grotesque old masque
>   Too loud we cannot sing,
> Or dance too wild or speak too wide
>   To praise a hidden thing.

It is the spirit of Christendom, as it was the spirit of R. L. Stevenson; but it is not the spirit of the age. In this sense Mr. Chesterton is reactionary. If universal nature made shipwreck to-morrow, yet would

> One wild form reel on the last rocking cliff,
> And shout: "The daisy has a ring of red."

Mr. Chesterton has stepped beyond the frontiers of poetry, to what M. Maritain in speaking of Rimbaud calls "the Eucharistic passion which he finds in the heart of life."

As a comment on one of his characters, he wrote: "He had somehow made a giant stride from babyhood to manhood, and missed that crisis in youth when most of us grow old." Mr. Chesterton himself is full of that child-like surprise and enjoyment which a sophisticated age supposes to be able to exist only in children. And it is to this more than ordinary awareness and freshness of perception that we may attribute his extraordinarily strong sense of fact. We can apply to him what he wrote of a young poet in one of his stories: "What are to most men impressions or half impressions, were to him incidents . . . The slope of a hill or the corner of a house checked him like a challenge. He wrestled with it seriously, until he could put something like a name to his nameless fancy." This profound humility in the face of reality is the very condition of honest art and all philosophy, and it explains Mr. Chesterton's imaginative sympathy with popular legends and proverbs: just as it is the reason for his energetic revival of tradition insofar as it dignifies and illuminates any present activity. In short, he is original in the only possible sense, because he considers everything in relation to its origins. It is because he is concerned to maintain our endangered institutions that he earnestly seeks to re-establish agriculture and small property, the only basis of any free culture.

But most of all does his strong sense of fact account for the recurrence of seeming paradoxes in his writings:

> The more plain and satisfying our state appears, the more we all know we are living in an unreal world. For the real world is not satisfying. The more clear become the colours and facts of Anglo-Saxon superiority, the more surely we may know that we are in a dream. For the real world is not clear or plain. The real world is full of bracing bewilderments and brutal surprises. Comfort is the blessing and curse of the English . . . For there is but an inch of difference between the cushioned chamber and the padded cell.

All profound truth, philosophical and spiritual, makes game with appearances, yet without really contradicting common sense. That is why Mr. Chesterton accuses the Victorians of believing in real paradoxes, such as expecting all men to have the same morals when they have different religions, or supposing that it was practical to be illogical. A little attention shows how he consciously causes a clash between appearances in order to attract attention to a real truth transcending such a conflict. There is no hint or hue of meaning amidst the dizziest crags of thought that is safe from his swift, darting, pursuit. We return safely and lucidly from the exhilarating chase of an idea to its logical conclusion. Such a world, rigid with thought and brilliant with colour, is the very antithesis of the pale-pink lullaby-land of popular science.

It is the difference between a cathedral window and blank infinity. That is why modern life, thoughtless and unpoised, has degenerated from a dance into a race, and history is regarded as a toboggan slide. But Mr. Chesterton has exposed the Christless cynicism of the supposedly iron laws of economics and shown that history is a road that must often be reconsidered and even retraced. For, if Progress implies a goal, it does not imply that all roads lead to it inevitably. And today, when the goal of Progress is no longer clear, the word is simply an excuse for procrastination.

It is scarcely necessary now, when philosophy and art have been revitalized by the study of medieval achievements, to explain that Mr. Chesterton does not want "to go back to the middle ages," and never did. "There is none rides back to pick up a glove or a feather." But the merest reference to anything prior to the Reformation starts a clockwork process in the mind of the nineteenth-century journalists who still write most of our papers: "Mr. Chesterton is a medievalist; and he is therefore quite justified (from his own benighted standpoint) in indulging as he does in the sport of tearing out the teeth of Jews, burning hundreds of human beings alive, and perpetually seeking for the Philosopher's Stone." Without these automatic and irresponsible reactions to anything resembling serious thought, there could not be that vast and increasing mountain of printed paper which indicates that progress is proceeding. For, as Stevenson noted, man does not live by bread alone, but by catchwords also. It all began with Luther's anathemas against Reason, and Descartes's expressed contempt for Aristotle and Aquinas.

The conspiracy, hatched at that time, to ignore history, which in practice meant the Middle Ages, had not been generally found out when Mr. Chesterton began to write. Certainly he knew there must have been something right about centuries whose architectural remains were admired by every class of mind. He was absolutely certain that people who were capable of an intensely significant use of colours, whose dress was as many-hued as the walls and windows of their churches, could not be as black as they were painted. So much he had in common with Ruskin, Rosetti, and Morris; but much deeper was his interest in the origins of that magnificent and complex culture. His was the intellectual interest of Newman rather than the aesthetic interest of Burne-Jones. "If we want the flowers of chivalry, we must go back to the roots of chivalry, Theology." And since it is always the world of ideas that determines the climate of sensation and opinion, the Troubadors, and Dante, and the Metaphysicals are today throbbing again with vital interest for us. Similarly the moral atmosphere of the Victorian time was prepared by Locke and Bentham and, though incohate, had stirred the anger of Keats:

> Fools! make me whole again that weighty pearl
> The Queen of Egypt melted, and I'll say
> That ye may love in spite of beaver hats.

Now Mr. Chesterton has never written a book to praise the Middle Ages, but he has written books to praise and explain the life of St. Francis and the thought of Aquinas. For, as he explains, "real conviction and real charity are very much nearer than men suppose." It is plain that he is literally a radical, because he goes to the roots of things. And it is for that reason that he is very hopeful for this generation, which has been forced back to roots and origins. Thus because it is sceptical even about scepticism, "the sophisticated youth, who has seen through the sophistical old men, may even yet see something worth seeing."

Although Mr. Chesterton has never entertained any desire to restore the Middle Ages, he shows that certain timeless principles were then understood which have since been foolishly forgotten. Though they were not the right place, they were the right turning and subsequent history has in a deep sense been an ignoble retreat from their difficult and untried ideas. It was a rout which distorted and diminished the Renaissance, and nullified its proud promise to us. Mr. Chesterton's concentration on history has been a splendid effort to rescue a civilization weakened by capitalism from the logical conclusion of capitalism, which is, either the servile or the communistic state:

> The highest use of the imagination is to learn from what never happened. It is to gather the rich treasures of truth stored up as much in what never was as in what was and will be. We are accused of praising and even idealising retrograde and barbaric things. What we praise is the progress which was for those retrograde things prevented, and the civilization that those barbarians were not allowed to reach. We do not merely praise what the Middle Ages possessed. It would be far truer to say that we praise . . . what they were never allowed to possess. But they had in them the potentiality of the possession; and

it was that that was lost in the evil hour when all other possession became a matter of scramble and pillage. The principle of the guild was a sound principle; and it was the principle and not only the practice that was trampled underfoot . . .

This tragic theme has found memorable expression in such poems as "The Secret People":

Smile at us, pay us, pass us; but do not quite forget;
For we are the people of England, that have never spoken yet.

For, equally with Dickens, Mr. Chesterton is the champion of the English poor. In equal degree he is a hater of class and of privilege, of cant and bureaucracy. But he is a great demagogue who has been shouted down by Publicity, that "voice loud enough to drown any remarks made by the public." He is the mouthpiece of the poor who cannot hear him. He is their memory and their poet, the cherisher of their traditions stamped out by misery, and the singer of virtues they have almost forgotten. And his sympathies are a proof of his splendid lineage:

I saw great Cobbett riding,
The horseman of the shires;
And his face was red with judgment
And a light of Luddite fires.

"Cobbett was defeated because the English people was defeated. After the frame-breaking riots, men as men were beaten . . . And Ireland did not get home rule because England didn't." This instinctive espousal of the cause of the oppressed and of the harassed and pitiable things is nowhere better expressed than in "The Donkey," which needs not quoting. There also will be found that inexpressible and mystic certainty, that the big battalions will one day be confounded by that weak and scattered remnant which has survived a hundred defeats. Yet Mr. Chesterton does not fight with any hope of success, but rather for the continuance of a cause and to witness to a truth:

In a world of flying loves and fading lusts
It is something to be sure of a desire.

It is probably his sympathy with the humble yet joyous traditions of England, together with his strong but sensitive feeling for her unrivalled roads and hills and villages, that has contributed to make him subtly and unmistakably English. He is not least English in his deep regard for morals, and a fondness for pertinently pointing morals even about morals: "We have grown to associate morality in a book with a kind of optimism and prettiness; according to us, a moral book is about moral people. But the old idea was almost exactly the opposite; a moral book was about immoral people." We have but to recall Hogarth and Fielding.

But in nothing is the peculiar quality of the autochthonous Englishman seen more clearly than in Mr. Chesterton's patriotism. To people unacquainted with the profound patriotism of Sir Thomas More, Johnson, Cobbett, and Dickens, it may be puzzling. For it is anything but an uncritical allegiance to the acts of professional politicians, which Johnson rightly designated as the last refuge of a scoundrel. Nor is it that still more pernicious physical and spiritual perversion that has disfigured Prussia since Frederick. For he heartily hates what England seems trying to become, and this produces "a sort of fierce doubt or double-mindedness which cannot exist in vague and homogeneous Englishmen." In his book *The Crimes of England*, he wrote:

> I have passed the great part of my life in criticising and condemning the existing institutions of my country: I think it is infinitely the most patriotic thing a man can do.

The high standard he sets for his own country makes him quick and generous in his recognition of the rights and virtues of others. And the French, American, and Irish peoples have no more discriminating admirer and interpreter than Mr. Chesterton. But like Socrates, he is a gadfly stinging his own countrymen into awareness of the crime of complacency:

> We have made our public schools the strongest walls against a whisper of the honour of England . . . What have we done and where have we wandered, we that have produced sages that could have spoken with Socrates and poets who could walk with Dante, that we should talk as if we had never done anything more intelligent than found colonies and kick niggers?

Mr. Chesterton opposed jingoism at the beginning of the century for the same reason that he opposes pacifism today. For both are craven moods that seek the exhilaration or security to be found in mass sentiment and unrealistic unanimity.

He believes in the ordinary man, and in no other sort of man. But unlike another very great journalist, Daniel Defoe, Mr. Chesterton has never failed to pay the ordinary man the compliment of reasoning with him. That is why he is such a poor salesman. For he does not wish to persuade without first convincing. His appeal is always to reason. In fact, that he turns a few cart-wheels out of sheer good spirits by way of enlivening his pages has annoyed a certain type of person, and is sure to puzzle a lazy or fatigued mind. Such, for instance, is his unparalleled power of making verbal coincidences really coincide. But the irreducibly simple language and the appeal to common experience are unmistakably directed to the ordinary person. Mr. T. S. Eliot, writing to the three thousand people who comprehend, according to his own computation, the total culture of the West, describes the poet's mind as "being a more finely perfected medium in which special or very varied feelings are at liberty to enter into new combinations." He says no more than Mr. Chesterton before him, who wrote that "nobody believes that an ordinary civilized stockbroker can really produce, out of his own inside, noises which denote all the mysteries of memory and the agonies of desire." The fact is that Mr. Chesterton has always that additional human energy and intellectual power which constitute humour.

That purely esoteric use of his powers which might have gone to the creation of fine art was made impossible by the appeal of a chaotic and turbid time to his great democratic sympathies. The extraordinary extent of his writing and discussions is proportioned to the desperate need for direction and unity in an age that has "smothered man in men." For external complexity has produced an insane simplification of thought, preying upon personal variety and spontaneous social expression:

> We have hands that fashion and heads that know,
> But our hearts we lost — how long ago!

What Mr. Chesterton has written of the power of St. Thomas to fix even passing things as they pass, and to scorch details under the magnifying lens of his attention, is strikingly true of himself. His is the power to focus a vast range of material into narrow compass; and his books though very numerous are extremely condensed. They might even be considered as projections of his mastery of epigram and sententious phrase. What had seemed a dull and formless expanse of history is made to shine with contemporary significance, and contemporary details are made to bristle with meaning. It is a great labour of synthesis and reconstruction in which Mr. Chesterton has been engaged. He has fixed his attention on the present and the past, because he is concerned lest our future steps be blindly mistaken. And a strong and growing group of like-minded writers indicates the impression he has made upon his generation. For there are many people who no longer regard Herbert Spencer as a philosopher, or think Mr. Chesterton a medieval buffoon.

Although his thunders of laughter may beguile some readers, there is no more serious master of debate and controversy. When his exuberant fancy may decorate an argument as a gargoyle embellishes a buttress, the buttress is there; and just as the buttress is there, so is the lofty edifice which it supports. There is a perfect continuity between his ideas even when they are most subtle; for he has seen modern problems from the beginning in all their complexity and connections, in other words, with wisdom. Therefore he has no nostrum and no novelty, no panacea and no private aim; nor is he deceived by his own metaphors. And nothing is more characteristic of him than scrupulous care in the definition of terms.

Mr. Chesterton has commanding vigour of expression, and appreciates the genius of the English language which is full of combative and explosive energy, especially found in short epithets: "A young man grows up in a world that often seems to him to be intolerably old. He grows up among proverbs and precepts that appear to be quite stiff and senseless. He seems to be stuffed with stale things; to be given the stones of death instead of the bread of life; to be fed on the dust of the dead past to live in a town of tombs." This passage may also be regarded as an instance of what some hold to be Mr. Chesterton's vice of alliteration. But he is doing something quite different from a Swinburne lulling the mind by alliterating woolly, caterpillar words. His energetic hatchet-like phrases hew out sharply defined images that are like a silhouette or a wood-cut. And these are of a piece with the rigorous clarity of his thought.

The artist in Mr. Chesterton has been far from subdued by the philosopher and controversialist. His poetry and his stories are as important as they are popular. It is because they are popular that very little need be said of them just now. But this part of his work is not easily appreciated in isolation from the more abstract portion. For instance, Mr. Chesterton regards the soul of a story as "the ordeal of a free man" . . . "There is no such thing as a Hegelian story, or a monist story, or a determinist story . . . Every short story does truly begin with the creation and end with the last judgment." The detective story won his praise from the start, because "it is the earliest and only form of popular literature in which is expressed some sense of the poetry of modern life." Such stories are "as rough and refreshing as the ballads of Robin Hood." They are based on the poetry of fact which Mr. Chesterton has expressed so well. "The romance of the police force is thus the whole romance of man. It is based on the fact that morality is the most dark and daring of conspiracies." That is why the inimitable Father Brown is a psychologist rather than a sleuth; and the culprit he exposes is shown to be a sinner rather than a mere criminal.

The stories of Mr. Chesterton are as colourful melodrama as can be imagined or desired. Like the old melodrama, they display this world as a battlefield and restore the colours of life. They are proof that "the finding and fighting of positive evil is the beginning of all fun and even of all farce." For in *The Napoleon of Notting Hill* and *Manalive* and the others, Mr. Chesterton enters faery lands to show that they are not forlorn. They contain a truly brave new world, rather unlike "the shape of things to come," in which very vivid people are etched upon a background of significantly contrasted colours:

> The broken flowerpot with its red-hot geraniums, the green bulk of Smith and the black bulk of Warner, the blue-spiked railings behind, clutched by the stranger's yellow vulture claws and peered over by his long vulture neck, the silk hat on the gravel and the little cloudlet of smoke floating across the garden as innocently as the puff of a cigarette — all these seemed unnaturally distinct and definite. They existed, like symbols, in an ecstasy of separation.

The most ordinary things become eerily and portentously real. Bodily gestures are stiff with spiritual significance, as in the old pageantry. And the deeps of the subconscious are entered, and monstrous facts from the borderland of the brain impress themselves upon us. As the modern jargon puts it, Mr. Chesterton has achieved an objective correlative for his thought and feeling.

The profound joy in Mr. Chesterton's poems and stories can be properly appreciated only when the suffocating materialism of pre-war days is remembered:

> *A cloud was on the mind of men, and wailing went the weather,*

and

> *Life was a fly that faded, and death a drone that stung;*
> *The world was very old indeed when you and I were young.*

But, liberated by faith and joy, Mr. Chesterton represents a very great increase in sensibility over the world that read the *Idylls of the King*. Any valuable extension of awareness is directly determined by the rediscovery of neglected truths, and there is much the same truth behind "The Ballad of the White Horse" and "The Wasteland." Many of Mr. Chesterton's poems have the directness of a shout or a blow, and at times he recaptures the startling simplicity of Chaucer through a combination of sanity and subtlety. Of his inspiriting songs it is unnecessary to speak. They could arouse spirits in a materialist Utopian.

And yet it is no contradiction to say that Mr. Chesterton is primarily an intellectual poet. This is too often overlooked even by those who know that his mind is full of nimble and fiery shapes, and that his wit is "quick, forgetive, apprehensive." He deserves the praise Mr. Eliot affords to Donne for the "quality of transmuting ideas into sensations, of transforming an observation into a state of mind." It is necessary only to refer to the great "Lepanto" or "The Donkey" as perfect achievement of this kind.

Had Mr. Chesterton been merely a quiet intellectual with an ordinary amount of energy, he would certainly have been an artist who was taken seriously by the three thousand cultured minds of Europe. The same might be said of Dickens. But in an age of shallow optimism, of crumbling creeds and faltering faith, he has walked securely and wildly, boisterously praising life and heaping benedictions upon decadents. He has become a legend while he yet lives. Nobody could wish him otherwise than as he is.

2

"The Great Difficulty About Truth":
Two Letters to Elsie McLuhan

[Written from Cambridge, England, Thursday morning, 5 September 1935]

Dear Mother:

Your alarm about my "religion-hunting" traits which you assume to be inherited from the most questionable part of my ancestry, is largely unfounded. Letters are of course fatal things when it comes to imparting a situation with its shades of emphasis. I need scarcely point out that religious enthusiasm (in which I am lamentably weak) has rarely directed the erratic and leaping feet of the inebriated one along the slow and arduous path that leads from a meeting-house to the Church — I mean the Catholic and universal Church, the visible body of Christ. Now religion-hunting even in its worst phases is yet a testimony to the greatest fact about man, namely that he is a creature and an image, and not sufficient unto himself. It is the whole bias of the mind that it seek truth, and of the soul which inspires our very life, that it seek that which gave it. The great difficulty about Truth is that it is not simple except to those who can attain to see it whole. The very definition of an enthusiast is that he has seized a truth which he cannot and would not if he could, relate to other truths of life. He is invariably unsympathetic and lacking in humanity. I have some elements of enthusiasm which have been more than occupied in hero-worship — e.g. Macaulay and Chesterton. Them days is gone forever but I shall always think that my selection of heroes was fortunate. Both were calculated to suppress effectively any tendency I had towards harping on *one* truth at a time. You may be sure that I shall make no inconsiderate step about entering the Roman communion — I shall probably take some years, because I am completely uneducated for the step. I am not even serious enough to be "contemptuous" of the probable effect on my worldly prospects. I believe they would not be altered save for small colleges originally of religious origin — perhaps Acadia, certainly Wesley. The Provincial U's would be indifferent, religion being at such an ebb in our land at present as to be considered a negligible factor. However I will not be a Catholic when I come to apply for posts. And I am waiting advice from Wheeler at present regarding what U's in Canada and U.S.A. to apply to, and *how* to apply to them. I therefore implore you to put aside your apprehensions. Religion is a personal matter and I shall not be visibly altered — tho I could wish for countless improvements — by such a change. The Catholic religion is the only religion — all sects are derivative. Buddhism and similar oriental philosophies and mythologies are not religions in any sense. They have no covenants and no sacraments and no theology. The very notion of "comparative" religion is ridiculous. Now the Catholic religion as you may be able to check in your own experience of it is alone in blessing and employing all those merely human faculties which produce games and philosophy, and poetry and music and mirth and fellowship with a very fleshly basis. It alone makes terms with what our sects have hated and called by ugly names — e.g. carnal which is delightfully near to charnel. The Catholic Church does not despise or wantonly mortify those members and faculties which Christ deigned to assume. They are henceforth holy and blessed. Catholic culture produced Chaucer and his merry story-telling pilgrims. Licentious enthusiasm produced the lonely despair of Christian in *Pilgrim's Progress* — what a different sort of pilgrim! Catholic culture produced Don Quixote and St. Francis and Rabelais. What I wish to emphasize about them is their various and rich-hearted humanity. I need scarcely indicate that everything that is especially hateful and devilish and inhuman about the conditions and strains of modern industrial society is not only Protestant in origin, but it is their boast (!) to have originated it. You may know a thing by its fruits if you are silly enough or ignorant enough to wait that long. I find the fruits and the theory of our sects very bitter. Had I not encountered Chesterton I would have remained agnostic for many years at least. Chesterton did not convince me of religious truth, but he prevented my despair from becoming a habit or hardening into misanthropy. He opened my eyes to European culture and encouraged me to know it more closely. He taught me the reasons for all that in me was simply blind anger and misery. He went through it himself; but since he lived where much Catholic culture remained and since he had genius he got through it quicker. He was no fanatic. He remained an Anglo-Catholic as long as he was able to do so (1922). His wife became a Catholic a few years later.

You ask about Marjorie and her folks — they know my mind very well. Marjorie is quite agnostic and would probably become a Catholic — in any case her reactions to Protestant morals and the dull dead daylight of Protestant rationalism which ruinously bathes every object from a beer parlour to a gasoline station, are my reactions. You see my "religion-hunting" began with a rather priggish "culture-hunting." I simply couldn't believe that men had to live in the mean mechanical rootless joyless fashion that I saw in Winnipeg. And when I began to read English Literature I knew that it was quite unnecessary for them so to live. You will remember my deep personal enjoyment of *Tom Brown's Schooldays* in grade 8. It brought me in contact with things for which I was starved — things which have since disappeared from England. All my Anglo-mania was really a recognition of things missing from our lives which I felt to be indispensable. It was a long time before I finally perceived that the character of every society, its food, clothing, arts, and amusements, are ultimately determined by its religion. It was longer still before I could believe that religion was as great and joyful as these things which it creates — or destroys. Look at the Bedouins the Arabs and Turks. Spain would have looked like Morocco if it had not expelled the Moors. There would have been no *Don Quixote*.

In writing to Red [his brother, Maurice] as I did I not unnaturally forget that he never has experienced any reaction to the culture in which he was reared — not one in a million does be it in China or Peru. *My* hunger for "truth" was sensuous in origin. I wanted a material satisfaction for the beauty that the mind can perceive. I still do. Unfortunately very few do. But I cannot but think that that whether they do or not they would be happier and more profitable servants if they felt otherwise. That is putting it mildly; for there is a true and eternal pattern for human life which the "progress" mongers wot not of. Blessed are they that find and follow that pattern. I never saw it more clearly described from the fact than in Balzac's *Country Doctor*.[1] I believe some of the Russian novelists adhere to it. All art is an attempt to realize it. It emanates from God himself. There is a vast gulf between the virtue of faith and dogmatic conviction. The latter is harsh intolerant feverishly restless and utterly unlovely. And yet faith is yet the first means of grace not in itself implying any spiritual attainment whatever. When you suggest that "a life of service" is superior to membership in the Church of Christ you say only what every Protestant conscious of exclusion from that membership says. It implies that the map of the universe was not radically altered by the Incarnation and Resurrection. It is like saying 2 and 21 makes 3. I long to serve and I know that in this muddled world there are so many opportunities that one need not worry lest one is left idle and useless.

> *The world is so full of a number of things,*
> *I'm sure we should all be as happy as Kings.*[2]

The deepest passion in man is his desire for significance. Significance in clothes, in labour, in gesture. It is the most frustrated passion where men are huddled together and taught to admire luxury. A life of service implies that one is serving something that is in the position of Lord and worthy of service.

> *But good grows wild and wide,*
> *Has shades, is nowhere none;*
> *But right must seek a side*
> *And choose for master one.* (Hopkins)[3]

The Americans serve "service." Like the rest of the world they have smothered man in men and set up the means as an end. It does not speak well for your discrimination as for your affectionate fears that you should confuse my position with the evangelicism of which you

---

1 A translation of Honoré de Balzac's *Le Médecin de campagne* (1833), part of his *Comédie humaine*.
2 Robert Louis Stevenson, "Happy Thoughts."
3 Gerard Manley Hopkins, "On a Piece of Music" (stanza 7). The last line correctly reads: "And choose for chieftain one."

have had experience. Nor do I believe that I am being unfair to Red in pointing out to him that there is an alternative which if he does not honestly face now he cannot but regret when increasing knowledge of that alternative and bitter experience with his present sect shall have mingled in later years. I have an uneasy suspicion Mother that you regard the United Church [of Canada] as an almost respectable profession in which oratory and humanitarian rhetoric can win the applause of good solid prosperous folk. You view with horror the idea of introducing religion into those auditoriums so well designed to exclude it. Let me tell you that religion is not a nice comfortable thing that can be scouted by cultivated lecturers like the Pidgeons. It is veritably something which, if it could be presented in an image, would make your hair stand on end. Hence the fate of those poor uneducated undisciplined devils who stumble upon some of its "horrors" (they cannot administer the sacraments to themselves nor to their followers) while remaining inaccessible to its resources. Such was Bunyan and countless others. It is no wonder that men unable *thus* to see God and to live, quickly rationalize their beliefs as has happened in all the older Protestant sects. Men must be at ease in Zion if they are to pay more than a flying visit. The seventeenth-century Protestants abandoned the world and the flesh to the Devil and packed up for Zion. They found the climate there impossible and returned to earth only to discover that the Devil had been making hay. That is the origin of predatory laissez-faire commerce:

> Industrialism establishes a state of slavery more corrupting than any previously known in the world because the master is not a man but a system, and the whip an invisible machine. With this it is impossible to enter into any but inhuman relations, and in such an inversion of humanity all the instincts become perverted at their source.[4]

There are two points to be cleared. First I shall not rush into the Church where even angels tread reverently. Therefore my worldly prospects will continue just as they are. Second, I wish to take no unfair advantage of Red. No matter what he decides in the matter. I wish only to present the matter at a time when it should be faced.

---

4   Osbert Burdett, *The Beardsley Period: An Essay in Perspective* (1925), page 268.

Since I cannot discuss it with him in person I recommend that he pursue this course: As soon as he can, discover what Protestantism is and in what points it cannot possibly agree with Rome. Let him lay these points before a Churchman (i.e., a priest) and let him discuss them with him. Let him then present the Churchman's replies to Dr. Pidgeon or any theologian of the Protestant communion and see what is retorted in the matter. Maurice [Red] has chosen to become a minister in the Church of Christ.[5] There can be no question of a career in such a choice. Abnegation is its definition. Such a choice unaccompanied by apostolic vows of chastity and poverty becomes almost meaningless. This whole question can be decided by reasoning, provided one is not loath to employ reason. But the matter decided (whichever way) affects the destiny of the soul. Let us leave it for now.

I have been most pleased with the snaps. I think you are getting a stummock Mother! Rags looks good to me. How I would like to have him here awhile.

Last Sunday I was to the Willisons for dinner at 1. Then we listened to Elgar's first symphony on their gramophone and chatted and read around their fire till tea, after which we went to church. The first time I have been to *church* (outside of chapel) since I came. It was (evensong) [at] St Clement's, which is "Very High."[6] In the course of a brief sermon I was ashamed to be told that there were two St Augustines (one of the sixth and one of the eighth centuries). The second was the one who came to England. The first the great theologian and author of the *Confessions*. We went to the Fellows' garde at the Hall afterwards which we had entirely to ourselves. It was a lovely night and I wished heartily that you were here then to enjoy it. It is clear that the presence of twenty-five or thirty great parks and gardens in close but hidden proximity raises each one to a higher power of peace and beauty than merely one could impart. I am going to write two or three articles for the [Winnipeg] *Free Press* which even if published won't fetch me a penny I fear — "Cambridge in Vacation Time" is already written. Monday I had supper with the Crawleys. Last night I went to see *East Lynne* played at the Festival.[7] Since there was a large town

---

5   Maurice had decided to enrol in Emmanuel College, University of Toronto, and become a minister of the United Church of Canada.

6   St. Clements, a parish church of Cambridge.

7   A dramatization of the melodramatic and sensational romance (1861) by Mrs. Henry Wood (1814–1887).

audience they did not give it the burlesque touches that students demand. But it was funny enuf. Think what fun some of our "serious" sex problem plays will provide for the next generation!

This morning I had two teeth filled — can't be helped. This afternoon I spent watching the town regatta. Jim Odams got beaten in sculling — close race. Ted and Kath [Willison] are in London looking for a house and have left me their key so that I can go listen to Elgar's first symphony on their radio. It is a Promenade concert from London directed by Sir Henry Wood — six weeks of the best music every year.[8] It starts in ten minutes so I'm off. Will read over there.

I feel utterly ashamed to think of using your thrice-earned money — well something shall be done before long. This next year will offer some relief for you — I mean the scholarship. I feel very badly to think of having caused you pain by my words and thoughts — you must know that I love you all more dearly every year —

Marshall

---

8 The English conductor Sir Henry Wood (1869–1944) founded in 1895 the popular summer programs of Promenade Concerts in London.

[Written from Cambridge, 12 April 1936]

Dear Mother:

Judging from some excerpts I believe you might find some excellent material in Max Beerbohm's "Zuleika Dobson" [1911]. She may merely be a character in a story of a different title but could easily be traced because Max is an exquisite and not a voluminous writer: "Zuleika Dobson was not strictly beautiful. Her eyes were a trifle large, and their lashes longer than they need have been. The mouth was a mere replica of Cupids bow . . . No apple-tree, no wall of peaches, had not been robbed, nor any Tyrian rose-garden, for the glory of Miss Dobson's cheeks. Her neck was imitation marble. Her hands and feet were of very mean proportions. She had no waist to speak of."

I don't know (Owen?) Merediths aux Italiens but imagine that it is very daring for you to say a good word for them these days![9]

Regarding your use of Phelan[10] on my behalf, I am of course not exactly elated. But there was nothing disreputable in the proceeding. I think there is latent in my mind a fear to exert myself full on *any* occasion lest I should have to admit the result to be my best; and that best not good enough. I have a strong sense of superiority that is utterly incommensurate with my abilities — by superiority, I mean superior *ability to do*, not superiority of personal value. It is the fact that goads me on when one hundred invitations of diversion, which would be welcomed by more pleasant people, vainly offer themselves. My very ordinary mind having been stimulated somewhat beyond the ordinary by whatever queer motives, soon had to admit that there was no merely personal or even human end to which such effort was owing — the utter transience and confusion of human affairs at their stablest being evident even to casual curiosity. Most people admit the

---

9 George Meredith spent a brief period in Italy as a war correspondent in 1866. Italy shocked world opinion in 1935 when Mussolini's troops invaded Ethiopia.

10 Father Gerald B. Phelan (1892–1965), whom Elsie McLuhan knew, was at this time Professor of Philosophy at St. Michael's College, University of Toronto, and in the School of Graduate Studies. He was President of the Pontifical Institute of Mediaeval Studies from 1937 to 1946, the year he moved to the University of Notre Dame. On 29 January 1936 (diary) McLuhan had been "immensely gratified by a note of appreciation (of my GK article)" from Phelan. Elsie McLuhan had perhaps offered to speak to Father Phelan about the possibilities of a teaching position for Marshall after he graduated from Cambridge. Later in the year Phelan would have a preliminary role in McLuhan's conversion to Roman Catholicism — a goal towards which McLuhan was moving when he wrote this letter. To his brother Maurice he had written on 11 April: "Had I come into contact with the Catholic Thing, the Faith, 5 years ago, I would have become a priest I believe."

natural growth of religious consciousness at this point — a growth usually blighted by various demands and sophistications of social life. You perceive no doubt some gruesome analogy between Roy[11] and myself. An immense distaste for spiritual perversion and incontinence would have kept me neutrally agnostic forever unless there had come opportunities for knowledge of things utterly alien to the culture — the grim product of a life-denying otherworldliness — that you know I hated from the time that I turned from our pavements and wheels to boats and sails.

I could never have respected a 'religion' that held reason and learning in contempt — witness the 'education' of our preachers. I have a taste for the intense cultivation of the Jesuit rather than the emotional orgies of an evangelist — or a poet like Shelley and even Browning in part.

I quite realize Red's difficulty — but I am far from increasing it by criticizing *now*, before he has even begun his 'theology' courses. I don't pretend to superior reasoning powers in these matters. I simply *know* of certain things which I didn't know two years ago and which you have never had an opportunity to know.

I was skipping through Morton's "In His Steps"[12] (what a sickening title!) after dinner today — (a very good dinner of cauliflower, roast fowl, Yorkshire pudding, etc., plus Xmas pudding!). I certainly found the *information* fascinating but am out of patience with Morton's trick of giving you the exact colour tone and amount of emotion with each *thing* that confronts him. It is like a cinema where you are the most passive of passive receptacles until you 'cat' over some particularly fulsome slab of stuff. When I came to his good samaritan stuff with the starving dog, I 'catted' (i.e., puked). It was simply awful. You feel as though he really could not distinguish between a spiritual being and an animal — a result of spiritual disorder and derangement. Had he reported this from France it would not have been so bad. But on *that* soil where the fact of the terrible spiritual stature of man is present in the mere reference and description — it was awful!

Almost as bad was his absurd journalistic presence at the ceremony of the Black Monks on the roof of the Church of the Holy Sepulchre.

---

11 McLuhan's uncle Roy (McLuhan) was a Jehovah's Witness.

12 This book was *In the Steps of the Master* (1934) by H. V. Morton. The title McLuhan gives was that of a bestselling inspirational novel by Charles M. Sheldon, *In His Steps: What Would Jesus Do* (1896). The references conform to passages in Morton's travel book.

The more beautiful or wonderful the *thing* (and things alone, not emotions about things, are wonderful), the more inevitably remote and inadequate is Morton to its comprehension. He never knows when to have done with reporting raptures. But there is no need for me to enumerate the undeniable body of excellent stuff (almost entirely cribbed from better writers whom his readers are never likely to consult) which stands outside my strictures.

Jean Farquhar's[13] death is very bad news — a tragic family indeed.

It is very selfish of me not to take time to comment on your own very interesting doings lately. I am most pleased at the pleasure and acknowledgements you receive. Occasionally I catch an oblique glimpse or illumination of Canadians, or some vivid memory is aroused and, I must confess, that at such times my heart sinks at the task awaiting the educator. But education is really 90% domestic in nature. The mere formal educator cannot transform the radical modes of life of which he is usually only too natural a product. My life in Canada will be a continual discontent. My task as a teacher will be to shake others from their complacency — how is it possible to contemplate the products of English life (i.e., Literature) without criticizing our own sterility —

> We are the unfruitful fig-tree
> A land so prosperous to men and kine,
> That which were which, a sage could scarce define!

Believe me dear Mother, most lovingly

Yours,
Marshall

---

13 The Winnipeg lawyer Jean Farquhar was a family friend.

3

"Spiritual Acts":
Letter to Corinne Lewis

[Written from St. Louis, Missouri, Sunday afternoon, 21 January 1939,
to his fiancée, nearly two years after his conversion]

[No complimentary opening]

Another time you may relax, Darling!

You can write such gratifying letters when in a weakened, fatigued state!

Stay that way. However you are probably repenting the foible by now.

You ask by the way whether I go to daily Mass. No. But, really, during vacation it does seem the least that one can *do*. You see, to hear Mass and/or to receive communion are spiritual *acts*. Not merely acts of worship but acts which have definite, specific merit. This merit can be applied to any other person either on earth or in purgatory. The merit of these acts does not, and this is crucial, proceed from the person performing the act. Since human merits, all of them in their entirety from the beginning of history, are not sufficient to compensate for the tiniest sin. For even the tiniest sin constitutes an act of spiritual rebellion against God. The tiniest imaginable sin is thus infinite in its enormity since it is a sin against an infinitely good, the only

Absolute Being. Thus the merit, to return to the first point, of spiritual *acts* is derivative. It is derived from Christ. The infinite merit of His Incarnation, His infinitely humbling Himself, was alone sufficient to 'liquidate' all human sins for all time. But the subsequent acts of His life have a mysterious value (a mystery is, strictly, not something queer or hidden, but something unfathomably and inexhaustibly rich in meanings) which *naturally* (in their very nature) dwarf every historical event and every philosophical or scientific truth.

So in going to Mass and assisting at that bloodless sacrifice, one is simply applying the merits of Christ either to oneself or, as the phrase goes, to one's "friends and benefactors," known or unknown. And nothing could be more natural when it is realized that the Church is strictly a society, though supernatural in character.

Let me point out some immediately obvious conclusions or implications attaching even to the brief suggestions here. First, since all sin is infinitely horrible and insulting to God (we are dependent creatures, owing our entire being to Him), Catholics are *taught*, and generally recognize, that one man is quite as great a sinner as the next. Knowing himself to be essentially imperfect he readily conceives charity for the imperfections of others. But charity for the sinner is quite compatible with intense repulsion from the sin. Moreover, he realizes that any moral virtue which he or anybody may achieve is directly owing to the mercy of God and the merits of Christ. He knows that he can take no credit for any goodness he achieves. And in reverencing the saints, and relics associated with them, the Catholic is venerating the *signs* of God's *favour* towards a creature.

Another important Catholic attitude follows. There is no sense of strain such as arises in Calvinistic quarters where the means of grace are denied, and either a deliberate effort of "the will to believe" is insisted on or else mere predestination is taught.

More important than any other single difference between Catholic attitudes and others is perhaps that the Catholic does not "fear" God, but has every reason to love Him. The *first* thought which a Catholic has of God is that which a man has for a *real* friend. It is only his second thought which may suggest to him how little he deserves such friendship. Taking this fact, together with the social nature of the Church, it is easy to see why Catholics speak so freely and naturally of their prayers and devotions.

There is nothing proper to human nature which is not perfected and assisted by the Church. Every human faculty finds its true use and function only within the Church. That is hard for Protestants to realize, because religion with them is so commonly a matter of restrictions and prohibitions. The Church, on the other hand, is primarily concerned with *action*. Since potency can only become real through act. The Protestant has, or had, a half-truth. He starves on a half loaf, foregoing his rightful heritage, much as the paranoiac imagines his dinner to be poisoned.

This brings up a dozen other matters. One doesn't take the Protestant errors very seriously after one has looked into a dozen or so similar heresies which sprang up in the third and fourth centuries — there were heresies before the third as well as after. And to understand orthodoxy, some study of the history of the Church is necessary.

Orthodoxy is intellectual honesty as regards divine things. Heresy is intellectual and spiritual lying — lying to God Himself. It is thus the most hateful of all sins. The one most bitterly punished by an orthodox state or polity. But there are no longer any orthodox states. This makes it difficult for us to sympathize with historical times when heresy was "persecuted."

Now, a man like Luther was a heretic. He lied to God. He knew the truth. But subsequent Lutherans etc. were never told the truth, and they were denied the sacraments which led to an 'inferior' awareness of the truth. Thus, it requires some considerable 'luck' or effort on the part of a Protestant today to rediscover orthodoxy. That is why most converts tend to be intellectuals, people with special knowledge of history and philosophy. It is true, for example, that a majority of Protestant ministers (even non-Anglican) in America today are *intellectually* convinced of the claims of the Catholic Church. But one can readily appreciate their *practical* obstacles to becoming Catholics. Furthermore it is possible to be intellectually convinced and yet to have no spiritual grace or *motive* to assist one. This latter, in such instances, is lacking simply because the person refuses to pray or to ask for it.

To return to the 'poisoned food' of the paranoiac — I refer, of course, to the Eucharist. Luther used to fall in a fit when celebrating Mass — he was terrified by the actual presence of God owing to his really terrible defection from God. But, perhaps oddly, heresy never begins by attacking dogma. At the time of the Reformation nobody ever denied the reality of God's Presence in the Mass, *at first*. The 'reformers' lied in their hearts, but they pretended to be concerned only with the correction of abuses *within* the Church. Gradually, by appealing to the cupidity of Kings and Princes, they produced schisms, and schisms, such as the Anglican, were soon widened by heresy. But note, the heresies were imposed *from the top*. The *vast* majority of Englishmen were as horrified as they were helpless when the Mass was abolished. There were at least five serious but badly organized revolts. But meantime the aristocracy was bought off by the enormous bribe of monastic lands, and the English people were deprived of the sacraments. At first they thought it would be only for a few years . . . Human weakness accomplished the rest. Today England is returning to the faith.

I just read a most interesting book by Clara Longworth, countess de Chambrun, *Shakespeare Rediscovered*.[1] She produces an enormous amount of evidence to show how *all* of Shakespeare's friends were Catholics, from Richard Field, his printer, to the Earls of Southampton and Essex, his patrons. Even his friend Whitgift, the Archbishop of Canterbury, was a profound Catholic sympathizer. Of course, it has long been known that his father and mother were staunch Catholics, and that his father was ruined, as were the rest of English Catholics, by the enormous fines imposed for non-attendance at Anglican services. Shakespeare himself had to pay about $2,000.00, in our money, to the local Anglican bishop for the privilege of being married by a priest. He was finally driven to London by the persecutions of Sir Thos Lucy (of "humorous" fame).[2] Lucy was one of the most prominent harriers of Catholics of the day.

I merely mention this as an instance of the complete and sordid silence which official English history has imposed on all these long known facts.

You speak, Corinne, of the sufficiency for your present needs of your present beliefs. I fully understand that. As I mentioned, I felt no *need* of Catholic dogma or belief even after I was received into the Church. If ever there was a self-sufficient mind or person (and of course there can never be such, since we are *created* beings) it was I.

---

1   Clara Longworth, comtesse de Chambrun (1873–1954), *Shakespeare Rediscovered: By Means of Public Records, Secret Reports and Private Correspondence Newly Set Forth as Evidence of His Life and Work* (1938).

2   There is a tradition that Sir Thomas Lucy (1532–1600), acting as Justice of the Peace at Stratford-on-Avon, prosecuted Shakespeare for deer-stealing in 1585 and that the poet wrote a ballad about it — an incident that is said to have precipitated his departure for London.

But I came to know so much about orthodoxy that it was impossible to retain my intellectual integrity any longer except by acting. I saw quite clearly that my only alternative was atheism — active hatred of the Church. For, after a certain point one either moves rapidly towards the Church or, equally rapidly, away from it.

I don't think it is unfair of me to talk about these things to you. But I must say, that I am anything but *eager* to do so. For I am more than a little afraid that you may become discouraged. And, since our free will is the most fundamental character we possess (it being insep-arable from the rational nature), I feel the utmost repugnance to influencing another person, except where readiness to inquire, examine, or consider, is obvious.

However, you should know that, in the event of a 'mixed mar-riage,' the non-Catholic is obliged to receive a certain minimum of instruction about the Church, and to agree that the children, if any, should be reared as Catholics. In point of fact, most mixed marriages are not too successful. But neither are most marriages, people being what they are!

Having been a Protestant most of my life, the idea of marrying one seems much more natural to me than it does to a "cradle Catholic." And obviously, the ideal marriage for a convert is with a convert. But life-long Catholics look with intense repugnance on marriage with Protestants. And this I have discovered somewhat to my surprise.

You and I are faced with one of those situations (which fortunately are not very numerous in one lifetime) which cannot possibly be *ade-quately* judged beforehand. It strikes me as a colossal gamble, or rather, a very great adventure. And personally I am considerably exhilarated by the risks! This exhilaration may compensate for the absence of "romance"! The greatness of the adventure perhaps con-sists partly in the fact that as a Catholic I can marry only once! But, as with being born, perhaps once is quite sufficient! In the Church, you know, there is a great heightening of every moment of experi-ence, since every moment is played against a supernatural backdrop. Nothing can be humdrum in this scheme. Every least act of the mind has infinite significance. (Dostoevsky, by the way, is one of the few novelists who has succeeded in *realizing* this in art. In the world of Passos, on the other hand, no act has any significance. There are *no* standards beyond those of immediate sensation. Passos himself rec-ognizes this, and, in consequence presents the situation not despairingly but satirically.) And just as there is nothing good or true which is not Catholic, so there are a great many things which can be had only by the Catholic. Needless to say, however, most Catholics are too lazy or too feeble to use what they possess. And particularly in America where the main currents of life are profoundly anti-Catholic, the average Catholic is too timid, too overawed by the surrounding material "splendour," to feel able to be anything but an 'interior' Catholic. As the "splendour" rapidly becomes ludicrous and stupid the Church will press forward in America. This is happening now.

You speak quite truly of my lack of "worldly" ambition. *Perhaps* this lack in me is simply a lack of competence for such success. But please don't imagine that I despise such competence, I am prepared to do all I can to achieve a reasonable "standard of living." My trouble, of course, is that I now enjoy such a high standard of living (most students can have pleasures that no money can ever command) that I am loath to sacrifice my intellectual standards to achieve a more popular success. The question then arises, can I reconcile the two things? Is it possible to achieve success through sheer excellence? Well, I know many who have done so. But many more, who are equally excellent, do not. And my unyielding, independent temperament is agin me here. I simply can't bring myself to curry favour among men whom I consider inferior in ability. But I can be utterly congenial with people whom I know to be equal or superior — and with inferiors from whom I expect nothing, or on whom I depend for nothing. Really, Corinne, I'm not boasting about this. It is not, perhaps, entirely creditable to be this way.

Nor do I see how the most marvellous possible wife (do you recognize yourself!) could do much to alter this. But she could undoubtedly do a very great deal to help a man along the road to excellence. I am very aggressive, very ardent in anything I do; but I need *drive*. There are any number of ways in which you could help me. But I hope you know that I would never ask or require it. It is quite obvious, though, that if you were not to help me, but simply expected things to happen by magic, we would fail miserably.

So far as money is concerned. I have never been tempted to spend more than I have. My *personal* expenditures always have and always will be small (books perhaps a slight exception here!). I have never been able to understand why a man earning a fixed stipend should concern himself about money. My "instinct" is to turn all of it over to the other partner in the enterprise! This I have heard is the traditional European method. It strikes me as utterly natural. Isn't it queer, at first glance, that in America of all places, where women are ostensibly the *only* object of "money-making," that men should "budget" them? It is of course merely another evidence that the American male has an *essential* contempt for, as well as fear of, women.

Well, I've arranged my year's leave of absence with Father McCabe.[3] So it's Cambridge now, without query. It will be ever so much more satisfactory to have the Ph.D.[4] And besides, it will give me a most refreshing year, and one in which to get a job of "scholarship" done, or at least on the way to completion. Most of my work is going to be critical, I can see. One *must* get things into print, you know, in order to command attention and salary. Good teaching goes for nothing in our universities today.

Incidentally, don't concern yourself over the "regrettable incident"[5] cited in the last letter. There was nothing *scandalous* about it!

Thought you might enjoy two of my freshmen's exam papers. I didn't choose the topic, and think it a poor one. Their prepared themes are much better than this, naturally.

By the way, could you send back the Passos[6] as soon as you have done with it? Hate to stop this. Do send some more letters like the last one! You are dear to me beyond thinking, Corinne —

Yours,
Marshall

---

3   Father William H. McCabe, S.J., was Chairman of the English Department at Saint Louis University.

4   McLuhan's Ph.D. thesis, accepted by Cambridge in 1943, was "The Place of Thomas Nashe in the Learning of His Time." The Elizabethan pamphleteer Thomas Nashe (1567–1601) — who had been a student at St. John's College, Cambridge — wrote several dramas and satires in the decade before his early death, along with the first picaresque romance in English, *The Unfortunate Traveller; or The Life of Jacke Wilton* (1564), a tale of adventure that includes much literary parody and pastiche. The thesis (as explained in McLuhan's abstract) focused on the conflict that existed in the world of sixteenth-century learning between those who were for or against the patristic method — based on grammar, dialectics, and rhetoric — in theology and formal expression, particularly on the quarrel between Gabriel Harvey (c. 1550–1631), who turned his back on classical rhetoric after leaving Cambridge, and Nashe, who became "a daring exponent of the traditional patristic program of learning and eloquence." The thesis also includes a history of the trivium, the medieval university course of grammar, rhetoric, and logic.

5   This might refer to the fact that Mrs. Lewis had a party for McLuhan while he was visiting Corinne Lewis in Fort Worth to which she also invited several young men friends of Corinne's, including one who had hoped to marry her.

6   The trilogy *USA* (1938) by John Dos Passos.

PART
2

The Church's Understanding
of Media

4

Communication Media:

Makers of the Modern World

I enjoyed that introduction, because it was apparently malicious — in a friendly way. I can tell you right off that there is no place that I'd rather be talking, or anybody that I'd rather be talking to, than right here, to you. I'm going to be fairly brief. I have a few notes here to begin with, a few headings on this memo sheet to open up with.

Let us start directly with a mention of what I consider to be an experience which we all share, all the time — the global-village atmosphere of the twentieth century. Whether you conceptualize it or whether you verbalize it, you live in a global situation in which every event modifies and affects every other event. Not at some *remote* time, not long after the first one, but at the *same* time. In other words, whatever happens today affects everything that happens today TODAY, not tomorrow.

Now, the way and degree in which these events interpenetrate varies. And the degree to which they enter the minds of decision-makers varies. But in the world about us, the endless decisions that are being taken by many kinds of people are taken habitually in an atmosphere in which everything happens at once.

∞ *Lightly edited transcript of an informal address, given at the twelfth annual Seminarians' Conference, St. Michael's College, University of Toronto, 29-31 August 1959, and published in the volume,* Communications and the Word of God, *by St. Michael's College, pages 9-22.*

You can see a rather strange and bizarre image of that process in changes that have taken place in Bay Street [Toronto's financial district] firms. For example, one firm (which I visited precisely to find out what changes have been occurring in recent months) called Harris Associates, which provides international service for investors, has recently made radical changes in their office space. All of the top brass now sit in a room facing each other, and the lower executives have private offices. The lower members of the executive staff are permitted private space because their immediate inter-association and decision-making is not so important. But those men who have to make the big decisions minute by minute as the teletypes work — those men have to be looking straight at each other all the time. They call this the partners' room. The eight partners sit at the single table all day: formerly they had private offices where they could read memos à la Parkinson's Law and write notes to people, read newspapers and so on. But now the decisions they have to make are speeded up to such a degree that private offices are impractical.

But this global-village world of ours is entirely the result of the force of telegraphic, teletyped communication — information that is moving at a relatively instantaneous rate. This increasingly terrifies ordinary people in the community. The general atmosphere in which they live is one in which total global information presses upon them daily as a continuous environment bringing with it all of the dangers in decision-making. They have no feelings about this: it's just their environment, the climate in which they live.

Now I'll shift away from that to the arts and what they have to do with the situation in which we exist. One thing which characterized the finer arts — poetry, painting, music — areas with which we're all familiar — for more than a century, but certainly for the past century, has been a continued insistence on their relevance to daily living. There has been quite an impressive chorus of urgent requests in all fields that we take seriously the arts as basic social factors of enlightenment and guidance and training.

This mounting urgency in the arts has a core that is, I think, related to the concept of relevance. The artist no longer suggests that art is something that you can take or leave, that it's for some people and not for other people: the artist insists on his absolute relevance. I'm sure this note was never heard in the Renaissance, or at any time before now. The concept of relevance is a twentieth-century concept. The antithetic concept, the one really opposed to it, is that of perspective, point of view. Perspective is irrelevant. Relevance is over-all and concerns all, and has nothing to do with temperament, bias, preference, etc.: it has an objective quality of need and urgency.

Now, I don't think that the artists have done very well in verbalizing their insistence; but let me mention in this regard the words of Gilson in *Painting and Reality*. There he mentions that, after Giotto in the thirteenth century, painting increasingly assumes the task of reporting the outside world, of providing precise information about external things, and it abandons the previous aim of painting which had been merely to be a thing. Up until Giotto, says Gilson, painting had been a thing, not about something, not a report, not information — just a *thing*. From Giotto to Cézanne, art tends, he says, *to be* nothing — but *about* things. Pictorial information; from many points of view. The rise of perspective is contemporary with or coincides with this same stress. After Cézanne painting once more becomes a thing, no longer a report about things. It is just *thing*, and you know how baffling this is to many people. When they come across a painting or sculpture and can't identify its correspondence with some external object they feel they're being cheated. This idea that a painting doesn't correspond to or report about some *thing* still baffles people.

Well, Cézanne and his followers, or those who followed after him anyway, had, I think, quite adequate reasons for abandoning perspective and pictorial space in favour of formal space in which, say, a pair of shoes is allowed to create its own world and is not reported from another world or stuck into a space with other objects. The simple discovery that was made in all the arts around 1860–1870 was that things have formal character and are quite able to speak for themselves. The artist's role is not to stress himself or his own point of view but to let things sing and talk, to release the forms within them.

This began in [Gerard Manley] Hopkins. Father Hopkins was trying desperately to say this, but all he succeeded in doing was inventing a couple of very quaint terms like "instress" and "inscape" and "sprung rhythm." All these terms mean the same thing: they mean that the *thingness* of things must come through them at you and must not be reported or described.

The testimony of the artist in the past century and a half cannot, I think, be easily indicted as philosophically-biased or as emanating from within a school of philosophy. It is a kind of existential testimony to pressures and exigencies and urgencies to which they reacted totally. One way of putting it would be to say that the artists took up the cause of formal causality about 1800 after the philosophers had abandoned it — and that goes for Catholic philosophers too. They also abandoned it. Formal causality disappeared, according to reports I have had from philosophers, about Descartes' time as an object of serious interest. It continues to be referred to but, as an object of serious concentration, formal causality disappears with Descartes. I can explain later why I think that may have happened, but that isn't my point.

My point is that the artists, with the romantics, in a most earnest manner took up the cause of formal causality. Only, they talked about formal causality as if it were art in which the forms of things began to be insisted upon as having something to say to man and, above all, that they had the power to train human sensibility. Not the power to impose systems of thought but to train human sensibility. All of the romantics in all fields have been harping (and "harping" is a good word) on that theme — that art has the power to train human sensibility, to give you eyes, to give you ears.

Alexander Pope, in the 1720s, published first drafts of *The Dunciad*. That amazing work is an epic song announcing universal disaster to the world:

> She comes! she comes! the sable Throne behold
> Of Night primeval, and of Chaos old!

The darkness he saw settling over the earth and the European spirit was the darkness of books. The first lines of the [original] poem are

> Books and the man I sing, the first who brings
> The Smithfield muses to the ears of kings

— kings who substitute the best-seller for taut, oral counsel in the ears of monarchy. *The Dunciad* is an epic to the disaster of books, mass-produced books, swarms of books, settling upon the human spirit. I'm not saying that Pope was right; I'm simply saying that he offered this testimony in 1720.

Shortly after, within ten years, the poets took up that song. The romantics with consistent voice denounced literary culture for the next century and more as a darkener of the human spirit and simply said that if you're going to have eyes and ears, if you're going to have any vitality at all, you'll have to ignore it. These are the sentiments, too, of Wordsworth and Coleridge, of Shelley and Keats and the pre-Raphaelites, even of Ruskin. They began to talk instead in terms of the old medieval language of the Book of Nature. Any book except the printed book was better for the spirit of man. This common, unified testimony came from all the artists. But it took a strange turn in our time.

Artists — people like Pound, Joyce, and Wyndham Lewis (Mr. Eliot is a little more prudent, but he meant the same things as these others did), and Yeats, of course — began to insist that if society was to be saved in even an elementary way it would only be by putting artists in charge. They said that the reason was the need to orchestrate many interests, to create a new harmony, a new equilibrium. Specialized interests were heading towards disaster and disorganization and collapse: an artist alone could navigate through these times. Well, at the present moment, this idea is shared by the top men. The artist in many fields, in industrial design, in motivational research, in executive training, in executive life itself, is going back into the control tower very fast. And that's no trickle: they're all going back.

Don't ask me if this is a good thing. I don't feel that any person is able yet to make value judgments of that sort. Our job is diagnosis and observation prior to judgment. But I have noticed over and over again that when people ask in the middle of some effort to chart an actual development, "Is this a good thing?" they always mean, "Is this a good thing for me?" "How does it affect me? — I'm a doctor." Or "How will it affect me? — I'm an architect." They don't mean, "Is it good?" They mean, "What will it do to me?" It took me years to find out what they really meant by this strange constant request for value judgment. It's a Protestant sort of fixation, this "Is it a good or a bad thing?" It comes from an obsession with efficient causes at an applied moment. The actual obsession with efficient causality — what you call activism — is basic to the Protestant outlook.

To return to art and formal causality for the moment: a formal cause exerts its pressure non-verbally and non-conservatively. Any substantial form impresses itself upon you without benefit of awareness or conscious attention on your part. You can be conscious about it if you like, but a tree, grass, stones, the world of forms in which we live impresses us steadily and constantly without intermission, without benefit of words or thoughts. They are total in their action upon us. It doesn't matter what theory we may have about them: their effect upon us is quite independent of any thought we have about them.

It is the same with a work of art. The meaning of a work of art, as the artists of past centuries can tell us, has nothing to do with what you think about it. It has to do with its action upon you. It is a form: it acts upon you. It invades your senses. It re-structures your outlook. It completely changes your attitudes, your wave-lengths. So our attitudes, our sensibilities, are completely altered by new forms, regardless of what we think about them. This is not an irrational statement, or a philosophical notion. It is a simple fact of experience.

I am prepared to say that the new media of communication are forms — not simple ones, but complex forms. But they are forms. And their effect upon us is that of forms, not of ideas or of concepts. The editorials in a newspaper have nothing to do with the effect of the newspaper on you. Whether it is *Pravda*, the *New York Times*, or the *Toronto Daily Star* makes no difference as far as the formal, causal pressure of that newspaper on those concerned. Just why people should be so obsessed by what they suppose to be the content of these forms, and so completely unaware of the formal structure and the formal causes of such forms, I do not understand.

The artists have been telling us this in their own way for a long time. Don't be taken in by the so-called content of a work of art because it is just a sugar coating to slip past your conscious awareness to let the real work of art do its work upon you unimpeded. Artists have been telling us this for centuries. Hopkins said it, and everyone since Hopkins: the so-called meaning is a way of lowering your guard so the form can work upon you. And the artist who sharpens his work to a high and good moral purpose gets past the guard of a good many people with the form. He even gets past his own guard: he is often the victim of his own strategies. So why is it impossible to take one thing at a time in the world we live in? The global village is not a place where one thing happens at a time. Everything happens at once. What we must have, therefore, is a means of coping with an all-at-once world. The artist and philosopher can perhaps help here.

A formal cause — let me just anticipate a little: we can go into more depth later — as it exists in an actual technical situation has a profound proportion to our senses. It is impossible for man to create any form of technology which is not proportional to the senses whether it is a telephone or radio or print, or any other language.

Or put it this way: they say that it is impossible that there could ever be a scientific concept that is not embedded in the vernacular tongue of the scientist, and that has not been embedded there for many centuries. You cannot conceive a form of scientific hypothesis which is not part of your own language, implicit in that language. All the mathematics in the world are externalizations of certain linguistic patterns. What the poets were saying — now more widely appreciated — was that the language itself embodies the greatest body of scientific intuition possible. The proportionalities in things, and between things and our senses, and so embodied in language itself, are inexhaustible.

The particular technology of a time releases some of that inexhaustible store of analogical intuition and experience which IS language. So television releases within language a whole body of resources which has been bound up there for centuries. But this does not depend upon concepts. It has to do with sensibility and observation — analogical perception, right in the structure of language itself.

Let me mention another basic matter in this connection. In an all-at-once order of the electronic type, where information moves instantly and en masse, the only possible form of intelligible order is auditory. Harmony can be made of a great mass of seemingly disconnected fragments, but it is impossible to have visual order made of a vast unassorted mass of data, as is typical of every moment of experience in the electronic age: you cannot fill it all in.

Look what happens to the newspaper page under the impact of the telegraph. When the telegraph began to exert direct pressure upon the structure of news, from about 1850 and certainly thereafter, the news began to flow in so fast that it was impossible to give it visual order or any kind of perspective or point of view. If you are going to receive reports from news services from around the entire globe you cannot ask or expect your reporters around the globe to have a single consistent point of view. At the same time, what they send in is quite useless because it cannot be ordered into a single day's news unless it does have a single point of view. You as editor cannot assemble it under a single date-line at high speed unless it has some form of consistency. So they hit upon what is known as objective reporting — which has nothing to do with objectivity. It means get rid of all feelings, all attitudes; just report in neutral form and we will assemble these neutral blocks into a mosaic. But you cannot have your daily mosaic if your authors have private points of view.

Now consider your local papers. The *"Tely"* [the Toronto *Telegram*] and the *"Star"* [the *Toronto Daily Star*] follow that format of the absolutely crazy kaleidoscopic mosaic. The *"Globe"* [the *Globe and Mail*] tries desperately to retain the old pre-telegraph literary style of point of view. But a newspaper with a point of view is a literary product: it is not telegraphic. The *New York Times* and *Pravda* are pre-telegraphic: the Soviet Union will have nothing to do with the telegraph as a newspaper influence. They resist to the utmost the effect of technology in areas that affect public opinion. All I am saying is this: people in our world automatically discovered the relevance and inevitability of *auditory order* and the irrelevance of *visual order*.

The ordinary kid in the classroom today has this enormous built-in bias. In the world he lives in, *auditory order* is the only kind he has ever experienced, whether from a newspaper, television, movie, or top-sixty, or anything else. *Auditory order*, an all-at-once sort of "being with it," harmonizing equilibrium and so on, he understands. But when he is presented with *visual order*, in which a subject is given to him in visual terms, one thing following another, he finds it absolutely meaningless. And teachers don't seem to understand why children should feel this frightful conflict between these two kinds of order.

I don't think the matter is limited to children, although it has become pathological by the fifteen-year level. After all, television is ten years old [this is 1959], so an average fifteen-year-old has grown up entirely on television. There should be quite a difference between the mentalities of a fifteen- and a twenty-year-old: there should be quite a cultural gap in those people.

Let us look at this matter of *auditory order* and *visual order*. The Middle Ages were not visual: they were oral in their ideas of things. There was no perspective, no point of view: it was all-at-once, mosaic. Their concept of order and their concept of learning was oral; everything happened at once. You gradually penetrated a field deeper and deeper, but you took the whole field simultaneously. The idea of taking one thing at a time and of there being a natural sequence in which to present order was inconceivable to them. It would be like trying to present to a primitive African a page of print and explaining to him that all those marks were words that he spoke every day and that they followed each other in those lines. It would be fantasy. Show the same African a picture or a snapshot of himself: it would take quite a while to explain the relation between him and those strange shapes on the card. Without training, he can't see a picture or adopt a point of view. Whether you hold it upside-down or sideways makes no difference to him at all.

There is no upside-down until you learn to read and write: psychologists have at least shown this. Until you learn to read and write and notice letters on a line right-side up, there is no horizontal or vertical axis in the visible world. Cave painters used no horizontal or visual axis. They painted. They would be just as happy painting on this microphone head as anywhere else, such as back here or under here, and they painted one picture on top of another and all around — like the levels of meaning in Scriptural study in the Middle Ages. There was no question that one meaning should follow another; they were all together, all over the place, all through each other.

The pre-literate man lives in a world that is auditory in that way. Everything penetrates everything else. Everything is at once. He doesn't sort things out and put them in places; he lives in an all-at-once world because he lives by ear. It's only after long periods of literacy that people begin to trust their eyes and begin to follow the structure of planes and lines and lines of force that the eyes experience. The eye is to the pre-literate man a very inferior organ.

Likewise, I think that you'll find that the average student today regards the classroom as a very inferior means of experience and not as a possible source of order at all. So when you present him with a curriculum structured visually, with subjects ordered side by side each in its special compartment, and that follow one another, I think you'll find exactly zero results in teaching. Don't ask me if this is a "bad thing." It is a very "bad thing" for us who have been trained in a visual order, but then we wouldn't survive five minutes in a thirteenth-century classroom. We couldn't cope with their ways of handling experience in a rush, everything at once, every facet, all sides — the total encyclopedia of knowledge all at once.

The sixteenth-century humanist, after a century of print, turned on the schoolman and said "Words, words, words, words . . . shut up!" because, after reading print for a century he had come to think of words as following each other distinctly, visually. The schoolman had become to him an absolutely grotesque character, a barbarian who just yattered and nattered on and on. Such, within a hundred years of

Gutenberg, was the normal reaction of the humanist to the auditory man.

The sixteenth-century discovery that there was such a thing as visual order has been the subject of much comment by Fr. Walter Ong in his recent works, particularly in his *Ramus, Method and the Decay of Dialogue*. He details the rise of this visual habit of ordering knowledge and the consequent decay of dialogue in forms of instruction and forms of learning. To come back to our own time: a form like this microphone has brought back dialogue in familiar forms like panels and round-tables and so on. The very fact that we're here, talking in this way, testifies to the power of this thing in the community at large.

Here's a curious thing: if a newspaperman interviews an expert of any sort, the newspaperman is not expected to know anything about the subject. He's just the "man-in-the-street" talking to the expert, and his job is to listen to the noises the expert makes for some newsworthy item and to spell that out in his medium. Everybody complains, upon being quoted in the press, "But I didn't say that." Naturally not, because the newspaperman's job is to translate whatever you said into his medium, for the ordinary guy. But in a radio interview, an ordinary guy talking with an expert makes for poor dialogue. This instrument [tapping the microphone] returns us to the dialogue form in which experts talk to experts. For entertainment or effective presentation, there's no use just asking a few vague or silly questions of, say, an expert analyst on armaments. From the point of view of public acceptance you've got to have someone who understands the subject.

In other words, the all-at-once electronic media compel us back to the dialogue form. In terms of formal causality, the dialogue is a necessity of education today. The old idea of presenting packaged information one-thing-at-a-time, visually-ordered, is completely at variance with our electronic media. I'm talking about their formal structure.

Let me mention another overall factor. The written word (print aside) is a detribalizing force. Why does writing smash the tribe wide open and segment it into individuals? This happened in the Greco-Roman world — in fact it was the Greco-Roman world. The lines of the famous roads that made the empires were literally paper-routes; when papyrus ended, they ended. Innis has documented this in *Empire and Communication*. With written, transportable communication you can organize the most remote outpost: you can have the same pattern of organization in Spain, Africa, Greece — everywhere at the same time. But you cannot do this orally. Aural structure goes as far as you can hear, and that is the size of the village compound — until this mike comes along and then you can hear everywhere at once and everywhere at once becomes a village. Here and now we have a fantastic culture-clash of formal causes absolutely antithetical.

What, for example, are some of the detribalizing factors in writing? In the first place there is the psychological effect from giving a visual form to the spoken word. There the formal cause is not paper or parchment. The great formal factor is the simple translation of the audible into the visible, and the human consequences that derive from that act of translation are enormous. The fact is that you pay attention to written words in a new way. You inspect them statically and develop the habit of segmenting or arresting the movements of the mind. This gives man the power of withdrawing from that auditory structure which is the tribe. He just breaks off. He withdraws into a private world created by his ability to inspect static aspects of thought and information.

I'll mention in passing that, because of its static aspect, the written word inspires the human mind with doubt. This is the habit of the eye inspecting writing: black-white . . . yes-no . . . maybe yes–maybe no. Scepticism is the very form of written culture. There are no doubters in an auditory society (from a missionary's point of view this can be pretty devastating). This is the world we are moving into: auditory order once more gives people a complete and total togetherness of assertion. No doubts. And individualism of course will be at a very heavy discount, because what does it mean? It is a visual form of ordering. Togetherness and collective forms of structure are the only possible forms of social order. Some of you here may know a lot more about this than I.

It has often struck me that the Nazis were the victims of radio in the sense that radio had the power to retribalize that unfortunate part of the world which had been made literate later than most parts of Europe. Admiral Speer said at the Nuremberg trials that the cause of Nazism was the teletype, the telephone, the radio. He said they made it possible to bypass all the formal social structures, all the formal orders written by responsible people. Anybody could pick up the telephone and talk to anybody. This, he said, destroyed totally the civilized forms of German proceeding.

In our world, the telephone has completely restructured the character of management and decision-making, and in those sheets [handed out beforehand] you'll find a passage from Peter Drucker in which he explains the tremendous revolution taking place in the world of managers. He describes the change but does not try to diagnose a cause. The change he describes is from visual to auditory order. When someone like [William H.] Whyte [Jr.] says, in *The Organization Man*, that these are "bad things," he confuses the issue terribly. He brings alarm without understanding, smoke and heat without light. Again, for some strange reason the Protestants prefer moral alarm to understanding. A strange, tremendous, self-righteous charge they get from being morally alarmed! The one thing they detest is the slightest understanding.

I see a name noted here which I would like to mention before I ask for questions: Mircea Eliade. His book, *The Sacred and the Profane*, studies two kinds of space and two kinds of time. Eliade considers archaic man, pre-literate man, on the one hand, and Western man, literate man, on the other. He says that, for Western man, time is continuous and homogeneous, and space is likewise continuous and homogeneous. But for pre-literate or archaic man, no two times or two spaces could be alike. Now this is the point: for the auditory man, no two times, no two spaces could be alike. Each is unique. Everything has its own structure. This is what brings the stress on existentialism.

In terms of eye and ear, both are completely right, but when one begins making value judgments about the other — as Bergson did — the trouble begins. Bergson simply went over to the ear side of things and denounced the visual order as the enemy of all Being. You can see what enthusiasm he was able to rally behind him. As long as you take a firm moral stand in the Western world you will rally a great number of people to your cause regardless of how deficient you are in understanding the situation.

Wyndham Lewis tried to answer Bergson and the ear men in terms of the eye order. Lewis spent his whole life simply saying Western man is an eye man: if he abandons the primacy of the eye in structuring his experience he is finished. Lewis spent his whole life in a magnificent rebuttal of the ear men of his time — and got nowhere because he was not a moralist. He didn't know how to rally that great backlog of Protestant moral fury to support his hypothesis.

5

Keys to the Electronic Revolution:
First Conversation with Pierre Babin

Pierre Babin: Doctor McLuhan, you are recognized as a specialist in mass media and for having devoted yourself to analyzing their effects on our cultures. Your research brings to light the analogous situations brought about in the history of human communication, and especially brings to light the upheavals produced in the West by the advent of print. As a professor of literature and art history, you have always been interested in cultural mutation and in its psychological and social roots.

Allow me to address myself today more specifically to the man and Christian that you are. As a Christian, have you examined the effects that such a context has on the Church and, more precisely, on faith?

Marshall McLuhan: I would prefer that most questions of that sort be dealt with by theologians, but they do not seem to be interested. I do not think that the powerful forces imposed on us by electricity have been considered at all by theologians and liturgists. My conversations at St. Michael's College give me the impression that nothing has been looked at in this area, in spite of its importance. These great movements have gone unnoticed.

Theologians have the impression, I imagine, that everything will

∞ *From* Autre homme, autre chrétien à l'âge électronique, *Lyon: Editions du Chalet, 1977. Translated by Wayne Constantineau.*

return to normal in a very short time. Well, no! Things will not re-stabilize. At the speed of light, in a culture that changes from day to day, when we can live a century in ten years, when every day of our lives we can pass through at least a hundred years of historical development, then we have to adapt our psychic and physical lives so that they change at the same rate.

The task horrifies us. We are not designed to change at such a pace. Alvin Toffler called it "Future Shock": "We are going too fast, we cannot adapt." At this speed, we cannot adapt to anything. Our entire mode of thought is based on equilibrium: "Things will return to normal," we think. But equilibrium is a principle inherited from Newton. No balance is possible at the speed of light, in economics, in physics, in the Church, or wherever . . .

Babin: Is there nothing left to do but to be carried away by the current? Have you not yourself searched for the keys to understanding change and thus take away its frightening character of blind and absurd fatality?

McLuhan: I think that, in effect, we can start by examining one by one the powerful and fundamental causes of these changes, researching them seriously. Then we would find some astonishing structural forms that allow us to introduce order into the chaos of contemporary experience.

Babin: If I follow you correctly, in order to understand what is happening today to faith and the Church, we need to find, in the history of culture and in our other sciences, supple frameworks along which cultural forces and phenomena organize themselves. Isn't that what you have done with Gutenberg and the invasion of print in the sixteenth century?

McLuhan: Yes, I have worked a long time on that. I even became a Catholic while studying the Renaissance almost exclusively. I became aware of the fact that the Church was destroyed or dismembered in that era by a stupid historical blunder, by a technology. Medieval culture based on manuscript allowed for a style of communal life very different from the mass community which appeared with print. The Gutenberg revolution made everyone a reader. From day to day, reading became accessible to anybody, thanks to the abundance of available texts.

In the manuscript era, texts were rare, which explains the small number of readers. Books [manuscripts] were very costly. A lot of time was required to make them and to read them.

The printed book accelerated the entire operation and, in doing so, completely modified the image of the old human community. In the same manner, in our time, we can say that the automobile, by its new type of acceleration, destroyed the traditional human community — even more so than print did. No one stays in one place long enough to strike up an acquaintance with anyone.

So Gutenberg was the first important step in the process of accelerating relations between people. Print provoked the development of nationalism, because, for the first time, everyone could see their mother tongue and not just hear it. In fact, people's consciousness of their national identity took root in a visual ground. The world of print is visual.

But, the eye isn't a unifying force. It tends towards fragmentation. It allows each person to have his own point of view and to hold to it. Gutenberg thus accents separation in space and in time. With the book, one can withdraw inward, in the egocentric and psychological sense of this term, and not, indeed, in the spiritual sense. The printed alphabet creates, in large measure, fragmentation.

Babin: According to you, the key, here, would have been the sudden passage from an oral and acoustic culture to a visual one. Can this key help us to understand what happened in the Church?

McLuhan: It is sure that making it possible for each reader to have exactly the same word in front of him at each instant had a considerable effect on doctrine. Each could thus think alone, look at it and invent his own particular point of view. Things did not happen this way in manuscript tradition, because the operation was much more acoustic than visual, and because transmission mostly came about orally.

The same goes for the scholastic method of discussion, the *questiones disputatae*. All of that was oral. But Luther and the first Protestants were "schoolmen" who were trained in literacy. They transposed the old method of scholastic discussion into the new visual order: they thus used the new discovery of print to dig the trench that separated them from the Roman Church. Furthermore, that is what gave the Protestant movement such impetus and power. This slide towards the visual also explains the appearance of sects. The word sect evokes visual fragmentation. Sects separated from one another according to visual criteria.

Recall the famous incident [in Hawthorne's novel, *The Scarlet Letter*] of the woman who belonged to a puritan sect in New England. She was convicted of adultery and branded with an "A." The idea of isolating her from the rest of the world with a scarlet mark characterizes those puritans who loved to classify people according to their opinions and attitudes. Suddenly, with Gutenberg, classification took on enormous importance, including classification of religious attitudes and dogma.

Babin: Given the shifting perspective from the oral to the visual, or its reverse, how do you explain what is happening today in the Church?

McLuhan: In order to understand this, we must place the Gutenberg incident in a much wider context, as the last stage of the visual in all of its domains.

Let me mention, first, that the Church came into being when the Greek phonetic alphabet was still in its first stages. Greco-Roman culture was still in its infancy when the Church came into being. Of course, this wasn't a simple historical accident, but an act of Providence. However, no one has studied this point in the history of religions. We assume that this goes without saying, and we do not even mention that it involves, for the Church, an event of exceptional importance. I have looked around for documentation on this subject, but very little exists, barely a few articles here and there.

But pre-Platonic Greek culture, that is to say, pre-alphabetic, was based on the magical use of speech: it also furnished man with a particular theory of communication and psychic change. The pre-Socratics, Heraclitus in particular, were acoustic people. They lived in a world abounding with voids, gaps, and intervals. For them, things stirred, intersected, and reacted on each other.

When the alphabet arrived, there suddenly surfaced thinkers like Parmenides and the first logicians who wanted to logically connect all beings. The man of the alphabetic age declared: all is static, all is fixed. That is visual man, logical man — Plato and Aristotle. It created an enormous revolution, but it is nevertheless true that it only affected a small number of people. The Greek population was tiny and only a few knew how to read.

That's how, paradoxically, the Church found itself embodied from its very beginnings in the only culture that preferred fixed and solid positions. The Church, which offers to man and demands of him a constant change of heart, wrapped itself in a visual culture that placed static permanence above all other values. This Greco-Roman culture, which seems to have been imposed on the Church like a shell on a turtle, doesn't allow for any possibility for a supple theory of change and of communication. It is this hard shell that stands between the Church and the other cultures of the world, all of which have accommodating, flexible, evolving forms.

Babin: But didn't you say, just a moment ago, that medieval culture was, as a whole, oral and acoustic?

McLuhan: Obviously, it is a paradox, a way of seeing things from several angles at a time. Paradox is quite normal in matters of religion. Using paradox made G. K. Chesterton famous: he always saw more than one aspect in a question. On the other hand, the orthodox person, in the etymological sense of the term, confines himself to one aspect only.

Remember that in manuscript culture very few people knew how to read and write; the vast majority belonged to an oral tradition. However, the hierarchy of the Church found itself being influenced more and more by writing. Rome in particular, in its role of authority, was oriented towards the visual, towards the written document, towards the type of authority that emerges from eye-based civilizations. That is why all the old Eastern (e.g., Greek Orthodox) Churches rejected it.

However, if it is true that the first effect of cheaply printed books was to create the illusion of self-sufficiency and private authority, its ultimate effect was to homogenize human perception and sensibility by making centralization possible to an extent previously unknown.

The Roman Church avoided as much as possible the individualizing effect of print, and, through a centralized program of educational, liturgical, and devotional uniformity, from the outset made the book a factor in collective experience.

But now an electric world is unfolding, acoustic in nature because it is instantaneous and simultaneous. It is formed as a vast global resonant unity. It ignores all forms of specialization, all fragmentation, all logic. Faced with this invasion, Greco-Roman culture cannot resist, and it is in the process of rapidly falling apart, abruptly and suddenly, so much so that we faced an unbelievable crisis. The Church is watching its cultural infrastructure crumble beneath its feet. When everything happens at the speed of light — at electric speed — the Greco-Roman world gives way. Doubtless the Church was always built for this civilization, but there is nothing in the new technology to sustain it. Of course, there will be a strong reaction when we catch our breath, but for now our young have been conquered by this electric world.

When you are on the air you are, in a way, everywhere at once. Electric man is a "super angel." When you are on the telephone you have no body. And, while your voice is there, you and the people you speak to are here, at the same time. Electric man has no bodily being. He is literally *dis*-carnate. But a discarnate world, like the one we now live in, is a tremendous menace to an incarnate Church, and its theologians haven't even deemed it worthwhile to examine the fact.

Babin: Do your interpretive keys, your probes, shed any light on the relationships between East and West?

McLuhan: Let us speak, first of all, about Eastern man in general. He chooses nirvana, the "void" or nothingness. For him, all the physical manifestations that science studies are bad, even the fact that he has some existence at all. He ignores private identity and, with it, the isolation of the individual as it is experienced by the alphabetized Westerner. For the Easterner, the human condition is focused on the group, the tribe, the family. According to Zen Buddhism, you have to immerse yourself in things and efface the self; you have to disappear. The Oriental opposes technology and innovation because he is acutely aware of their magical power to transform the world. He turns inward. His universe is of an oral and acoustic type.

The same characteristics apply to the Eastern Church as a whole. It, too, is acoustic in nature. It tends towards internalization.

However, over the last hundred years, the West has become increasingly interested in all forms of Eastern art, poetry, painting, and music. But at the same time that the Oriental began his march towards the West and towards externalization, the Orient, China and India in particular, began the process of abandoning the interior life in favour of external goals and objectives. What Orientals want now is quantity and assembly-line production. The Orient no longer wants to be oriental: they want our old way of life. They are prepared to give up everything they have in order to acquire our old nineteenth-century stuff, the clothes that we want to get rid of. We think that they have lost their heads because we want to be what they are and they want to be who we were.

Will we remain strangers, like people who pass each other in the night?

Babin: Could we use the same keys to interpret the schism that arose at the time of the Reformation?

McLuhan: Of course. As long as we remember that Protestantism had a doctrinal as well as a political side. The countries situated just outside of the Roman territorial orbit, that is, outside of Spain's, France's, and Italy's Latin traditions — almost all of them automatically became Protestant for reasons more political than doctrinal. What I mean is that in religious matters all "under-developed" or tribal nations consider themselves to be their own Popes.

I use the word *tribal*, here, without value judgment, but purely structurally, to refer to places where the oral tradition, decentralization, and cultural diversity based on the ear and physical contact, dominate. Switzerland, Germany, Scotland, England, Scandinavia, on the periphery of the Roman sphere, have had a lot of difficulty accepting the bureaucratic homogeneity and specialization of the Latin core. These relatively tribal communities, with their strongly paternalistic stress on the head of the family, were not inclined to submit to the dictates of the Latin people, largely dominated by writing and marked by a preference for centralism. We could expect from the Eastern community even less inclination to submit to the Church's bureaucratic centralism.

It is the resurgence of Protestantism in the contemporary Catholic church that prompted me to outline these events. Paradoxically, in the sixteenth century the printed book, with its accent on the visual, first impressed itself on, or found favour in, countries with oral traditions. We find the same paradox today in the world of Vatican II, where acoustic man reappears amidst the great nineteenth-century bureaucracies still maintained by our political, educational, and religious institutions. Acoustic or tribal man reacts like a deviant or Protestant, a rebel, when he opposes the centralized bureaucracies and legalistic hierarchies which we inherited from the alphabet.

Babin: Are the cultural and geographic phenomena of which you have spoken not rooted even in the make-up of the human being?

McLuhan: Precisely. Starting from my observations on poetry and music, I took a growing interest in the make-up of the two hemispheres of the brain. That is, I began to pay attention to them and to recognize their importance. It no longer involves a simple hypothesis, but a scientific discovery supported by anatomy and neuro-surgery.

Here is how scientists now characterize the two sides of the brain. The left hemisphere specializes in analysis; the right hemisphere, in global or holistic thought, with a limited aptitude for language. The right hemisphere governs the succession of words not so much as a logical sequence but as resonant interfaces. This hemisphere is, first of all, responsible for our orientation in space, our artistic enterprises, our artistic abilities, the image we have of our own body, the way we recognize faces. It concerns everything we take as a whole. Thus we recognize a face not by a particular trait, but by the face taken as a whole. The right hemisphere treats information much more diffusely than does the left hemisphere: information is distributed more vaguely. The right covers the *field* of perception in its entirety, whereas the left concentrates on one aspect at a time.

Gutenberg attaches itself to the left hemisphere; the oral, the acoustic and consequently the electric, to the right hemisphere.

It is only in the last few years that we have come to recognize the biological basis for these enormous cultural differences, and their link to anatomical particularities. Thus, the entire Western world — what we call civilization — from the Greco-Roman era onwards comes from the left cerebral hemisphere, if not entirely, then at least for the most part. The Gutenberg event gave a disproportionate push to visuality. It launched an era of left-brain dominance, that is, of logical, sequential, and visual control. This movement reached its peak with Newton. Afterwards, it quickly slid towards modern science, which is no longer visual. The subatomic particles of contemporary physics are, by definition, not visible.

Our world flipped around the year 1900. At that time Max Planck explained with quantum mechanics that matter isn't continuous, that the material world has no connections, that it is made up of, and held together by, resonant interfaces. This marked the end of Newton for whom everything was linked. It also heralded the appearance of Picasso and of Cubism with its technique of no longer looking at things from a single point of view but from multiple points of view simultaneously. Finally, with electricity, which is above all oral and acoustic, the right cerebral hemisphere rises to the surface.

Babin: When it was said "God is dead," did it not mean, at least in part, "Newton is dead"?

McLuhan: Without a doubt. The world that made sense according to Newtonian categories was quickly crumbling. But the God that this culture had adored, wasn't He a bit too much cast in the image of a particular type of man? Wasn't He too rationalized, a sort of divinity for deists?

In any event, we can say that the revolution in the Church came about as a result of a sudden hemispheric shift in the brain, and it occurred in the blink of an eye, a snap of the fingers.

Indeed, the solution lies in the complementary nature of the two cerebral hemispheres. For, anatomically, these two hemispheres are complementary, and not exclusive. Neither mode is more important except in transitional forms of awareness. It is culture that makes one or the other dominant and exclusive. A culture builds itself on a preference for one or the other hemisphere instead of basing itself on both. Our school system, like our Catholic hierarchy, is completely dominated by the left side of the brain. Vatican II was a very poor attempt to pass over to the right side. The result was mostly confusion. Ecumenism, too, I suppose, attempts to play both hemispheres equally, but it leaves me perplexed.

6

The De-Romanization of
the American Catholic Church

De-Romanization is a fact ever since the telegraph. Any speed-up of communication de-centralizes. Slow forms of communication centralize: information is localized and the decision-making takes place at the centre. All this is reversed by electric speed when information becomes available at the same moment everywhere. Decisions can be made at the periphery the same as at the centre. The President does not have to be in Washington; the Pope does not have to be in Rome.

But people fight desperately to hold old images, old shapes. New ones demand far more energy than people have. They flee into preceding situations because they feel at home there. People can't bear new forms. It's easier to go back with *Bonanza* that to take the hippies and the Beatles. Only artists are able to live in the present. Saints are artists, too. You never heard of a saint who lived in the past or future. Saints want to live in the present. That's why they are intolerable.

How did Romanization come about? Rome was entirely a product of technology — a bureaucracy, a classification system like a dictionary or a phone book. But in a world of electricity, classification gives way to involvement and men live the apostolate of pain. When you are involved in other people's lives, you are involved in their being,

∞ *McLuhan's introduction to* The De-Romanization of the American Catholic Church *by Edward Wakin and Fr. Joseph Scheuer, New American Library / Plume 1970, pages xi-xiii.*

their pain. When men discover the dimensions of suffering, they no longer classify. The big filing cabinet that is Rome lives by classification and must learn that old classifications have given way to involvement. Rome is going to have to liquidate its bureaucracy.

Ancient Rome fell when the Egyptians no longer sent papyrus and the Roman bureaucracy no longer had a way to communicate. It wasn't until the Renaissance, when the Chinese sent papyrus back to Europe, that Roman bureaucracy became powerful again. Then there was a vast clerical staff and centralized administration. Gutenberg stepped up centralization a thousand times and bureaucrats could achieve dimensions of centralization and bureaucracy not dreamed of by the Romans.

Until electricity, technology fragmented. The whole of Genesis is concerned with the attempt of man to build new technologies. When Cain, a "tiller of the ground," wanted to become more than a simple farmer, he slew Abel, the "keeper of sheep." When men began to build cities or towers, a technology of bricks — as in Babel — fragmented mankind. When man worshipped pagan idols, it meant the worshipping of tools. Enoch and Methusaleh were not so much persons as long-lived cultures, tribal kinship groups, or totalities — all of them fallen and fragmented. Men lost human respect, living as somnambulists hypnotized by their own technologies.

Under electric conditions, participation is inevitable. The visual monopoly is over; visual organization is over. Nothing "visuable" is twentieth century (I make no value judgments here). In the Catholic church, the new liturgy is an attempt to accommodate to electric forms. The Church is the only institution capable of coping with this situation and is not very keen on it.

A new doctrine is needed that should have been promulgated one hundred years ago: at the instant of Incarnation, the structure of the universe was changed. All of creation was remade. There was a new physics, a new matter, a new world. The doctrine would enable modern man to take the Church much more seriously. The moment God touched matter its very structure was altered, its potency was enormously enhanced. So was man's. Modern science is aware of this, not necessarily as revealed truth, but simply as truth.

The first Adam was an aesthete. He simply looked at things and labelled them. The second Adam was not. He was a maker, a creator. The human being sharing in the second Adam has the mandatory role of being creative. Passivity is not for man; creativity is mandatory.

Being wide awake is frightening, a nightmare. The problem of orientation means that drop-outs will only be at the top. The drop-outs will be the Cardinal Legers (who left his diocese to work among lepers). The higher up in the hierarchy the harder it is to get involved. We must get rid of the hierarchy if we want participation. But we don't have to wish for it. It's happening.

We are on the verge of the apocalypse. In fact, we are living in it.

7

"Our Only Hope Is Apocalypse"

(Edward Wakin) In the late 1960s, Marshall McLuhan announced that the "de-Romanization" of the Catholic Church "is a fact ever since the telegraph." The author of one of the century's most famous phrases — "the medium is the message" — explained that the "Pope does not have to be in Rome" any more than the President has to be in Washington.

Professor of English and director of the University of Toronto Centre for Culture and Technology, McLuhan remains an irrepressible punster of powerful insights, a compulsive inventor of one-liners, and an indefatigable commentator on change (eight books in process at the present time). Once an indifferent Baptist, the sixty-five-year-old McLuhan has been a devoted Catholic since coming "into the Church on my knees" in his mid-twenties.

Catholicism is clearly McLuhan's rock in the world. Between the euphoric 1960s and the disillusioned early '70s, between John XXIII and Paul VI, between clerical turbulence and lay agitation. McLuhan has stood on his rock as his reality amidst all the electric images. He still stands there, along with his characteristic arsenal of provocative commentary.

∞ From "Futurechurch: Edward Wakin interviews Marshall McLuhan" in
  U. S. Catholic, vol. 42, no. 1, January 1977, pages 6-11.

(**Marshall McLuhan**) The Catholic Church does not depend on human wisdom or human strategies for survival. All the best intentions in the world cannot destroy the Catholic Church! It is indestructible, even as a human institution. It may once again undergo a terrible persecution and so on. But that's probably what it needs.

(**Wakin**) Around this steadfast statement of faith swirl statements and observations that are not at all tranquilizing and certainly not comforting to the conservative Catholicism with which McLuhan seems to identify himself. His comments are explosive rather than systematic. They echo and they resonate — like the electric world which he is constantly exploring.

"Jump around," he said in handing me his latest book. "That's the way it's meant to be read. Don't read it straight through." The same applies to our exchange in his carriage-house office, in the cafeteria, and walking along the campus. Or as he adds: "I don't know what I think until I've said it." For starters, here are McLuhan's reactions to Vatican II and after.

(**McLuhan**) The nineteenth-century bureaucrats who assembled at the Second Vatican Council in 1962 were naturally as unaware of the causes of their problems and reforms as the representatives of the Church at the Council of Trent in the sixteenth century. There was not a single individual at the Council of Trent who understood the effects of print on the spiritual schism and psychic distress of the religious and political life of that time. At the Second Vatican Council, the participants paid no attention to the causes of their problems in their new policies and prescriptions.

(**Wakin**) The centrepiece of McLuhan's exploration of the causes of contemporary problems for church and state is *Understanding Media: The Extensions of Man*. In it, he expounds the theme that new technologies create new environments. For instance, just stop and think for a moment how much the car has changed our environment, our entire way of life. McLuhan calls the motorcar "the mechanical bride," and in this characteristic passage from *Understanding Media* provides an insight into how the car is more than a motor-driven vehicle:

"When the motorcar was new, it exercised the typical mechanical pressure of explosion and separation of functions. It broke up family life, or so it seemed, in the 1920s. It separated work and domicile, as never before. It exploded each city into a dozen suburbs, and then extended many of the forms of urban life along the highways until the open road seemed to become non-stop cities. It created the asphalt jungles, and caused 40,000 square miles of green and pleasant land to be cemented over. . . . The car, in a word, has quite refashioned all of the spaces that unite and separate men. . . ."

What McLuhan does is "probe" (his word) and provoke (my word) his listeners and readers to notice what they tend to overlook: how our inventions shape us. He likes to point out that we shape our tools and are, in turn, shaped by them. So McLuhan is always busy seeing hidden environments, including those created by mass media.

McLuhan sees humanity returning in an electric age to the pre-alphabetic stage of tribal life where "hearing is believing." When the alphabet came into the picture, "seeing was believing," and when print ushered in the Gutenberg Galaxy of moveable type, what dominated was a linear, uniform, connected, continuous way of approaching the world. In the nineteenth century, invention of the telegraph started humanity back towards an all-at-once life. The invention created a "global village" of instant communications, culminating in the satellite age which turned the world into a global theatre. Everyone in the world can watch everyone else instantaneously — you can't tell the difference between the actors and the audience. Indeed, McLuhan notes, the difference has vanished.

As to the Catholic Church, which is in the middle of all this change, McLuhan sounds optimistic in the long run, but extremely unsettling in the immediate future, for anyone with fixed images of the Catholic Church. But don't try to pin easy labels such as optimist or pessimist on McLuhan.

(McLuhan) I have never been an optimist or a pessimist. I'm an apoc-alyptic only. Our only hope is apocalypse. If you are asking about the ordinary secular climate of the Church, or its prospects as a secular institution, I should think the opportunities for survival are a heck of a lot better than those of the United States or any other secular insti-tution. Even in the secular sense, the Church has at least as much survival potential as any existing social or political institution, because, after all, is it not unaided at all times — even on the secular side — by supernatural means.

Apocalypse is not gloom. It's salvation. No Christian could ever be an optimist or a pessimist: that's a purely secular state of mind. I have no interest whatever in secular institutions as a place to have a nice or a bad time. I don't understand that kind of mentality. I guess it has taken me quite a long time to get to this state: it didn't happen overnight.

(Wakin) McLuhan explains why he thinks the leadership of the church is not with it. He sees the Catholic Church as wedded to the literacy of the West, and thereby handicapped in universality. This is clear once McLuhan outlines his views of what is happening to East and West — views that also offer an explanation of new interest in Eastern mysticism among Westerners.

(McLuhan) Never before has the entire world been organized on two patterns, both of which are in a state of interchange and simultaneous metamorphosis. The West is "going East" under the impact of speed-up of information movement. The speed of the electric circuit drives man from outer to inner interests, thus Orientalizing the West by means of its own technology. Meantime, the East is "going West" as it acquires more and more of the old Western "hardware" setup. The East, as well as Africa and Latin America, now seeks to create for itself the nineteenth-century world of consumer services and packages that the West is sloughing off via the inspiration of its electric circuitry.

The cradle of the Church was Greco-Roman literacy, and this was Providentially designed, not humanly planned. The fact that Greco-Roman culture has set apart the largest proportion of mankind from ever becoming Christian has never been discussed. It is taken for granted that missionaries will probably get the faith across by the written word.

But now we have suddenly a way of propagating information and knowledge without literacy. I would say it is a wide-open question whether the Church has any future at all as a Greco-Roman institution. It would be a good time to be Russian Orthodox: they split off from Rome because it was too literate. The Eastern Church is an "ear" Church; Rome was always very far along the visual road to visual power.

I would expect the hierarchy to have more to say on the Church's cradling in Greco-Roman literacy. This cultural heritage is expendable.

The trouble is that they just don't know the answers; they just don't know. There is nobody in the hierarchy, including the Pope, who knows these things. There is nobody.

(Wakin) When asked about his "apocalyptic" view of what faces the Catholic Church, McLuhan sees three trends dominating the global village — decentralization (and de-Romanization); software-prevailing (information dominating technological hardware); role-playing (rather than goal-chasing).

(McLuhan) The Roman hierarchy, after Gutenberg, had acquired a great deal of the organizational-chart patterns of specialism and rigidity. Improved written communication made possible the development of a huge Roman bureaucracy, transforming the Roman pontiff into a chief executive. Further improvement in travel and communication brought the pontiff into more immediate personal relation to his subjects. Today, even the President of the United States need not govern from Washington, D.C. What, therefore, is called the de-Romanization of the Roman Church is quite simply its electrification. When things speed up hierarchy disappears and global theatre sets in.

(Wakin) But in such a view is the Pope obsolete?

(McLuhan) The Pope is obsolete as a bureaucratic figure. But the Pope as a role-player is more important than ever. The Pope has authority. After all, if there were only three Catholics in the world, one of them would have to be Pope. Otherwise, there would be no church. There has to be a teaching authority or else no church at all.

(Wakin) Then there is the matter of the Catholic Church itself in a world where you cannot have goals. Instead you seek roles.

(McLuhan) You cannot have goals in an acoustic, non-visual world. You want a role: you don't want a goal. The Catholic Church has a role: salvation.

(Wakin) What of the institutional church in terms of decentralization and de-Romanization?

(McLuhan) The visual church is goal-oriented: its objectives are bigger collections, bigger missions, bigger everything. There is no need for institutional buildings at all. Everything can be performed in private places. At the speed of light you cannot have executives. You cannot have hierarchy. The job yields to roles and a role consists of multiple jobs. Institutionally, I would say, the Church is always out of place. Culturally as well. Sometimes way ahead; sometimes way behind.

(Wakin) What does the church do in the face of the breakneck pace of change in our technological era?

(McLuhan) One of the effects of innovation is somnambulism. When people are under a heavy strain psychically they tend to cave in, to turn zombie. Zombie-ism is a normal mode today for withstanding technological innovation.

(Wakin) What is the task of the church and is it doing it?

(McLuhan) That's one of the jobs of the Church — to shake up our present population. To do that you'd have to preach nothing but hell-fire. In my life, I have never heard one such sermon from a Catholic pulpit. You know, there is one fire-and-brimstone sermon in Joyce's *A Portrait of the Artist as a Young Man*, a very great one in my judgment. It brought a lot of people into the Church, including Thomas Merton.

(Wakin) Then is the church being too soft and accommodating?

(McLuhan) I would say so. Its strategies of survival; are not very well-designed. They seem to be fighting off the "group mentality" by pushing towards Protestantism and the extreme privatization of the Protestant faith. There I see nothing but failure. What they promulgate seems to be very badly suited. The attempt to adapt, say, rock music to the liturgy is very ineffective, and probably for many reasons. And costume was never as important in the history of the Church as now. The Church is going to private dress at a time when all the kids want to get into costume. They don't want private dress; they want costume and role.

(Wakin) What, then, of how the church varied before and after Vatican II? And how did it feel to raise a family during these two decades?

(McLuhan) I'm not a very useful person to talk to. I raised a family of six kids in that period — in the '50s and '60s — and they all left the Church except one. One out of six remains. Maybe some will come back some day. But there is a great disproportion between what the kids learned in the Church, and what they experienced, and what their needs are.

Our situation is unheard of — the changes under which we have been living. In this century, the changes occur at a speed which no human psyche or any human community can withstand, and we have not withstood it. We have failed. Our private identity has been dissolved. There are no more private people in North America. There are only groups.

(Wakin) In the McLuhan view of human history, the alphabet created private man, sitting alone poring over the printed page. What does this mean to a print-oriented church?

(McLuhan) That unique innovation, the phonetic alphabet, released the Greeks from the universal acoustic spell of tribal societies. Visual detachment via the written page also gave the power of the second look, the moment of recognition. This released people from the bondage of the uncritical and emotionally involved life. It also fostered the cult of private competition and individual emulation in sports and politics. The quest for private power came quickly.

Today, the alphabet is being wiped out. It is being wiped out electrically. The Church does not know that its fate is tied to literacy; she never has known this. She has taken it for granted because she was born in the middle of literacy.

(Wakin) What is the state of literacy in the Catholic Church today?

(McLuhan) The degree of literacy within the Catholic Church is not much — that is, within the hierarchy. Within the seminaries, I would say that the degree of literacy is very low indeed. Not as low as it had been in various periods of the Middle Ages. At the present time the levels of culture in the Catholic Church are on the *Reader's Digest* level. But that doesn't signal great danger. It is just a bit of a disgrace, like having one's fly open in public.

(Wakin) Is this related to the defection of Catholic intellectuals who have been so critical of the church?

(McLuhan) I never came into the Church as a person who was being taught. I came in on my knees. That is *the only* way in. When people start praying, they need truths; that's all. You don't come into the Church by ideas and concepts, and you cannot leave by mere disagreement. It has to be a loss of faith, a loss of participation. You can tell when people leave the Church: they have quit praying.

Actively relating to the Church's prayer and sacraments is not done through ideas. Any Catholic today who has an intellectual disagreement with the Church has an illusion. You cannot have an intellectual disagreement with the Church: that's meaningless. The Church is not an intellectual institution. It is a superhuman institution.

(Wakin) How does someone like Marshall McLuhan, professor, pundit, prophet of the electric age, feel in the Catholic Church he sees and experiences? Comfortable? Uncomfortable?

(McLuhan) I don't expect to be comfortable. The Church has never claimed to be a place of security in any ordinary psychological sense. Anyone who comes to the Church for that purpose is wrong: nothing of that sort is available in the Church. There never has been: it isn't that kind of institution. At the speed of light, there is nothing but violence possible, and violence wipes out every boundary. Even territory is violated at the speed of light. There is no place left to hide. The Church becomes a Church of the soul.

Christ said: "I bring you not peace but a sword." The custodian of civilized values and so on — that phase of the Church is all over, I'd say. Now we're on a life raft — a sort of survival operation. At the speed of light, now the normal speed of life — information's speed — there is no peace. The potential for teaching and learning in the Church was never greater than in the electric world. The Chair of Peter can jet around the world: it doesn't have to stay in Rome.

The new matrix is acoustic, simultaneous, electric — which in one way is very friendly to the Church. That is, the togetherness of humanity is now total. Everybody is now simultaneously in the same place and involved in everybody. The present Church demands an extreme unworldliness. But that's easy now. It is easy to be unworldly. What it means, though, is that everything we've been accustomed to is obsolete now.

8

"The Logos Reaching Across Barriers":
Letters to Ong, Mole, Maritain, and Culkin

[Written to Walter J. Ong, S.J., from Toronto, on 14 October 1954]

Dear Walter:

Please explicate sentence on p. 21 of your System Space and Intellect in Ren[aissance] Symbolism essay: "Out of it has come modern science, with the possibility it offers for increasing the subjection of matter and impregnation of matter by spiritual forces . . ."[1]

I've read a lot of Rosicrucian stuff lately and you make me wonder whether you have their thoughts in mind.

On p. 396 of Madame Blavatsky's *Isis Unveiled* (vol. I, New York, 1889)[2] she cites the traditional Pythagorean distinction between Fancy and Imagination, citing Wordsworth as obvious recent exemplar: "Imagination Pythagoras maintained to be the remembrance of precedent spiritual, mental and physical states, while fancy is the disorderly production of the material brain." In context this means that Imagination is contact with the Anima Mundi (e.g., Yeats) whereas Fancy is merely a portion of the Anima Hominis. That is Imagination

---

1 This is a quotation from the brief of a paper by Walter J. Ong, "Space and Intellect in Renaissance Symbolism," delivered at the Catholic Renascence Society Symposium in Philadelphia in April 1954. It was published in full in *Explorations* 4, February 1955.
2 The major book of Helena Petrovna Blavatsky (1831–1891), Russian occultist and co-founder in New York, in 1875, of the Theosophical Society.

concerns direct contact with divine archetypes whereas fancy is merely human and cognitive. As fallen spirits or devils men have their intellect which is of the earth earthy, presided over by the Earth mother, the White Goddess of Robt Graves, etc.[3] The intellect is the dark principle. But the imagination is mode of divine union for the *uncreated* divine spark hidden in our corrupt clay, etc. You are familiar with this aspect of the Old Religion, Gnosis, neo-platonism, theosophy, et al.?

I don't see how it is possible to teach English literature, or any European lit., without full knowledge of the "secret doctrine" for which the arts are the sole means of grace.[4] I realize now that my own rejection of philosophy as a study in my pre-Catholic days was owing to the sense that it was a meaningless truncation. Not that my present interest is due to any conviction of truth in the secret doctrine. Quite

---

3 Among the many works of poet, novelist, and essayist Robert Graves (1895–1985) was *The White Goddess: A Historical Grammar of Poetic Myth* (1948), which argues that the primitive Moon Goddess, the female principle, was the Muse of poetry.

4 In the early 1950s McLuhan's interest in Renaissance and neo-Augustan literatures (e.g., Pope and Swift, who were interested in Rosicrucianism and Masonry), as well as in modern literature, led him to undertake research into the effects of esoteric thought on the arts. Tracing the symbolism and rituals that were a means of transmitting gnostic and pagan religious thought in the Middle Ages and the Renaissance, he became fascinated with the role of Rosicrucianism and Masonry in the transition from the Renaissance to the Age of Reason, and with the continued presence of these themes and associated liturgies and symbols in modern art and literature — as reflected in such works as Eliot's *The Waste Land* and Joyce's *Ulysses*. As a Roman Catholic, McLuhan found much evidence that "secret societies" and "secret doctrines" — associated with gnosticism, Rosicrucianism, and Masonry — persisted among élites in the twentieth century and around him in the university. Following Wyndham Lewis's condemnation of the "freemasonry of the arts" in *Time and Western Man*, McLuhan protested — in the following letter (to Ezra Pound), as in other letters of the 1950s — what he felt was this continuing influence:

81 St Mary St
Toronto 5
Feb 28 / 53

Dear Pound
Last year has been spent in going through rituals of secret societies with fine comb. As I said before I'm in a bloody rage at the discovery that the arts and sciences are in the pockets of these societies. It doesn't make me any happier to know that Joyce, Lewis, Eliot, yourself have used these rituals as a basis for art activity.
   Monopolies of knowledge are intolerable
   The use of the arts for sectarian warfare! ugh.
   The use of the arts as a technique of salvation!
         as a channel of supernatural grace!
   The validity of the rituals is entirely in the cognitive order.
   Art is imitation of the process of apprehension.
    clarification of   "   "   "   .
Now that I know the nature of the sectarian strife among the Societies I have no intention of participating in it any further, until I know a good deal more. To hell with East and West.
                            — *McLuhan*

the contrary. It is rather to a sense of it as the fecund source of lies and misconceptions, e.g., Puritan Inner Light.

Can you think of any reason why Catholic students of philosophy and lit. today should not be given the facts about these "secrets"? I can find nobody here who can or will discuss the question.

Turrible busy! Keep in touch.
As ever in Christ,
Mac

[Written to John W. Mole, O.M.I,[5] from 81 St. Mary Street, Toronto,
on 18 April 1969]

Dear Father John:

Thanks for the issue of *Christian Communications*.

Am currently finishing off a book which I have to take to New York.

Your piece on me brings to mind that I am a Thomist for whom the sensory order resonates with the divine Logos. I don't think concepts have any relevance in religion. Analogy is not concept. It is community. It is resonance. It is inclusive. It is the cognitive process itself. That is the analogy of the divine Logos. I think of Jasper, Bergson, and Buber as very inferior conceptualist types, quite out of touch with the immediate analogical awareness that begins in the senses and is derailed by concepts or ideas.[6]

Best wishes with your work.
Yours in XTO,
[Marshall]

P. S. Have just read Maritain's *The Peasant of the Garonne* [1968]. 100% right as far as he goes. He is totally ignorant of the new electric environment as creating the world before which misguided Christians kneel. This strictly Luciferan product is ethereal and a highly plausible mock-up of the mystical body.

---

5 John W. Mole (b. 1911 in Durham, England) was ordained a priest in 1947 of the Oblate Order (Missionary Oblates of Mary Immaculate, O.M.I.). In 1960 he founded the Canadian Institute of Communications and edited its quarterly *Canadian Communications* (1960–1962). He also founded and edited *Christian Communications* (1960–1975). In 1969 founded the Institute of Social Communications, Saint Paul University, Ottawa, where he lectured on the philosophy of communications.

6 Discussed in Mole's articles were the German philosopher Karl Jaspers (1883–1969); the French philosopher Henri Bergson (1859–1941); and the Austrian-born Jewish thinker and philosopher Martin Buber (1878–1965).

[Written to Jacques Maritain on 6 May 1969, from Toronto]

Dear Monsieur Maritain:

Having read your Paysan [*The Peasant of the Garonne*, 1968] with much reward and approval, may I venture a few additional observations? The Gutenberg technology retrieved antiquity and junked the Middle Ages. The tensors of your electric technology (the environmental extension of our own nervous system) retrieves all the impoverished areas of the world, dumping them into the Western lap and simultaneously junking the nineteenth-century industrial hardware and its numerous descendants. Every new technology is an evolutionary extension of our own bodies. The evolutionary process has shifted from biology to technology in an eminent degree since electricity. Each extension of ourselves creates a new human environment and an entirely new set of interpersonal relationships. The service or disservice environments (they are complementary) created by these extensions of our bodies saturate our sensoria and are thus invisible. Every new technology thus alters the human sensory bias creating new areas of perception and new areas of blindness. This is as true of clothing as of the alphabet, or the radio.

James Joyce put the matter very simply in *Finnegans Wake* (page 81, line 1):"As for the viability of vicinals, when invisible they are invincible."[7] By "vicinals" Joyce alludes to [Giovanni Battista] Vico whose *Scienza Nuova* asserts the principle of the sensory and perceptual change resulting from new technologies throughout human history.[8]

---

7 A slight misquote (but the sense is retained): the line reads, "Yes, the viability of vicinals if invisible is invincible."

8 Giovanni Battista (Giambattista) Vico (1688–1744) was a grammarian and a professor of rhetoric at the University of Naples. His *La Scienza Nuova* (New Science), published in 1725, and *La Scienza Seconda* (1730, 1744) — which discusses history in terms of a natural cycle of growth, decay, and regrowth and reflects a concern with words and the poetics of words — had a great influence on thinkers in the nineteenth and twentieth centuries. McLuhan's interest in Vico at this time relates to his influence on James Joyce, who said of Vico, "My imagination grows when I read Vico as it doesn't when I read Freud or Jung." While Joyce's interest in Vico is seen in *Ulysses* in his uses of Homer and in several references — such as the Vico Road, Dalkey, in the "Nestor" episode — it is most apparent in *Finnegans Wake*, which was influenced by Vico's treatment of language, by his elaborate theory of cyclic recurrence (used by Joyce as a "trellis") drawn primarily from Vico's three ages — of gods, heroes, and men — and by such imaginative images in Vico as the divine thunderclap, represented in the Wake by a 100-letter word.

Hence the ancients attributed god-like status to all inventors since they alter human perception and self-awareness. Heinrich Hertz stated the same principle of complementarity and metamorphosis of our identity image in relation to technologies in his famous dictum: "The consequences of the images will be the image of the consequences."[9]

It was Aquinas who alerted me (I delighted in the phrase "Should old Aquinas be forgot," with its allusion to the Scottish song "Should Old Acquaintance Be Forgot and Never Brought to Mind") to the principle of complementarity inherent in all created forms. (In the Summa, I-II, Q. 113, a. 7, ad quintum.)

The same principle is stated in the *I Ching* that when any form reaches the end of its potential, it reverses its characteristics.[10] The matter is neatly illustrated in the joke about the caterpillar sceptically observing the flittings of a butterfly and saying: "You'll never get me up in one of those darned things!"

When the Gutenberg technology hit the human sensibility silent reading at high speed became possible for the first time. Semantic uniformity set in as well as "correct" spelling. The reader had the illusion of separate and private individuality and of "inner light" resulting from his exposure to seas of ink. The chiasmus of the process is given epic treatment in Alexander Pope's *The Dunciad*, whose closing lines sum up the liquidation of trivium and the quadrivium: "Art after art goes out and all is night."[11]

The speed-up of print permitted a very high development of bureaucratic centralism in church and state, just as the much greater speed-up of electricity dissolves the echelons of the organization chart and creates utter decentralism — mini-art and mini-state. Whereas the Renaissance print-oriented individual thought of himself as a fragmented entity, the electric-oriented person thinks of himself as tribally

---

9   Heinrich Hertz: "The images which we may form of things are not determined without ambiguity by the requirement that the consequents of the images must be the images of the consequents." From the Introduction (page 2) to *The Principles of Mechanics* (1956), translated by D. E. Jones and J. T. Walley.

10 The *I-Ching* (Book of Changes) was one of the *Five Classics*, the basis of Chinese education, which contains mystical speculations. McLuhan used a reprint of the James Legge translation of 1874.

11 This is line 640, Book IV, of *The Dunciad*, which ends with line 656.

inclusive of all mankind. Electric information environments being utterly ethereal fosters the illusion of the world as a spiritual substance. It is now a reasonable facsimile of the mystical body, a blatant manifestation of the Anti-Christ. After all, the Prince of this World is a very great electric engineer.

May I suggest that just as the Roman clergy defected in the Gutenberg era on the illusion of the inner light, even greater numbers may be expected to defect under the mystical attractions of the electric light. Since our reason has been given us to understand natural processes, why have men never considered the consequences of their own artefacts upon their modes of self-awareness? I have devoted several books to this subject. There is a deep-seated repugnance in the human breast against understanding the processes in which we are involved. Such understanding involves far too much responsibility for our actions.

I know of no philosopher who has ever studied the effects of technology on philosophical concepts, though the ascendancy of the eye provided by the phonetic alphabet obviously made Euclid and Plato possible. It is equally obvious that the degradation of the eye by the visceral extension electrically of our proprioceptive lives creates the attitudes of "involvement" and "participation" and the world of Existentiality. The nineteenth-century bureaucrats in charge of implementing Vatican II are quite helpless in the face of a world of instantaneous information. Since we are doing these things to ourselves, there is no earthly reason for submitting to them unconsciously or irrationally. Perhaps now, when things happen at very high speeds, a formal causality or pattern recognition may appear for the first time in human history. Analogy of proper proportionality, for example, is a mode of awareness destroyed by literacy, since the literate man insists on visual connections where being insists on resonance.

Let me speak to you of an occasion when you talked at the Royal Ontario Museum in Toronto on "The Longing for God." Throughout your address, you pronounced "longing" "lungeing." It had a very mysterious resonance. On consulting the big Oxford Dictionary I discovered that "lunge" means "a length of rope on which a horse is exercised in a circle." "Lunge" is the root and origin of "longing." Is not this a nice example of the reverberations of the Logos reaching across language barriers?

My first encounter with your work was at Cambridge University in

1934. Your *Art and Scholasticism* was on the reading list of the English School. It was a revelation to me. I became a Catholic in 1937.[12]

Yours, with many prayers,
Marshall McLuhan
P. S. Summa —

Et ideo in toto tempore praecedenti,
  quo aliquid movetur ad unam
formam, subest formae oppositae; et
  in ultimo instanti illius temporis, quod
      est primum instans . . .[13]

---

12 Maritain replied with a long letter (15 May 1969), written in French, agreeing with several of McLuhan's statements; expressing concern over the rapidity of change that did not allow time for adaptation and over the grave "troubles" the technological revolution was producing for some Catholics; but taking comfort in his belief that the endurance of certain doctrinal perspectives was surely a sign that they were superior to the times and founded on truth.

13 "And therefore in the preceding time, by which anything is moved towards a form, it is supported by the opposite form; and in the final instant of its time, which is the first instant . . ." (St. Thomas Aquinas, *Summa Theologica*).

[Written from to Fr. John Culkin, on 19 June 1975]

Dear John:

I just did a note to my friend, Fritz Wilhelmsen, Thomist at the University of Dallas. He is interested in working on St. Thomas's theory of communication, and I have pointed out to him that Aquinas designates his audience, the people he wants to influence and alter, in the Objections of each article. Then I realized that the audience is, in all matters of art and expression, the formal cause, e.g., fallen man is the formal cause of the Incarnation, and Plato's public is tha formal cause of his philosophy. Formal cause is concerned with effects and with structural form, and not value judgments.

My own approach to the media has been entirely from formal cause. Since formal causes are hidden and environmental, they exert their structural pressure by interval and interface with whatever is in their environmental territory. Formal cause is always hidden, whereas the things upon which they act are visible. The TV generation has been shaped not by TV programs, but by the pervasive and penetrating character of the TV image, or service, itself.

Imagine my amazement on picking up *Art and Scholasticism* [*and the Frontiers of Poetry*, 1962] by Maritain the other day to discover that he has nothing whatever to say about formal cause. He is a complete Cartesian subjectivist in by-passing the entire world of rhetorical elocutio. If you study Eric's piece on classical rhetorical structure in *Finnegans Wake*, you will see how basic classical rhetoric is in Joyce. It is equally relevant to T. S. Eliot, and Eric is the first to point this out. (By the way, he is going to the University of Dallas for a couple of years to work on his Ph.D. in that rather ideal academic environment where we both taught this spring for a few weeks.) This matter of formal causality and the environments created by the media is so big that I hope your new academic set-up will be able to take hold of some of it.

[Marshall]

9

International Motley
and Religious Costume

One of the most useful phrases for approaching the whole question of costume is International Motley. So far as I know the phrase originated in Ireland and refers to the costume adopted spontaneously by the young people of the TV generation in many countries. It refers to the conscious rearrangement of hair and attire to avoid the impression of "dress," for costume is not so much "dressing up for" people as "putting on" the public. The small demi-mask worn by the participants in a masquerade is a "put on" of the group. The wearer drops his private identity in order to assume a corporate identity. To wear such a mask is to submerge oneself, as it were, in the vortex of festive celebration and this is done by abandoning the specialism of private dress in order to enjoy the stepped-up group power and energy of a special corporate mood.

It would take a good deal of time and space to explore the meaning of the "put on" as it creates a liaison between individual and group, between the everyday and the special occasion or mood. There seems to be, however, one basic component or circumstance which relates individual and group in any "put on," and it may well be that it is a deep underlying grievance. Even in the case of the conventional strip-tease this is not lacking. The stripper takes off her clothes in order to

∞ From "International Motley and Religious Costume," Christian Communications, December 1972, issue no. 39.

"put on" her audience. Nudity is not nakedness, since the nude expects to be seen whereas the naked person does not. In fact nakedness is the "put off" of all power and dignity and social being. This fact draws attention to clothing as equipment and technology and power. Clothing, indeed, is weaponry and this fact is nowhere more noticeable than in the strip-tease act, where the weaponry of dress and respectability is cast aside only to involve the stripper in an even larger vortex of power than her dress allows, namely, her admirers. In a sense she *becomes* her admirers as much as any poet or performer in any medium can do.

In the case of the motley of the clown, this *figure* must be seen against the *ground* of the Emperor. The traditional image of *The Emperor's New Clothes* would seem to allude to the fact that emperors create whole environments. It is these environments that are invisible until some precocious infant challenges them, as in the case of the little boy on his first airplane ride who asked, "Daddy, when do we start to get smaller?" The jet traveller does not question the *figure* of the plane as it relates to the *ground*. From the ground, the plane gets much smaller. Why then should the *figure* of the plane remain the same? Why should the inside of the cabin of a plane not diminish as the ground becomes more and more remote? One reason is that an enclosed space is a visual space, and, as such, is static. The same little boy, in the open cockpit of a small plane, would not have asked such a question. The user of a jet plane puts on the plane as a costume of power as much as any medieval knight put on his suit of metal in order to become an irresistible human tank. The emperor's clothes are corporate social services whose character is concealed by their way of involving everybody, thus making themselves invisible. Such "corporate clothing" is familiar in phrases like "the King's highway," "the King's justice," "the King's English," "the King's press," etc. These corporate clothes, or social vestitures, are vast environmental weaponry such as enlists the total social energy of a whole population. Those who relate to these social services as officers or deputies of their power and influence also tend to be invested with costume rather than private dress. The judge in his robes, as much as the constable or policeman in his uniform, is a delegate of the corporate power created by the large social services. Thus, it is natural for the professions of law and learning, of military and medicine, to "put on" the public by indicating their involvement in a social role that is only incidentally personal. Insofar, however, as this "put on" is a kind of takeover of a corporate social role, it is inevitably represented as usurpation and deprivation by those who have to forego some of their private power and function in order to make this corporate role possible.

The religious who put on some of the available corporate powers of their society in order to function in a role are seen by many job-holders as usurpers. On the other hand, could it not be said that the religious who abandoned corporate costume in order to wear the private dress of the mere job-holder are abandoning their social function as much as any espionage agent? The confusion which exists at present, as between private or corporate dress for religious, may herald the advent of a time when all religious will become the underground. The mere fact that many feel the need to abandon the costume of social service and corporate ministry in favour of the anonymity of mere dress, may be a token of the time when the hidden environment of the Mystical Body may once more have to resort to an invisible ministry.

Earlier it was suggested that the "put on" that is costume is inseparable from the hidden ground of grievance. In the case of festivity and masquerades, such a grievance is obvious in the desire to escape from dull routine, but in the case of religious costume the ground of grievances may be simply the world itself which demands an encounter with the spirit. Eventually, such an encounter of world and spirit invites extremes, whether of gaudiness or poverty, joy or sorrow, in a kind of costume as a declaration of alienation from the world and its ground-rules. The mystic may have to take up the middle ground between gaudiness and poverty which is, or used to be, middle-class respectability. This is where "international motley" may be of some help in revealing a strategy of an anti-worldly kind. The dress of the TV generation is quite imaginative in contriving to "put on" the homogeneous establishment by announcing its alienation from the same. It is almost entirely a secular matter, however, since the young are replacing their alienation from a consumer world of aggressive values with a world in which participation in the social process is to become more or less natural.

What can be learned from the international motley of the anti-establishment performers in their variegated costumes is that there is no possibility of returning to private dress for those who are awake to the need for hostility to the values of the world. When Mr. T. S. Eliot arrived in the London of the early twentieth century, the art world was still dishevelled by the costume strategies of the aesthetes. He at once dissociated himself from these effete consumers of packaged art by flamboyantly presenting an image of rigorous neatness. Anybody who needs to indicate in his personal figure the rejection of the *ground* and ground-rules of an affluent society will be able to find various means apt to this end. The question remains open whether this could best be done by the individual or a consistent group. Again, we may take heed of the universal language of international motley, for the meaning of this would be much weakened if it were merely occasional and personal in its expression.

Insofar as religious orders have in the past adopted uniform dress, they tended to present themselves to the world as an image of corporate and almost military power. The clerical *habit*, in assuming the aspect of a military uniform, lost many psychological advantages. This dilemma appears strikingly in the case of the uniformed policeman. The uniform earns for the cop the name of "pig" — itself an archaic slang term for a policeman. But the same youngsters who detest the cop in his ordinary attire admire and imitate the motorcycle cop in his functionary attire, admire and imitate the motorcycle cop in his more spectacular costume. The latter may offer a cue to each religious that it may be the wrong time to dim down clerical attire just when something "far out" and very unconventional may be needed.

John Cage, in his distressed and faded blue jeans, points out that, in this extremely economical yet elitish costume, "I can stop my car on my way to or from a concert or lecture engagement and hunt for mushrooms in the woods." He has found this an all-purpose attire that admits him to the most elegant and esoteric company while continuing his bond with the most humble society. It "enables him to walk with Kings nor lose the common touch."

10

Electric Consciousness
and the Church

Hubert Hoskins: In various articles and in your books *The Gutenberg Galaxy* and *Understanding Media* and *The Medium Is the Massage*, you have probed a new way of envisaging technical media as what you call extensions of our human faculties and our consciousness, and I suppose millions of people by now have heard the slogan or expression, "The medium is the message." I take it you reject the idea that what is most effective for change is what used to be called the content of a communication: what really counts is not the what but the how.

Marshall McLuhan: Yes. It might be illustrated by saying that the English language is an enormous medium that is very much more potent and effective than anything ever said in English. Anybody who uses that medium invokes or resonates the totality of it even with the most trivial remark. Our own mother tongues are things in which we participate totally. They change our perception. So if we spoke Chinese we would have a different sense of hearing, smell, and touch. The same is true with printing, radio, movies, and TV. They actually alter our organs of perception without our knowing it. We are never aware of these changes.

∞ *An interview with McLuhan by Hubert Hoskins, originally published in* The Listener, *26 March 1970.*

Hoskins: And part of your argument, I take it, is that we have, in the West at any rate, passed through periods of culture — which you have described as literate or sequential or logical — in which men have become capable of abstracting themselves from this environment of individualizing, segregating, and so on. And these have been periods in which religion — for example, Christianity — has evolved in terms of verbalism.

McLuhan: I don't think it was accidental that Christianity began in the Greco-Roman culture. I don't think that Christ would have suffered under Ghengis Khan with the same meaning as under Pontius Pilate. The Greeks had invented a medium, the phonetic alphabet, which, as Eric Havelock explains in his book *Preface to Plato*, made it possible for men to have for the first time in human history a sense of private identity. A sense of private substantial identity — a self — is to this day utterly unknown to tribal societies. Christianity was introduced into a matrix of culture in which the individual had enormous significance: this is not characteristic of other world cultures.

Hoskins: Why is it that Christianity, which began in a preliterate and oral society, very quickly became deposited, became embodied, in propositions known as dogmas and so on — became a matter of very high definition, to use your own terminology? Do you regard this as a fundamental aberration?

McLuhan: These issues were all raised at the First Council in the quarrel between Paul and Peter. Paul was a cultivated Greco-Roman who wanted Christianity for the whole world. Peter thought that it had to be filtered through Judaic culture in order to be valid. Today all these ancient issues are alive again. One of the amazing things about electric technology is that it retrieves the most primal, the most ancient forms of awareness as contemporary. There is no more "past" under electric culture: every "past" is now. And there is no future: it is already here. You cannot any longer speak geographically or ideologically in one simple time or place. Now, today, we are dealing with universal forms of experience. So the fact that Christianity began in Greco-Roman culture really is of enormous significance. I don't think theologians have especially heeded this matter.

The effect of TV on the young today is to scrub their private identities. The problem of private identity vs. tribal involvement has become one of the crosses of our time. It was the big clash between Peter and Paul; I don't think it was ever more alive as a problem than right now.

Hoskins: Would you agree that the answer to Christianity for the private individual was the one which predominated from late medieval times onwards and reached its climax perhaps in the Protestant Reformation; and that ever since we have had this highly explicit, highly verbalized, propositional manifestation of what passes at any rate for the Christian revelation?

McLuhan: I am myself quite aware that there is a great contrast between perceptual and conceptual confrontation; and I think that the "death of Christianity" or the "death of God" occurs the moment they become concept. As long as they remain percept, directly involving the perceiver, they are alive.

Hoskins: But concept surely enters into the process at a very early stage. Take the fourth Gospel: is this where God begins to die?

McLuhan: The revelation is of *thing*, not theory. And where revelation reveals actual thing-ness you are not dealing with concept. The thing-ness revealed in Christianity has always been a scandal to the conceptualist: it has always been incredible. This issue is raised in the Book of Job, where faith and understanding were put at totally opposite poles. Job was not working on a theory but on a direct percept. All understanding was against him; all concept was against him. He was directly perceiving a reality, one revealed to him.

Hoskins: If what you are saying is right, I still don't see how such an activity as theology is possible even in theory.

McLuhan: I should think that it is very much a pastime, in the sense of a rehearsal of past times. It is not personal and direct confrontation. Theology is one of the "games people play," in the sense of its theorizing. But using direct percept and direct involvement with the actuality of a revealed thing — there need be no theology in the ordinary sense of the word.

Hoskins: What do you think of the kind of activity carried on by your colleague in Toronto, Professor Leslie Dewart? In *The Future of Belief*, I believe Dewart is arguing that there can be no future for most forms of traditional theism, for the wholly transcendent God. Do you think he's talking nonsense here?

McLuhan: No. I think he's just conceptualizing.

Hoskins: You regard this as a game?

McLuhan: Pure game.

Hoskins: A useless game?

McLuhan: Not necessarily more useless than any other game. Most games are a tremendous *katharsis* for pent-up emotions and frustrations. There has always been a great clash between works and concepts in religion. I think that theology can become a work, perhaps a part of the *opus dei*, part of the prayerful contemplation of God. Insofar as theology is contemplation and prayer it is part of the contemplation of the *thing*ness and the mysteries.

Hoskins: This is using the term "theology" in a rather unusual way.

McLuhan: Theology should ideally be a study of the *thing*ness, the nature of God, since it is a form of contemplation. But insofar as it is a theoretical or intellectual construct, it is purely a game, though perhaps a very attractive game. It can be played equally with any oriental theology: it has no more relevance to Christian theology than to Hindu theology.

Hoskins: I'm not quite clear about your distinction between concept and percept. If I were to say that the traditional Christian doctrine of the Incarnation can be expressed in the phrase, "Christ is the medium and the message," is that a percept or a concept?

McLuhan: It is a percept because, as Christ said over and over again, it is visible to babes, but not to sophisticates. The sophisticated, the conceptualizers, the Scribes and the Pharisees — these had too many theories to be able to perceive anything. Concepts are wonderful buffers for preventing people from confronting any form of percept. Most people are quite unable to perceive the effects of the ordinary cultural media around them because their theories about change prevent them from perceiving change itself. It never occurs to people that a satellite environment can alter the perceptions of the entire human race. They have no theory that permits them to obtain such a concept of metamorphosis. In fact, we *per*ceive the satellite environment whether we *con*ceive it or not. The percept is what does the work in changing our experience and our organs of perception.

The satellite environment has completely altered the organs of human perception and revealed the universal pollution.

Hoskins: Do you think that these modifications of consciousness which you see taking place are going to open up a new world of perception, so that religious experience as the perception of revelation is something which society will be able to realize much more concretely? In future, will there be worship? And what kind of worship? Will it be made concrete in liturgy?

McLuhan: The need for participation in groups and social forms always requires some code whether verbalized or in the form of costume and vestment, as a means of involvement in a common action. Today, for example, the plain-clothed priest or plain-clothed nun presents a sort of CIA or FBI scandal. It is one of the ludicrous hang-ups of our time. What the young are obviously telling us is this: we want beards, we want massive costumes and vestments for everybody. We do not want any of this simple, plain, individual stuff. We want the big corporate role. The young have abandoned all job-holding and specialism in favour of corporate costuming and role-playing. They are in the exact opposite position of Hamlet, who lived in an age when roles were being thrown away, and Machiavelli and individuals were emerging. Today, Machiavelli has been thrown away in favour of role-playing once again. The Church, that is, the administrative bureaucracy of ordinary human beings, is never very much aware of what is going on. A bureaucracy has to maintain its function regardless of change, and it always persists long after it's irrelevant. As a bureaucracy, the Church today is, in a way, a comic set of hang-ups and is no more relevant in its strategies than Don Quixote was when confronted with Gutenberg.

Quixote rode madly off into the Middle Ages, hoping that it was the future.

Hoskins: Do you see any prospect of its becoming relevant? Or of its adopting a program?

McLuhan: I think one of the factors that is of compelling relevance in our time is the speed of change. At electric speeds, patterns become so clear that even bureaucrats begin to get the message. This is new, though. Things used to change gradually enough to be imperceptible; today the patterns of change are declaring themselves very vividly because of the speed at which they occur. That is what pollution comes from: pollution is merely the revelation of a situation changing at high speeds. We now regard all our institutions as polluted because we can see that they have many patterns that have nothing to do with the function they are supposed to perform.

So the young become intolerant. They become aware, through the speed of information, of all the knowledge that only adults were privy to in the past. Then the young simply move in as actor rather than as audience: participation today is a universal pattern in which audience becomes active. There is no more audience in our world. On this planet, the entire audience has been rendered active and participant.

Naturally, religion undergoes tremendous changes under these conditions. And administration undergoes tremendous changes: all forms of authorization and administration and teaching and every sort of political and military establishment are altered by this fact. It is very high speeds and access to universally available information that make this awareness possible.

Now, its effect on religion is as drastic as its effect on military or other objectives. All forms of sham, all forms of irrelevance, all forms of routinized repetition are swept aside, and along with that clean sweep goes this wiping-out of the old private identities of centuries of cultural heritage. How much we can survive without any private identity is, I think, a question for religion to consider. "Is there life before death?" somebody once asked. It has become a much more relevant question than the old one about life after death. If there is no longer such a thing as a private individual because of our electric culture of total involvement, then the question of life after death becomes irrelevant. Individualism, in the old nineteenth-century sense, has been scrubbed right off our culture, and many people find themselves completely bewildered by this change.

Hoskins: Might not Christianity offer us some hope of reconciling the individual with the collective?

McLuhan: Christianity definitely supports the idea of a private, independent metaphysical substance of the self. Where the technologies supply no cultural basis for this individual, then Christianity is in for trouble. When you have a new tribal culture confronting an individualist religion, there is trouble.

Hoskins: You yourself believe in the divine revelation. It cannot be ephemeral? It is indestructible?   .

McLuhan: It doesn't matter at all what people think about it.

Hoskins: Well, it matters in the sense that it is for people.

McLuhan: It matters to them; it certainly would affect their future, or their future existence. But as far as the society of men is concerned, the private opinion about any of these matters is quite insignificant. The revealed and divinely constituted fact of religion has nothing to do with human opinion or human adherence.

Hoskins: So what you are really saying is that, as you see it, the Church as an institution has no relevant future.

McLuhan: In its merely bureaucratic, administrative, and institutional side, I think, it is going to undergo the same pattern of change as the rest of our institutions. In terms of, say, a computer technology, we are heading for cottage economies, where the most important industrial activities can be carried on in any little individual shack anywhere on the globe. That is, the most important designs and the most important activities can be programmed by individuals in the most remote areas. In that sense, Christianity — in a centralized, administrative, bureaucratic form — is certainly irrelevant.

Hoskins: Suppose we envisage the church as a community, founded upon the Christian myth of revelation in Christ: what future for that?

McLuhan: The word "myth," in this connection, of course, is properly used because it is the Greek word for "word"; the *mythos* is "word," *logos*. Myth is anything seen at very high speeds; any process seen at a very high speed is a myth. I see myth as the super-real. The Christian myth is not fiction but something more than ordinarily real.

Hoskins: Exactly. But what I am asking is: do you see any prospect of the Church's being transformed from a traditional kind of institution into a mythical community or a community based on this myth?

McLuhan: The Church has in various periods consisted of hermits in very scattered huts and hovels in all sorts of backward territories. It could easily become this again, and in the age of the helicopter I see no reason why the Church should have any central institutions whatever. So any of the visible forms of the church could undergo total transformation and dissipation, but this would have no relevance to the central reality and thingness of the revealed and divinely constituted Church. Naturally, people who share such awareness of divinity enjoy their community; they enjoy being together. So in that sense, nothing is ever going to prevent Christians from congregating. But the forms in which they will congregate and organize their activities and help one another — those are capable of indefinite transformation. But I don't think that they are of much importance, not so long as the divine fact — and that includes, as far as I am concerned, the divine sacraments — is available to communities and to the Christian faithful. As long as there is the means of communion, social and divine, there is an indefinite number of forms in which it can be achieved. It just happened that with the coming of very heavy technologies after Gutenberg the Church began to get very heavily centralized, railway-style. But in the age of the aeroplane, railway-style centralism, which favours very centralized bureaucracies, big nation-states, and so on, is dissolved. The Church's massive centralized bureaucracy is certainly *passé*.

Hoskins: What changes do you envisage coming about through the advent of a "global village" situation, where culture in various stages of development — culture with quite diverse histories and quite diverse presents — are flung together? How do you envisage this as affecting the immediate future of Christianity?

McLuhan: This has already happened. Because of electric speed, we have had the entire "primitive" or "backward" world thrown into our Western life — and the direct responsibility both to feed and to teach. Many of these areas, like Biafra or North Vietnam, had been Christianized by missionaries.

Hoskins: I was thinking more of the ancient cultures of the East.

McLuhan: They, too, have had much contact with Christianity at various times. India was one of the first Christianized areas, so her presence today in the Christian community is as real as any Western one's. I don't think that there are any geographic or ideological barriers left to a Christian community. An Indian or a Negro or a Korean beside you in Church is no more strange than members of your own family.

Hoskins: I was thinking, though, of the great cultures which I think you would hesitate yourself to call religious at all: the anthropologies, as I believe you call them, Hinduism, Buddhism, and so on.

McLuhan: I don't think of them as religious except in an anthropological sense. They are not, as far as I am concerned, the *thing* — revealed divine event — at all. They have all the fascination of any other massive cultural achievement. They were rendered obsolete at the moment of the Incarnation and they remain so. They are *Games People Play*. There is nothing to prevent any one of them becoming an incidental means of illuminating some aspect of Christian community. We co-exist with all these forms as we co-exist with all the languages of the world. They are in fact part of the cultural languages of the world. They are part of the technology of the word — which again are languages.

Hoskins: I'd like to just read you a passage in *Understanding Media*, one of those rare passages in which you appear to predict, or even to prophesy. It reminded me when I read it of the closing part of *The*

Phenomenon of Man by Teilhard de Chardin, although you refer in this passage to Bergson's critique of language and consciousness:

> Languages as the technology of human extension may have been the Tower of Babel by which man sought to scale the highest heavens; and today, computers hold out the promise of instant change of any code or language into any other code or language. The computer promises, in short, by technology, a Pentecostal condition of universal understanding and unity.

Now are you here predicting, are you prophesying, are you trying to say something historical, or trans-historical, are you trying to say something that lies beyond history?

McLuhan: Well, I think that we live in post-history in the sense that all pasts that ever were are now present to our consciousness and that all the futures that will be are here now. In that sense we are post-history and timeless. Instant awareness of all the varieties of human expression reconstitutes the mythic type of consciousness, of *once-upon-a-time*-ness, which means all-time, out of time.

It is possible that our new technologies can bypass verbalizing. There is nothing impossible about the computer's — or that type of technology's — extending consciousness itself, as a universal environment. In a sense, the *surround* of information that we now experience electrically is an extension of consciousness itself. What effect this might have on the individual in society is just speculation. But — it *has* happened: it isn't something that is going to happen. Many people simply resort instantly to the occult, to ESP, and every form of hidden awareness in response to this new surround of electric information. And so we live, in the vulgar sense, in an extremely religious age. I think that the age we are moving into will probably seem the most religious ever. We are already there.

11

"A Peculiar War to Fight":

Letter to Robert J. Leuver, C.M.F.

[Written from Toronto on 30 July 1969]

Dear Fr. Leuver:[1]

I would like to clarify some of Mr. James Parker's observations on war.[2] He was kind enough to draw attention to some of my notes on the subject.

There seems to be a general unwillingness to consider the impact of technological innovation on the human sensibility. The reason that Joyce considered Vico's *New Science* so important for his own linguistic probes was that Vico was the first to point out that a total history of human culture and sensibility is embedded in the changing structural forms of language. Today we are very conscious of slang as a frontier of linguistic change and response to the new service environments created for our senses by electronic information. Even old forms like "dig," "gutsy," "groovy," indicate a large shift from the "cat's pyjamas," and "hot mammas," and "I'll tell da world" of the 1920s. The '20s were going corporate and tribal fast enough under the huge speed-up of information movement by radio. But their slang is still visual and square (i.e., Euclidean) compared to the tactile, haptic,

---

1 Father Robert J. Leuver, C.M.F., was Editor, *U. S. Catholic*, Chicago.
2 James Parker, "The Joys of War," *U. S. Catholic*, August 1969.

proprioceptive, and acoustic spaces and involvement of the slang of the TV age.

Because total new environments are always hidden from perception (e.g., the satellite environment of the earth which for the first time makes the earth the content of a man-made container), people not only ignore them but assume that they have no effect upon them.

Plato and Aristotle were quite unaware of the ways in which the phonetic alphabet had created a new primacy of visual or Euclidean space. They imagined that their sudden preference for connectedness or analytic reasoning and clarification had arisen from their own conceptual activities merely. Eric Havelock's *Preface to Plato* records the sudden revulsion against the bardic modes of education with the coming of phonetic literacy. Today we have returned to the bardic tradition through the universal use of the [sung] word both in ads and entertainment. In fact, the poets had fervently moved in this direction from Blake, Wordsworth, and Coleridge forward. The poets merely preferred the bardic to the more ludicrous extremes of mechanism that had been perceived by Swift and Pope. *The Dunciad* is a dismissal of the crushing impact of an excess of printed matter on the human intellect.

With Gutenberg the first mechanization of a handicraft was by segmentation of the scribal process, demonstrating the powers of rapid repetition to create mass production. Gutenberg wiped out scholasticism and scribal culture almost overnight. In the same manner that TV uses movies, Gutenberg used the old medieval content as his programming. Soon his technology created a new environment that altered the human sensorium drastically, providing the presses with individual authors eager to express fragmented opinions, or what we later began to call "private points of view." Just as there was nobody in the ancient classical world to notice the effects of the phonetic alphabet and papyrus on the human psyche and social organization, so there was nobody at the Council of Trent who noted that it was the form of printing that imposed a totally new formal causality on human consciousness. In the sixteenth century and after, many God-fearing readers were sure that the "inner light" emanated from the black ink of the printed page. It was the same speedy form of repetitive print that not only revolutionized education in the Renaissance but created the "Romanization of the Catholic church" which is now being de-Romanized by an even greater speed-up of the electric information environment.

Nobody at Vatican I or II paid any attention to the causes of the new "needs" for the church of our time. The "need" of any period is always the puppet-like response to a new hidden service environment that shapes the awareness of all occupants of the same environment, whether they are directly involved in it or not. The motor car, for example, changes all the spaces in housing and urban arrangement. Using a motor car has nothing to do with the effects of the new spaces upon human perception.

Going along with the total and, perhaps, motivated ignorance of man-made environments is the failure of philosophers and psychologists in general to notice that our senses are not passive receptors of experience. Each of our several senses creates unique modalities of space which have been ignored by psychologists in all periods. They prefer to study the mechanisms of the senses rather than the worlds created by them. The work of Edward T. Hall (*The Silent Language* and *The Hidden Dimension*) has directed attention to the amazing variety of social spaces created by different cultures of the world. He does not try to relate the diversity of these spatial forms to technological impact on our sensibilities.

Back to war and Mr. Parker. Every human being is incessantly engaged in creating an image of identity for himself. The image differs with the stages of youth and age, but even more it differs with the technological service environment within which this image-making activity proceeds. The tribal and more Oriental mores of the TV generation is rooted in a response both to the iconic TV image and also to the new satellite environment of the earth. The latter has transformed the earth into a global theatre in which jobs and dress become an anathema, and each seeks to "do his thing," to achieve a unique role with a unique costume. That the entire planet should become show business on a twenty-four-hour basis is not only inevitable now, but it creates "challenges" for all levels of the establishment on a scale that will gradually obliterate consciousness.

When a new problem becomes greater than the human scale can cope with, the mind instinctively shrinks and sleeps. Today, for the first time, things happening at the speed of light also illuminate even the inveterate human somnambulism, forcing pattern recognition and intelligibility on the most reluctant. It is not brains or intelligence that is needed to cope with the problems which Plato and Aristotle and all of their successors to the present have failed to confront. What is needed is a readiness to undervalue the world altogether. This is only possible for a Christian. Willingness to laugh at the pompous hyperboles and banalities of moon-shots may need to be cultivated by some. The "scientific mind" is far too specialized to grasp very large jokes. For example, Newton did not discover gravity, but levity, not earth-pull, but moon-pull. To this day no scientist has a single clue as to what "gravity" is. In the eighteenth century it was defined as "a mysterious carriage of the body to conceal the defects of the mind." The comedy of science as presented by Swift in the third book of *Gulliver's Travels* (Laputa, the floating island) employed the principle of levity to enlarge the gaiety of nations.

In Christian terms, the components of Mars, or the rest of the systems of the cosmos, can reveal nothing comparable to the dimensions of experience available to the most grovelling Christian. Christians, however, have a peculiar war to fight which concerns their identity. The Christian feels the downward mania of the earth and its treasures, and is just as inclined to conform his sensibilities to man-made environments as anyone else. When the secular man senses a new technology is offering a threat to his hard-won human image of self-identity, he struggles to escape from this new pressure. When a community is threatened in its image of itself by rivals or neighbours, it goes to war. Any technology that weakens a conventional identity image creates a response of panic and rage which we call "war." Heinrich Hertz, the inventor of radio, put the matter very briefly: "The consequence of the image will be the image of the consequences."

When the identity image which we enjoy is shattered by new technological environments or by invaders of our lives who possess new weaponry, we lash back first by acquiring their weaponry and then by using it. What we ignore is that in acquiring the enemy's weaponry, we also destroy our former identity. That is, we create new sensory environments which "scrub" our old images of ourselves. Thus war is not only education but also a means of accelerated social evolution. It is these changes that only the Christian can afford to laugh at. People who take them seriously are prepared to wipe out one another in order to impose them as ideals. Today there is no past. All technologies, and all cultures, ancient and modern, are part of our immediate expanse. There is hope in this diversity since it creates vast new possibilities of detachment and amusement at human gullibility and self-deception.

There is no harm in reminding ourselves from time to time that the "Prince of this World" is a great P.R. man, a great salesman of new hardware and software, a great electrical engineer, and a great master of the media. It is His master stroke to be not only environmental but invisible, for the environment is invincibly persuasive when ignored.

War has become the environment of our time if only because it is an accelerated form of innovation and education. If war, according to the Hertzean principle of complementarity, is the natural result of shifting loyalties and identity images, we can use the same Hertzean principle to understand other conundrums. For example, affluence creates poverty, just as the public creates privacy; that is, where there is no affluence there may be hardship, but no poverty, and where there is no public, there may be solitude, but no privacy. These are matters that I have discussed in the *Dew-Line Newsletters* at length. The principle of complementarity is indispensable to understanding the unconscious effects of technologies on human sensibility since the response is never the same as the input. This is the theme of *The Gutenberg Galaxy* where it is explained that the visually oriented person stresses matching rather than making in all experience. It is this matching that is often mistaken for truth in general.

The hallucinogenic world, in environmental terms, can be considered as a forlorn effort of man to match the speed and power of his extended nervous system (which we call the "electronic world") by intensifying the activity of his inner nervous system. This is somewhat like the use of the fast motor car as a way of fighting back at the overpowering scale of high-rise and metropolitan buildings.

Please don't regard this as anything more than a few random responses to Mr. Parker.

Sincerely yours,
[Marshall]

12

Religion and Youth:

Second Conversation with Pierre Babin

Pierre Babin: Do you think that in the electric age Christian faith has to be approached in a new way?

Marshall McLuhan: A little over a year ago I read *L'Eglise et moi (The Church and I)*, published by a French publisher. I was struck by one of his observations concerning catechism. Basically, the author said, we teach catechism as though we were trying to get people to swallow a nut without first breaking the shell. We can't taste the nut, only the shell. And, he added, that's what happens when you make children learn catechism by heart. It doesn't give them a taste for doctrine but only makes them swallow it.

Catechism is something that our TV generation can no longer tolerate, because — as a result of Gutenberg — it is basically a visual form. Young people have acquired an extreme sensitivity to things that involve more than one sense at a time. They have become polyvalent. That is why they like to make their own clothes and huddle close together.

For example, the youngest of my sons presently lives in a commune 150 miles from Toronto with a group of people who all enjoy their careers but want to get back to earthly roots.

∞ *From* Autre homme, autre chrétien à l'âge électronique, *Lyon: Editions du Chalet, 1977. Translated by Wayne Constantineau.*

Babin: How do our young people relate to the electric environment?

McLuhan: Just now, our youngsters have been completely taken over by the electric world, which is acoustic, intuitive, holistic, that is, global and total — a new world that has obsolesced our old scientific world with its quantities, its size, our over-industrialized First World. Young people prefer the Third World because it is more oral and acoustic. It invites them into total immersion, and it doesn't lean towards goals or objectives but focuses only on a certain quality of life.

Babin: Could we call this a return to mysticism?

McLuhan: I think so. Gutenberg emphasized the process of outering and Marconi marked the start of its ebb. At the speed of light, the inner trip is all that's left. Young people prefer Zen Buddhism to our Western form of spirituality. They want to be immersed in things and lose the individual self, which is a by-product of the alphabet and the visual world that flows from it. The Eastern Church, especially the Slavs, traditionally tends towards the inner trip: from that comes the importance to young Westerners of Dostoevski and similar authors.

Here, let me digress. We have lately seen an astonishing renewal of interest in medieval studies by our TV generation. The Institute for Mediaeval Studies at St. Michael's College is forced to turn away two out of every three applicants. They have a profound empathy for this period which is so different from the literary medievalism of the pre-Raphaelites, Newman, or Chesterton. They jump into the Middle Ages like a disk jockey sampling musical styles: they can play it by ear.

Babin: What kind of environment are teenagers looking for?

McLuhan: First, today's teens hate bigness. That is a peculiarity of electric speed where you have everything happening at once, in the same place. Instead of expansion or explosion, you have a sudden contraction or implosion. "Small is beautiful" is their motto. The fact that the entire world is at their fingertips shapes their thinking. So they start to ask questions. "Why do we have giant expressways?" "Why do we have to keep going faster on them and in bigger and bigger vehicles?" "Why do we need railway tracks?" "Why all of this?" The usefulness of all this seems to escape them. A big church, for them, falls in with big schools, the big this and big that . . . And they say: "Enough!"

The small group that they long for retrieves the family, a unity founded on relationship or kinship, or on age similarity. Group membership demands a total involvement in each other, and these groups are formed in an auditory context, a musical environment. The form is simultaneous.

Babin: Aren't these closed groups like sects?

McLuhan: We find, instead, a tribal mentality. Sects were founded on visual predominance, while these small groups are based on aural considerations. So they have quite a different structure and meaning. We could use, here, the terms diachronic and synchronic. Diachronic is the opposite of structure. It is a simple, linear, historical, "one-thing-at-a-time" description. Synchronic is cultural; it means all-at-once. The small group is synchronic. It tries to attain all the values of collective life at once. Our kids want nothing to do with groups separated by distinctions of visual values and interests.

Babin: But don't young people today also like big gatherings like Woodstock in the U.S.A. and Taizé in France?

McLuhan: This is, in fact, one paradox among many. The "instant city" and the large gatherings of music fans were made possible by linking media to the microphone. In these cases, electric media combined with modes of individual transportation, which are also media and attract even more attention. Thanks to electric media and to the great mobility of the audience, this kind of mass assembly was able to mushroom.

I've noticed that the real goal of those who go to these gatherings isn't obvious; it could be about isolating oneself by losing oneself in the crowd as much as it could be about satisfying any communal needs.

Another paradox: while our past spirituality was made up of external manifestations, like individual dress and designated places of worship, the new spiritual form seems to emphasize group and inner experience. So, in these music festivals, young people have discovered a new social ritual, a renewed attraction for role playing by adopting group language and costume. Paradoxically, again, the current interest in Zen stems from the movie *Easy Rider*. This kind of spirituality can develop on the highway. The idea of breaking away from the adult community is attractive to adolescents. They respond to the poetry of movement and their idea of community is radically different from that of any other era. To become an errant knight or a nomad is easy today thanks to the telephone, the car, and the jet. With jets and similar forms of transportation, a new kind of human association comes into play. Teens are drawn to the image of the pioneer's covered wagon heading west. They see in it a community on the move where people have to deal with all kinds of difficulties. They like the idea of being in new situations and having to face unexpected problems daily.

In this regard, the TV generation is not a consumer generation. They are opposed to the style of life offered by a consumer society. They don't want to buy pre-packaged goods. "Do-it-yourself" is their formula. The problem with catechism is precisely due to the fact that it is pre-packaged goods. And they don't like it.

Babin: The Church's main mission is to communicate the message of Jesus. I willingly accept that this message isn't a package, but how can it be communicated as a living reality?

McLuhan: Our youth has already chosen and accepted its masters. I mentioned disk jockeys earlier, in relation to the Middle Ages. Teens accept, without hesitation, their top-ten tunes. And a disk jockey has the answers to all the questions that you ask yourself in catechesis.

Or they go find themselves a guru. Zen is all the rage. They snap up anything that refers to Zen, including motorcycle maintenance!

What counts today is the image that authority presents, and not the doctrine that it may want to get across. Christianity is all about transforming the image that we have of ourselves. In the secular world, when we have lost our identity or when we want a new one, we go to see a psychiatrist. For eighty dollars an hour you get a new sense of your life. Well, the psychiatrist is a new model for the catechist. He is a new type of teacher. He conducts a seminar for you personally, like a tutor in the British school system, a private counsellor. Catechism probably should be reformatted as individual counselling instead of being designed for large groups.

Babin: Do you expect those responsible for the communication of faith to become spiritual masters?

McLuhan: Look what happened to the scholastics after Gutenberg: they were out of touch and they quickly disappeared, or else they turned Protestant. Today, it means that religious teachers have to become mystics and live with the group, or else they'll be out of touch. They'll have to transcend themselves and operate from their right cerebral hemispheres.

Babin: In this regard, what about the Church's traditional insistence on having its own Christian schools to communicate the faith?

McLuhan: Think of Ivan Illich's book on schools, *Deschooling*. He says that since there is now more information outside of schools than inside, close them! I think he is going a bit too far. It is much better to bring the information inside. The answers to all problems, including religious problems, are already there, outside the classroom. Everyone in the human community has access to them.

I've just finished writing a book of exercises with some teachers that could be useful to us in teaching the faith [*City as Classroom*, Toronto: Book Society of Canada, 1977]. It proposes organizing students into small teams and sending them out into the city to investigate specific situations. They would, for example, go find developers and promoters to ask them detailed questions about what they were building. "How long will it take you to erect this office?" "What effect will it have on the existing buildings and on the community's established activities?" Then these teams would report back to the class and discuss their findings. Thus, they go out and come back in, alternating diastolic (expanding) and systolic (contracting) movements.

Babin: That suggests an active and democratic process. Instruction wouldn't be handed down from above. If you applied that to the teaching of faith, would you not be putting at risk the Church's voice of authority?

McLuhan: Obviously. But Church authority has to take on entirely new forms. Young people accept the authority of disk jockeys because they tune them in to what is in the wind or in the air, where they can vibrate in unison. The new ways of thinking and speaking, the new styles to which everyone conforms, are acoustic. The new way does not consist of seeing then doing, but of tuning oneself to the proper frequency, the right wavelength. It's our whole idea of communication that has changed.

In a connected, coherent world (that is, Newton's world), communication operated via connections and links. In the electric world, there are no connections, only separate levels that vibrate together or are in disharmony. We have discovered in our time that touch consists of tuning the sense organ to the frequency of the object itself, maintaining a constant interval between the organ and the object. If we want to grasp the object and squeeze it, we are no longer dealing with contact (and interval) but with connection.

To express their idea of communication, the kids use terms from the electronic and acoustic worlds: to be right on, to be with it, to be in, to catch the right vibes, turn on, and tune in. And that is the message of St. John's Gospel: "May those who have ears to hear, let them hear" [actually Matthew 11:15], that is, tune in to the right frequency. Most people, however, do not have ears for hearing, but only for listening. To listen is to blinker yourself, to restrict the eyes, as it were. To grasp the way the words arrive, what the speaker is saying. But to hear is to put yourself on the same wavelength as the speaker.

Christ himself uses this metaphor. He speaks of listening as opposed to hearing. The scribes were "listeners," they looked at texts. "It is written . . . but I say unto you . . ." But they understood nothing. They had no ears for hearing, but only for listening. The same situation repeats itself today: you may have all the necessary titles and degrees but be on the wrong wavelength.

Jesus also says: "My sheep know my voice. I know my sheep and they recognize my voice. But if you cannot hear me you are not part of my flock" [paraphrase of John 10:27]. He repeats several times in the Gospel of John, essentially: "Most of these people do not belong to my flock, they are on the wrong wavelength. If they hear my voice, it is because the Father has tuned them to the proper frequency. He programmed them from within to hear me." St. John repeats it constantly. The Father has given me certain people who hear me, the others are content just to listen; they don't tune their receivers. They grasp nothing. To them it's all a great mystery!

Babin: Your famous phrase, "the medium is the message," can we apply it to the present question? Usually we think that the message is Christ and His Gospel, and that the medium is the Church. If it is so, how can we say that the medium is the message?

McLuhan: Let me begin with your first question which deals directly with the problem of communication.

Here I want to use the vocabulary and fundamental ideas of Gestalt psychology. In Gestalt, reality presents itself to the mind as a *figure* detaching itself from a *ground*. We notice the *figure* first and most often it dominates our whole field of consciousness. However, the ground is at least as important and often is even more important, especially in the areas that concern us. I wasn't aware of Gestalt theory when I first talked about the medium being the message, and I hadn't yet discovered the significance of the two hemispheres of the brain.

Take a simple example. If you speak of the car as a medium, you are no further ahead because the car is no more than a *figure* detaching itself from a service environment of expressways, oil companies, automobile assembly lines, etc. The real medium, in the case of the car, is the totality of services it creates, or, better yet, the huge change that it creates in the human community. The car as figure is not the message.

For North Americans, the hidden *ground*, the real message, of the car is what it does with our sense of privacy. The effect is different in Europe, but the car for us has been largely created to insure our privacy; in other words, the car's message is privacy, intimacy, and solitude. Privacy is made possible by the large network of highways, the biggest architectural structure in the history of the world which, by contrast, makes the pyramids and the Great Wall of China seem small. The car itself is no more than a *figure* in this service environment.

The same *figure/ground* gestalt structure applies to the Gutenberg press and all other media: the "medium" is not simply a *figure*. And a radio program is only a *figure* on a service *ground*: thus the program isn't the message. The real message is what we call the secondary or side-effect of the medium, not its obvious effects. Side-effects are always hidden, like the ground. We are not aware of them. That is also the essence of Gestalt psychology: the *figure*, the gestalt, is visible while the *ground* remains invisible. Human perception encourages us to pay attention to the *figure* (a painting) and to ignore the *ground* (its frame, the wall, etc.).

This is especially true in the West. The Third World has quite a different approach.

Babin: You spoke of secondary or side-effects. How do you explain that they appeared more important than the direct effects when what is at play is the communication of a message ?

McLuhan: You are thinking in terms of efficient cause, like everyone in the Western world since it was foisted on us by Aristotle: such and such a cause produces such and such an effect. A car transports a man faster than his feet, radio provides instant information. So in the case of efficient cause: the cause necessarily appears prior to the effect, which is contrary to approaching it from formal cause. Efficient cause depends on the left cerebral hemisphere's concern for an abstract element which is also what the *figure* from Gestalt psychology is. Now in the electric age, at the speed of light, we need to process these things through the right hemisphere, that is, holistically, using formal cause. And in formal cause the effects appear before the causes. It is crucial that we use this approach. We need to know in advance what the effects on the users will be before we build the particular medium.

Take cancer for example. Medical science believes that we can get rid of its effects by suppressing its efficient cause. But here is a case where the classic scheme of things no longer works; the cause of cancer resides in the general lifestyle of the person, beyond any particular efficient cause or factor. To cure cancer, we need to examine our total way of life, for example our taste or habit for certain colours or aromas which induce us to add chemical ingredients to food, such as food colourings. They are all known to be carcinogenic but none of them is so directly. We could say that our lifestyle is the underlying cause of cancer (the formal cause), not the food colouring (its efficient cause). In formal cause, the most important effect — in this equation, the one proceeding from lifestyle — appears as a secondary or side-effect (while medical science concentrates on the obvious effect — the one linked to efficient cause).

Here's another example, one closer to our subject. When we're in a frame of mind that draws mostly on the left hemisphere, we instinctively ask: what is the content of the radio program? That's what we think is the message, the direct and obvious effect of the radio, which we believe to be the most important thing. However the content isn't the message. The real message is all the secondary effects produced by the services and disservices that the medium demands. And these are the social and psychic changes that the medium causes in the lives of its users (the formal cause).

If you want to change the effects of radio and eventually protect yourself from them, you shouldn't overly focus on the content, the radio program. The effects have already produced themselves regardless of radio's content. But, let's be frank, in the current mental context (left-brained) these matters are very difficult to accept.

Babin: You are aware that the Church has organizations which concern themselves exclusively with media. For example the OCIC for cinema, and the UNDA for TV and radio. What role would you give to these organizations?

McLuhan: I have already given you the answer. Whether you refer to the media or the Church, their leadership is entirely preoccupied with providing the best possible content. However, they miss the really important points. What you print has very little importance: the effects of print are exactly the same whether one prints "good" or "bad" books.

Babin: But if I push your idea to its limits, applying it to the Church itself, one could conclude that it isn't worth spending a lot of time working on the "message"?

McLuhan: Isn't the real message of the Church in the secondary or side-effects of the Incarnation, that is to say, in Christ's penetration into all of human existence? Then the question is, where are you in relation to this reality? Most people prefer to avoid the question by side-stepping it. The message is there but they want no part of it. So they eliminate it by plugging into another channel. They hypnotize themselves with the *figure* so as to better ignore the *ground*. They prefer to study the words rather than the questions that Christ asks everywhere, and of every human being.

I think that Gestalt's *figure/ground* dichotomy presents us with a useful way of speaking and understanding. The cognitive agent — to speak like Aristotle and Thomas Aquinas — is on the level of the efficient cause, not on that of formal cause. He concerns himself with the "content" of Christianity, not with its true message which consists of being plugged into a person. Generally, when you teach the content of the faith, you seldom go beyond its efficient cause. The formal cause is your manner of being, and all the baggage that accompanies your message.

As a result, to teach catechism as a given or as content is to limit oneself to only half of Christianity. The formal cause — the ground that is perceived unconsciously — is not words, but that part of the faith which operates in our lives. The two should be united.

In Jesus Christ, there is no distance or separation between the medium and the message: it is the one case where we can say that the medium and the message are fully one and the same.

Let me give you another example. Look at the following photograph: it is a well-known reproduction from a Chinese photographer. At a time when he was struggling with some religious questions, this man photographed a landscape of melting snow, in a cemetery with the black earth appearing here and there. When he developed the negative, he was stupefied to notice the face of Christ, and he converted to Christianity on the spot.

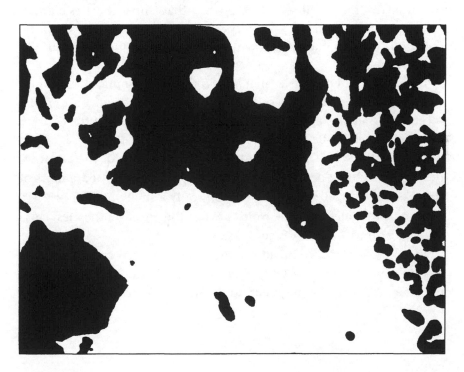

Babin: I am looking at the photograph and I must admit that I see nothing of the sort.

McLuhan: I believe that you have looked at the background as though it were the figure, and, as a result, you saw nothing. So is it with most people when they study a medium: they focus on a medium's program, they grasp only its content. But the vehicle, the entire array of services necessary just to have a program — all of that escapes them. The Oriental, the man from the Third World, is better prepared than we to use the proper approach. Think of traditional Chinese painting which seems to be made up of voids, intervals, and blank spaces, and which for us may have no discernible meaning.

Babin: This Chinese photographer has thus seen Jesus in his totality, as medium and message, and he was transformed because it-suddenly-struck him, spoke to him from within.

McLuhan: That is exactly what I wanted you to notice. To say that the Word became flesh in Jesus Christ is the theological affirmation; it's the *figure* (in the gestalt sense). But to say that Christ touches all men — beggars, hobos, misfits — is to speak of *ground*, that is to say, of the multitude of secondary effects which we have such great difficulty in perceiving.

In fact, it is only at the level of a lived Christianity that the medium really is the message. It is only at that level that *figure* and *ground* meet. And that also applies to the Bible: we often speak of the content of Scripture, all while thinking that this content is the message. It is nothing of the sort. The content is everybody who reads the Bible: so, in reading it, some people "hear" it, and others don't. All are users of the Word of God, all are its content, but only a small number of them discern its true message. The words are not the message; the message is the effect on us, and that is conversion.

In other words, if you read the Bible, how do you read it? Does it pass into your daily life? Only then do you get the message, that is, the effect. Only in that moment do medium and message unite.

PART
3

Vatican II, Liturgy, and the Media

13

Liturgy and the Microphone

"The Bible Belt is oral territory and therefore despised by the literati." The resolution of this paradox depends on noticing that literate culture has, since Flaubert and the Symbolists, itself become structured by oral factors. At instant speeds of information, all structures partake of an acoustic dimension, for auditory space means hearing from all directions at once, involving many levels of awareness. The matter has been memorably put in T. S. Eliot's description of "the auditory imagination":

> What I call the "auditory imagination" is the feeling for syllable and rhythm, penetrating far below the conscious levels of thought and feeling, invigorating every word: sinking to the most primitive and forgotten, returning to the origin and bringing something back, seeking the beginning and the end. It works through meanings, certainly, or not without meanings in the ordinary sense, and fuses the old and obliterated, and the trite, the current, and the new and the surprising, the most ancient and the most civilized mentality.[1]

∞ Originally published in The Critic, vol. 33, no. 1, October–November–December 1974, pages 12-17.

---

1   A quote from Eliot discussed often by McLuhan. T. S. Eliot, essay on Matthew Arnold, in *The Use of Poetry and the Use of Criticism* (London: Faber and Faber, 1933), page 118. See also in this book, pages 122 and 143.

Mr. Eliot is here pointing to the revolution in language and consciousness that occurs when we move from the plane of the simultaneous interplay of multiple factors and experiences. That is why southern culture in the U.S.A. has dominated the twentieth-century arts, both popular and esoteric, both jazz and literature. Eliot has also indicated why the southern idiom has become the avant-garde form of twentieth-century consciousness., when he pointed to Mark Twain as the one who had "purified the dialect of the tribe" by "up-dating" the English language. The poet's cultural role is similar to that of the bridge-builder, language being the stream of unconscious tradition which must be bridged again and again:

> It is possible, on the other hand, that the influence of Mark Twain may prove to have been considerable. If so, it is for this reason: that Twain, at least in *Huckleberry Finn*, reveals himself to be one of those writers, of whom there are not a great many in any literature, who have discovered a new way of writing, valid not only for themselves but for others. I should place him, in this respect, even with Dryden and Swift, as one of those rare writers who have brought their language up to date, and in so doing, "purified the dialect of the tribe."[2]

The updating that Dryden and Swift did in the Newtonian age consisted in their throwing aside traditional schemes of rhetoric and Baroque eloquence, in favour of a direct, colloquial simplicity adapted to the clockwork universe devised by the new astronomy and the new physics. Two centuries later, Mark Twain was engaged in relating the corporate life of the English language to the telegraph age and the telegraph press, an operation in which he was assisted by Charles Dickens and Mr. Jingle. *Huckleberry Finn* carries us into a world of semiliterate idiom and dialect, of oral slang and twang, suited to a corporate stream of consciousness, and inseparable from life on the Mississippi. It is a theme which gets much attention in *Four Quartets*:

> *I do not know much about gods; but I think that the river*
> *Is a strong brown god — sullen, untamed and intractable*

---

2   T. S. Eliot, *To Criticize the Critic* (London: Faber and Faber, 1965), page 54.

Like the hidden levels of human tradition and consciousness, the river challenges the bridge builder:

The problem once solved, the brown god is almost forgotten
By the dwellers in cities — ever, however, implacable . . .

Eliot was born and raised in St. Louis and steeped in the Mississippi environment. He speaks of the river:

His rhythm was present in the nursery bedroom,
In the rank ailanthus of the April dooryard . . .

In *Crowds and Power*, Elias Canetti observes that the river has many features in common with the crowd:

> A river is the crowd in its vanity, the crowd exhibiting itself. This being seen is as important as the element of direction. There is no river without banks; its bordering verdure is like a lane of people. All riverlike formations, such as processions or demonstrations, want to be seen. They show as much as possible of their surface, extending as far as they can and offering themselves to the largest possible number of spectators.

Mr. Eliot was intensely aware of the symbolism of natural forms, and *Four Quartets* makes much of not only the river, but of the sea. Canetti's thoughts about the river seem to have relevance to the entire role of southern-American culture in the contemporary world of jazz and rock, as well as in the work of Mr. Eliot and James Joyce, for whom the oral traditions of the American south and of Ireland have been central facts.

How the "Bible Belt" enters the world of jazz and rock has become a major theme of cultural historians — who are nevertheless baffled by the fact that the avant-garde forms of experimental jazz and rock originate in the deep south rather than in the industrial north. It is a fact of the greatest relevance to the students of liturgy. It points to one of the most traumatic developments in current liturgy, namely, the visitation upon Catholic congregations of bureaucratic process. The liturgy of the Eucharist now exists in a "vernacular" form, ordered by committees whose relation to the English language has much of the dead character of a computer's. Minus the oral dimension of collo-quial idiom and rhythm, the vernacular can be a wasteland and a spiritual desert. The rhythms of the Latin Mass were easygoing and permitted a good deal of meditation; the vernacular pace is more intense with far less opportunity for meditation.

Throughout the twentieth century, the role of the microphone has been to intensify the place of the vernacular in our public and social lives. If Gutenberg had given great new salience to the vernacular in its visual forms, the microphone has created an entire new acoustic world by means of the vernacular. In *The Responsive Chord* (Anchor Books, 1973), Tony Schwartz discusses acoustic imagery with full recognition of the video or TV image, explaining that TV has the power to use the eye as if it were an ear. That is, the TV image is not only audile-tactile in its structure and texture, but it has the means of multi-directional coverage which the unaided eye does not. All of the electric media of our time have tended towards the strengthening of the vernacular in its most colloquial and non-literary forms. The world of the Watergate investigations put this trend into a position of intense public awareness by giving salience to the fact of the recording of private human voices as matters of the utmost political importance. "Bugging" is broadcasting in reverse, as it were; instead of directing the beam towards the individual, the private individual becomes the broadcaster and secrecy becomes show business. In the same way, flips between private and public participation occur when the vernacular is present via the microphone in the Mass. The audience and the mike merge, with the vernacular creating a kind of "sound bubble" which involves everybody. This is the nature of acoustic space, which is con-stituted by its centre being everywhere and its margin being nowhere. Without the microphone the speaker is at a single centre, while with the microphone he is everywhere simultaneously — a fact which "obsolesces" the architecture of our existing churches.

∞

In technological terms, the vernacular has had two major amplifica-tions, one visual and one auditory. In the sixteenth century, Gutenberg gave new visual intensity to the vernacular in a way that created many new forms of specialist division psychically, politically, and spiritually. What might have seemed, in the sixteenth century, a "spontaneous" demand for a vernacular liturgy, was inseparable from the Gutenberg technology which created simultaneously intense individualism and intense nationalism. In liturgical terms, the new stress on preaching was inseparable from the popularity of printed sermons and the opportunity for textual exegesis in the pulpit. The intense new visual stress favoured a celebrant facing a congregation across a table/altar. This practice was accepted by the Reform churches and rejected by Rome. The visual experience naturally excludes metamorphosis and transubstantiation, for visual or Euclidean space is the only static sensory mode known to man.

In his *Ramus, Method, and the Decay of Dialogue*, Walter Ong, S.J., explained how the printed word tended to suppress dialogue, while pushing scholastic forms of classification into the classroom. Print not only created a multiplicity of new divisions between "subjects," but it intensified nationalistic divisions in terms of the vernaculars which suddenly became major political forces. In the twentieth century, the microphone reversed a great many of the visual characteristics of the printed vernacular. The telegraph had already created new forms of the printed word, in the newspaper and in poetry alike. By making it possible for information to be gathered simultaneously from every quarter of the globe, the telegraph press took on a mosaic and essentially acoustic character of simultaneity that occurred in Symbolist poetry as well.

Merely to illustrate how essential the microphone is to our ordinary lives, were the microphone to be removed from the entertainment world of the night club, the concert hall, the radio, and TV, the entire situation would be altered. Indeed, without the microphone there could be no radio or TV or telephone. Rudy Vallee began by singing into a megaphone, which is strikingly different from "soul singing." The "soul" singer, unlike the "torch" singer, seems to disappear inside the mike, while the microphone singer appears to be projecting himself through his medium.

The microphone is inseparable from some form of amplification by which the relation to the public is altered. PA systems attached to microphones have developed such strikingly different characters as Ghandi and Hitler, Bing Crosby and Winston Churchill. The hardware/software complementarity is evident in the fact that the microphone permits us to do more with less. One of the more recent areas in which the mike has made its power of transformation evident

is that of liturgy and ritual. Many people will lament the disappearance of the Latin Mass from the Catholic Church without realizing
that it was a victim of the microphone on the altar. It is not practical
to say Latin into a microphone since the mike sharpens and intensifies the sounds of Latin to a meaningless degree. That is, Latin is really
a very cool form of verbal delivery in which mutter and murmur play a
large role, whereas the mike does not take kindly to humming indis-
tinctly. Another effect of the mike at the altar has been to turn the
celebrant around to face the congregation. By the same token, ampli-
fiers which are placed in the church to create sounds from all directions
at once make the church architecturally obsolete. In a word, the mike
makes worshippers demand an intimate and small group of participants. On the other hand, the microphone, which makes it so easy
for a speaker to be heard by many, also forbids him to exhort or be
vehement. The mike is indeed a cool medium.

The microphone in the studio has created a totally new kind of
musical situation. The possibility of using many mikes simultaneously
and recording different qualities on multiple tracks makes possible
a new mix of sounds. Meantime, the "performer," say a pianist like
Glenn Gould, is thinking less of the public that used to be in a concert
hall, than of the composer, on one hand, and the sound engineers,
on the other hand. The ideal of "hi fi" really indicates a new concept
of composition rather than performance. If the jazz musician composes in the act of performing, the mike and studio situation bring
into existence both new composition and new performance.

∞

Another musical dimension made possible by the mike is the "instant
city," a gathering of music fans for a specific occasion of performance
by one or more bands. Here the mike is drawing attention to the other
media that permit rapid movement in space which make for new
kinds of audiences, a preview of which had taken place at Bayreuth at
the Wagner music festival, where culture was transformed into a high
religious ritual. High mobility on the part of the audience makes of
music festivals a new social ritual which, in turn, is transferred to film
and recording. In all of this, the audience itself becomes a major performer. Naturally, the audience as performer represents a feature of
all sports, much more so since electronic coverage of these events.

Paradoxically, the bullfight, which had declined in popular esteem during the period of radio, acquired new dimensions of popularity and participation with TV. TV monitors drew great crowds into the streets to watch bullfights on TV while the cost of seats in the arena skyrocketed. The kind of sensory satisfactions enjoyed in each of these situations is quite unlike the others. As an example, the odors of the bullring are notably absent in broadcasts, although they are a great feature of the actual scene.

The role of the mike in religious broadcasts since the first days of radio has been as important as it has been in political life and organization. (The image of Amy Semple MacPherson, like that of Billy Graham, would scarcely have existed without the microphone.) When TV arrived, radio stations were bought up in large numbers by Bible schools and religious sects. Today, for example, the entire Watergate affair is intimately linked with the world of the microphone and the recording, creating a new acoustic dimension in politics which is direct conflict with the press, the constitution, and the printed word. To an extent unknown in any other country, the political life of the U.S.A. is postulated on the printed word. Its legal and political institutions presumed the printed word from the start. They also presumed a public primarily related to the printed word, so that when radio and TV entirely upset this balance in politics and in other areas of the establishment, the psychological distress has been as great as it has been mysterious and confusing. Few, if any, have heeded the causes of this major upheaval in social and political life which results from the switch from visual to acoustic bias in daily experience. Likewise, the disturbances within the Church and the liturgy are, in a large part, to be understood in relation to this vast reversal of form and content which occurs when a whole people is suddenly flipped from visual to auditory experience. In terms of the use of the microphone in the liturgy, it may be observed that acoustic amplification overloads our auditory sensory channel, diminishing the attention span of the visual and private experience of the liturgy, as well as of the architectural space, isolating the individual in a kind of "sound bubble." Private identity is reduced and "equalized," as it were, to its surroundings, by this resonance. Hymn-singing provides a similar paradox, since the individual effort of singing actually becomes a means of merging with others. Perhaps the Catholic reluctance to vocalize communally relates to the habitual use of the Mass for private meditation. These are multi-leveled and complex matters which cannot be dealt with in a short space. The meditative individual in his "sound bubble" is naturally irritated by the strident and amplified vernacular voice of the celebrant. Latin had kept him at a corporate distance, for Latin is not a private medium of expression. The vernacular is strongly horizontal in its thrust and embrace, whereas Latin tended to the vertical and the specialist aspiration. The microphone on the altar and in the pulpit has brought changes to the liturgy of considerable extent. We need only imagine the present situation, minus the microphone, to sense its importance. The coming of the microphone was gradually discovered to be incompatible with the use of Latin which is a corporate, low-definition form of mutterings in its ritual use.

∞

Without reconstructing the history of the decision to shelve the Latin Mass, one can see the matter in parallel form in the discovery by the preacher that the microphone is incompatible with vehement exhortation or stern admonition. To a public that is electrically participant in a completely acoustic situation, loudspeakers bring the sounds of the preacher from several directions at once. The structure of our churches is obsolesced by the multi-directional media speaker system, and the older distance between speaker and audience is gone. The audience is now in immediate relation with the speaker, a factor which also turns the celebrant around to face the congregation. These major aspects of liturgical change were unforeseen and unplanned and remain unacknowledged by the users of the microphone system in our churches.

The ordinary evolutionary and developmental attitude towards innovation assumes that there is a technological imperative: "If it *can* be done, it *has to be* done"; so that the emergence of any new means *must* be introduced, for the creation of no matter what new ends, regardless of the consequences. Lineal and revolutionary ideas of development naturally derive from visual culture, which is no longer the form of the electric and acoustic age. What had been seen as inevitable, in visual and lineal terms of development, appears to the electronic man as merely one of many possible programs. The electronic man starts with the effect desired and then looks around for the means to those effects, whereas the old visual culture had accepted all the available means as a kind of destiny or irreversible fate which drove him towards ever-changing patterns, regardless of the cost.

Without attempting to evaluate the advantages and disadvantages of the visual world whose structure had dominated recent centuries, it is important to know that visual structure is not compatible with the free play of information and simultaneous patterns of experience. Under visual conditions, to have a goal or objective is by no means the same thing as anticipating effects. The builder of a church or a university may well begin with some idea of the effects he wishes to create, but at very high speeds of traffic and of both population and information movement the most august structures may cease to be service environments within a single life span. Even before such obsolescence occurs, those in charge of these services may inadvertently introduce subsidiary techniques which upset the entire structures. Thus, in this century the telephone has rendered the organization chart of many big businesses quite inoperative, and the microphone has introduced effects into the liturgy which nobody had expected or planned.

∞

One of the biggest paradoxes of our time is the universal disease of being unwanted. Greatly increased mobility simply erases the forms of human community as we have known them. Most of us meet many people daily for the first and only time, while seeing many of our older friends but rarely. On the other hand, electric information brings us into very close association with all of the people on this planet. Like the congestion in our cities, this new electronic involvement of everybody in everybody creates the effect of a "population explosion." The same electric means which involve us in others in depth, almost eliminating space and time in our lives — these same means also deprive us of most of what had been considered private identity and individuality in recent centuries. It is natural to be blinded to the loss of identity when we are deeply and newly involved in the lives of many others. Whether private "identity" and individuality has any permanent importance beyond the world of social change is a matter for theologians. What we can consider is the immediate experience of this loss of the sense of identity as it manifests itself in life and liturgy.

One of the immediate consequences of weak identity is moral

permissiveness and slackness. The correlative of this is the demand for rigorous standards of public behaviour. Again, loss of private identity means loss of strongly envisaged goals and objectives, accompanied by an eagerness to play a variety of roles in the lives of other people. The need to be "wanted" by others comes with loss of private identity and also of community. In a world of rapid movement and change, everybody is a nobody, and the greatest head of state, when off-base, could be mistaken for a flunky. In liturgical terms, loss of identity means loss of clerical vocations, and moral permissiveness means loss of the need to go to Confession. Whereas many used to go to Confession and relatively few to Communion, now very few go to Confession and most go to Communion.

∞

The Watergate episode is full of lessons for the liturgist, for it represents a blind struggle to maintain Gutenberg private values, on the one hand, and the total involvement of electronic environment, on the other hand. Personal freedom and individual rights to privacy and dignity, in accordance with the written code, have been challenged by the Watergate episode, which has reversed all secrecy into show business, and all privacy into broadcasting. The turning of the inside outside, and of the outside inside, exactly parallels the power of the TV medium which threatens to reverse the American way of life. Whereas North Americans had for centuries gone outside to be alone and inside to be social, TV has brought the outside into our intimate social lives, and taken our social lives out into the public domain. The Loud family episode, in which the intimate personal lives of the family group became "show biz," parallels Watergate which transformed the backroom political intrigues into "show biz." Both have personally involved the entire nation in a reversal of values and the abolition of goals by flipping us into public role-playing. Parallels for the liturgical reversals which have taken place under electric auspices can be found in every other sector: in education, politics, and commerce.

14

Liturgy and Media:
Do Americans Go to Church to Be Alone?

Is twentieth-century man one who runs down the street shouting, "I've got the answers. What are the questions?"

How much of sixteenth-century Protestantism was political ploy and how much doctrinal conviction?

Was it only the tribal periphery of areas outside the Latin core and the ground design of Spain, Italy, France, that became Protestant?

Is life in the magnetic city (the Megamachine) compatible with the survival of the Greco-Roman tradition?

Is Western civilization inherent in the Church or only attached to it?

Is the private, civilized, and phonetically literate man merely a transient artifact of human origin?

∞ Originally published in The Critic, vol. 31, no. 3, January–February 1973, pages 14-23; plus further thoughts in the next issue of the same magazine, vol. 31, no. 4, March–April 1973.

Is there an insoluble conflict between the role of the Church to change man and the power of the Greco-Roman rational culture to invent and hold him fixed?

Has the Greco-Roman culture of the Church deprived Oriental and African man of Christianity?

Under the instant pressures of electric media, does Western man become discarnate and inward while the East becomes extrovert?

Has the Church today missed the meaning of the communication revolution as it did in the sixteenth century?

What is the ecological responsibility of the Church for the restraint of secular innovations in technology?

Why has Western man, and why has the Catholic Church, no theory of communication of secular psychic change?

Has the Church itself been responsible for much of the secular technology that has shaped the Western psyche? (See Lynn Whyte's *Machina ex Deo*.)

Do the decentralized patterns of electric culture commit man to a diversity of life and liturgy styles more divergent than those of the Greek and Roman Churches?

Must the Greco-Roman Church take a stand against the inner tribal and discarnate dynamics released by the electric information environment?

Is the Catholic concern with the *figure* of the liturgy any reason for ignoring the *ground* of the liturgy? Why cannot Hans Küng study the telegraph as *ground* for the infallible decree of 1870?

Is renewal in the Church also disintegration?

Can Christian renewal ignore the disintegration of the
business, educational, and political establishments that
are the *grounds* of the renewal?

Need the Church discard traditional roles and costumes
just when these modes of performance are being discovered in the secular world?

One of the unique features of the North American outlook is the invol-
untary and unconscious habit of going outside to be alone. This gesture
is as natural to us as going inside for company and community. Some
of the consequences of these spatial ways of seeking our deepest satisfactions of privacy and society are not new in America, but they are
almost unknown in any other part of the world. In Tokyo, as in Paris,
or Buenos Aires, or in London, people typically and habitually go out,
whether to dine or to shows or to church, in order to be with people.
Everywhere else, save America, people go home to be alone. Home is
for privacy all over the world, except in America. There is little privacy in the American home. And this is said not to evaluate but to
draw attention to some very remarkable human patterns old and new.
For even the long-established American habit of seeking privacy outside the home, and preferably out-of-doors, is less characteristic of the
young today. The young are shedding the established forms of seeking
privacy outside and community inside the house.

In matters of liturgy and worship, Americans have not been comfortable with the European distribution of space, or, for that matter,
with European programming of space. Traditional church architecture
relates as little to American needs as do European forms of liturgy. But
where culture is concerned, Americans have long been consumers of
the imported "quality" product. One of the results of going out to be
alone is that the individual is fated to consume what has been prepared
elsewhere by a group. Europeans go out not to consume products but to
participate in a process of social making and exchange. They dine out
for conversation and new acquaintance, as they visit the play or concert in order to criticize performance and to observe the participants.

I am going to mention some specific examples of the differences
between American and European attitudes, first because they are differences that hold quite well as between American and other cultures,
and second because these differences are now disappearing among

young Americans. America is becoming producer- rather than consumer-minded, and this relates to media on one hand, and to liturgy on the other.

Faced with a special assignment to speak to a congress of British advertisers, I finally chose to begin with the American dislike of ads in movies. Most Americans would resent an encounter with large commercial ads in a playhouse or even in a movie. When a "short" turns out to be a sponsored ad, Americans think of getting their money back from the box office, but Europeans are quite blithe about such intrusions in movies and theatres. Yet they fight strongly against the same ads appearing on radio and TV where they invade the privacy of the home. Americans don't like ads at home or on TV, but settle their grievances with such jokes as: "Why do station managers have to have very small hands?" The answer sends some people up the wall: "Small paws for station identification." But there is a sequel which mollifies the visually oriented who writhe under the pun: "What is the longest word in any language?" It is, of course, "A word from our sponsor." American intolerance of ads in movies or theatres is matched by their instant irritation with conversation or vocal comment while performances are in progress. This is felt as an invasion of privacy.

It is, of course, impossible to get a full consensus on these matters of space and private sensibility, for individuals differ a good deal. Moreover, most people don't like to discuss or even think about such general but hidden patterns of behaviour that concern their own private lives. Since these attitudes are deeply set and also relate to liturgy, I shall try to illustrate them indirectly and in neutral areas. Thus the American car is quite unlike those of other countries, for the American finds in his car the ultimate means of "going outside to be alone," and the dream of "the open road" is near to the American heart. In scope and mass the highway in America is a monumental vortex of corporate engineering that far overshadows the Aztec pyramids. And the American car is typically a large space far in excess of the needs of the lonely motorist speeding to and from work. By contrast, the cars of other lands are mere toys or playthings used festively, like motorbikes, and regarded as pets. Perhaps it is in relation to the car that it is easiest to see the why and how of the American "extrovert," the man who is alone when outside, the man who is a lonely crowd and never more so than when in a traffic jam, in town or on the highway. Paradoxically, it has been found that many Americans are quite happy in traffic jams, for here they are least accessible of all. The psychological case against public transit in America is a strong one.

An even larger and deeper factor in the American quest for privacy out-of-doors is in the contrast between American speech and the speech patterns of other cultures. When Americans are outside, in public, they use a private or personal speaking voice. We are unique in the use of natural voices without the "standard" elocutionary effects of acquired prestige tones, such as the educated European takes for granted. To speak without regional dialect or without the put-on patina of manifest elocution has been possible for the American alone. Even the speech of Brooklyn and the south seem odd to us. The traces of Brooklyn and southern group or dialect speech are just sufficient to remind us that Professor Higgins, the elocutionist of Shaw's *Pygmalion*, is retained in order to scrub off such regional voice features. Professor Higgins could barely eke out a living in a drama school in America. In a word, the absence of class speech in America owes very much to our going out to be alone and to be just "me myself and I."

But to go out to be alone also means that Americans tend to be job-holders and private goal-seekers rather than role-players, and this is also a matter that concerns participation liturgy very much indeed. For liturgy calls for a considerable degree of immersion of the private psyche in the corporate life, just as it demands a "putting on" of group image. Since the young have recently found new impulse in the direction of role-playing by adoption of group speech and the putting-on of corporate costume, it may provide some light if we take a look at the jazz and rock scene, for these are areas of spontaneous corporate rituals. Piggy-backing on fast transport, rock musicians have introduced the "instant" city, Woodstock-style. The camp meeting has mushroomed, via electronics, but whether these forms of going outside are for the purpose of being alone or to fulfil communal needs is not obvious. The character of the participants has changed as much as the performance. When Hindus meet in vast numbers they speak of having a mystic experience of *darshan*. Our own larger gatherings tend to be for games and contests rather than for mysticism, but rock has brought a new character to our togetherness. Since rock also interests liturgists very much, it is relevant to take a look at its structure and some of its effects.

∞

The Sound of the City: The Rise of Rock and Roll is the title of Charlie Gillett's study of rock (Outerbridge and Dienstfrey, New York, 1970). Gillett notes that in our century "a remarkable proportion of the important stylistic changes in American popular music has stemmed from the southern states" (page 199). In the same way, a remarkable proportion of the stylistic changes in twentieth-century poetry have stemmed from Ireland. Both in Ireland and the American south there is a major hidden factor that may help us to understand both of these manifestations of art. Ireland and the American south possess a virtual monopoly of oral tradition in English speech, and in both areas the origin is "Elizabethan" English. When speech historians simulate Chaucer's English, it sounds very "Scottish," and when the BBC performs Shakespeare in the speech style of his time, it sounds very "Irish" indeed. This is not to say that Chaucer had any Scottish connections or that Shakespeare had any interest in Ireland. In the same way, the American south has a variety of traditional English dialects and an overriding rhythm that is corporate and oral. That is, the rhythm is not borrowed from or found on the written page, but belongs to what T. S. Eliot called the "auditory imagination." It is helpful for the student of rock to know how the oral rhythms of English affect the entire structure of "meanings" in language:

> What I call the "auditory imagination" is the feeling for syllable and rhythm penetrating far below the conscious levels of thought and feeling, invigorating every word: sinking to the most primitive and forgotten, returning to the origin and bringing something back, seeking the beginning and the end. It works through meanings, certainly, or not without meanings in the ordinary sense, and fuses the old and obliterated, and the trite, the current and the new and the surprising, the most ancient and the most civilized mentality.[1]

The auditory imagination is much muted in a merely literary culture when the oral tradition has been overlaid by mountains of print.

Let me pause to disclaim any concern about trying to assign relative values to speech and writing. I am trying to find out some of the hidden bases of liturgy and popular speech and entertainment, since public worship and corporate speech and song are closely intertwined.

---

1 See also McLuhan's discussion of this quote on pages 107 and 143 of this book.

Speech is the encoded form of the collective perception and wisdom of countless men. Speech is not the area of theory or concept but of performance and percept. Poetry and Song are major means by which speech is purified and strengthened, and poetry and music are extensions of speech, so it is not by chance that most of the English poetry and song of the twentieth century have come out of Ireland and the American south. T. S. Eliot would have been the first to insist upon his debt to W. B. Yeats and James Joyce. In his review of *Ulysses* in *The Dial* (November 1922), he wrote:

> In using the myth, in manipulating a continuous parallel between contemporaneity and antiquity, Mr. Joyce is pursuing a method which others must pursue after him. They will not be imitators, any more than the scientist who uses the discoveries of an Einstein in pursuing his own, independent, further investigations. It is simply a way of controlling, of ordering, of giving a shape and a significance to the immense panorama of futility and anarchy which is contemporary history.

And apropos his acknowledgment to Yeats as having anticipated Joyce in the use of the continuous parallel, it is explained by Yeats himself in his essay on *The Emotion of Multitude* in 1903:

> I have been thinking a good deal about plays lately, and I have been wondering why I dislike the clear and logical construction which seems necessary if one is to succeed on the modern stage. It came into my head the other day that this construction, which all the world has learnt from France, has everything of high literature except the emotion of multitude. The Greek drama has got the emotion of multitude from its chorus, which called up famous sorrows, even all the gods and all heroes, to witness, as it were, some well-ordered fable, some action separated but for this from all but itself. The French play delights in the well-ordered fable, but by leaving out the chorus it has created an art where poetry and imagination, always the children of far-off multitudinous things, must of necessity grow less important than the mere will. This is why, I said to myself, French dramatic poetry is so often rhetorical, for what is rhetoric but the will trying to do the work of the imagination? The Shakespearean drama gets the emotion of multitude out of the subplot which

copies the main plot, much as a shadow upon the wall copies one's body in the firelight. We think of *King Lear* less as the history of one man and his sorrows as the history of a whole evil time. Lear's shadow is in Gloucester, who also has ungrateful children, and the mind goes on imagining other shadows, shadow beyond shadow, until it has pictured the world. In *Hamlet*, one hardly notices, so subtly is the web woven, that the murder of Hamlet's father and the sorrow of Hamlet are shadowed in the lives of Fortinbras and Ophelia and Laertes, whose fathers, too, have been killed. It is so in all the plays, or in all but all, and very commonly the subplot is the main plot working itself out in more ordinary men and women, and so doubly calling up before us the image of multitude. Ibsen and Maeterlinck have, on the other hand, created a new form, for they get multitude from the wild duck in the attic, or from the crown at the bottom of the fountain, vague symbols that set the mind wandering from idea to idea, emotion to emotion. Indeed all the great masters have understood that there cannot be great art without the little limited life of the fable, which is always the better the simpler it is, and the rich, far-wandering, many-imaged life of the half-seen world beyond it. There are some who understand that the simple unmysterious things living as in a clear noon light are of the nature of the sun, and that vague, many-imaged things have in them the strength of the moon. Did not the Egyptian carve it on emerald that all living things have the sun for father and the moon for mother, and has it not been said that a man of genius takes the most after his mother?

Eliot, Yeats, and Joyce offer the liturgist today these major insights into the needful restructuring of any performance that is to create a corporate harmony from the anarchy of contemporary experience. The fact that Charlie Gillett can refer to rock as "the Sound of the City" means that rock is the technological sound of Megalopolis translated through the English language. The fact that it is the English of the American south relates to its oral tradition which has been the basis not only of country music and ballads (including the Cowboy songs) but of the well-established tradition of Baptist hymns, such as nourished the art of "Satchmo" Louis Armstrong. American jazz and the blues (it has long been recognized) originated in the popular church music of the American south. What has not been understood is that the hidden *ground*, not only of jazz and rock, but of all music, must be the common dialect. Technical innovation in the human environment disturbs all levels of personal perceptual life and must find its resolution through the common measures of speech. Speech, as it were, is the great corporate and organic medium which digests and orders the chaotic inputs of daily experience. Here is the conscious organ of the auditory imagination where multitudes of changes and adjustments are made every day, as well as in the purgative dreams of the night.

$$\infty$$

I have tackled an enormous theme in approaching liturgy and the media, and it is possible only to brush against its vast patterns. When it is grasped that public worship naturally requires the dominant medium of speech itself, it is also possible to see why alteration or innovation strikes to the psychic core by the resonance in the auditory imagination. The Latin liturgy, for example, had a long history of interplay between written and oral, learned and popular forms. The Latin was, and is, grounded in the vernaculars much as any musical art form has to be as well. The interplay between the Latin Mass and the vernacular participant is not additive. The Latin is not added to the experience of, say, the English congregation. There is already much Latin in the English tongue, and the parallel action between English and Latin in the Tridentine Mass is of the order indicated in the Yeats comment on "The Emotion of Multitude." The interface of the two tongues creates a powerful, dramatic tension far above either of them.

There is a difficult area of jazz and rock that concerns dance rhythms. A consensus exists about the fact of Negro dance rhythms in jazz and rock. It needs much study and I can merely hint at how it could be approached. It is familiar to many people that jazz and rock cannot be sung satisfactorily in any language but English. Even in the 1920s jazz went far to make English a world language, sung in Peking, Berlin, Moscow, Paris, and London alike. Sung in any other language, the performer seems to be putting on an alien costume, seeking to complete with his hands and body what is omitted from the speech rhythms. I am going to venture another hypothesis based on the fact that most languages have no prosody of feet, such as iambics and trochees, but only syllables. English, and in some degree German, have prosodic, or foot, stresses, rather than the syllabic stress that is typical of most tongues. Father Hopkins, the English poet, may have been trying to substitute syllabic for prosodic stress in English poetry, just as Frank Lloyd Wright seems to have substituted American space for European space in architecture. At any rate, English rhythms seem to be able to accommodate Negro dance in jazz and rock songs while other languages have had to leave these dance rhythms out of their translations of jazz and rock. In Denmark, I have heard, there has been an attempt to use three languages at once for rock.

If it is a principal function of music to assimilate the changing sounds of the technological environment of human sensibility by passing them through the relatively stable medium of language, then it becomes possible to glimpse some of the problems of interrelating music and speech and liturgy. It is also easier to see why no ordinary group of well-intentioned innovators could hope to produce either participation or worship or solace by improvised liturgical experiment. The prolonged intensity of stylistic work done in the rock world alone points to the size of the problem of relating popular experience to the liturgical environment. rock is not added to the city. It is the city in musical translation. If the translators are doing a poor job, it may be due to their inadequate grasp of the medium of English.

In *Four Quartets*, where the social functions of music and speech make a principal theme, Eliot cites Mallarmé:

> *Since our concern was speech, and speech impelled us*
> *To purify the dialect of the tribe*
> *And urge the mind to aftersight and foresight,*
> *Let me disclose the gifts reserved for age*
> *To set a crown upon your lifetime's effort.*

Eliot is careful to point to the corporate, spoken language as "speech," and "dialect," and "tribal," because these features of language are much beyond the range of the written or printed word. It is this total body of speech as shaped by the experience of all ages which is the concern of the poet:

> *For last year's words belong to last year's language*
> *And next year's words await another voice.*

When this total body of speech is alienated from those in charge of liturgy, the worshipper is deprived and befogged in his spiritual gestures.

∞

I opened these observations with the suggestion that in the space patterns of America people go out to church to be alone. Americans are thus confused by being saddled with, or overlaid by, ideas of self and society and of prayer and worship that derive from Europe where people go outside to be with people and inside to be alone. I did not venture even to ask why Americans experience space and one another in a style radically different from the rest of mankind. The reason may have something to do with the fact that the U.S.A. is the only place in the world where Western man had literacy from the beginning. The preliterates of America were the Indians whose primal culture is now shared by the young TV generation. Another factor in the unconscious American attitude to self and society may be the obvious frontier and the emptiness of the environment. The feeling of stepping outside into "God's country" and the feeling of owning it all are not natural to those who dwell in densely populated areas of the world.

The *why* query in this matter was foremost in my mind recently when a Japanese came to visit. He was a theological student working on communications and liturgy, and I asked his opinion about these matters of the unique American relation to space. He agreed at once that the Japanese, different in so much else, shared the European attitudes to space, privacy, and community.

As we considered possible causes for these contrasting attitudes, I raised another related question to this able Japanese theologian. Why, I asked, does the Western world, unlike the Orient, shun all investigation of the psychic and social effects of technology? He had no hesitation in replying: "Because you feel the study of technological effects on people to be an invasion of your privacy." Much reflection on his remark has confirmed its relevance. Neither Plato nor Aristotle nor Aquinas nor any traditional Western thinker has thought it worth investigation. There is no theory of how psychic constitution is altered by the impact of man's own technologies. Lewis Mumford in *The Pentagon of Power* echoes Gordon Childe when he writes in passing: "Man is his own supreme artifact." Mumford has no theory of communication or psychic change, but Eric Havelock's *Preface to Plato* (Harvard University Press, 1963) does have such a theory. He derives the private identity image of the civilized Greeks from the unique character of the technology of the Greek alphabet. No preliterate man ever experienced the peculiar isolation and individuality of the Western literate man. The pre-Christian Hebrews did not have it. The Oriental does not have it now.

This is not to make any value judgments whatever. The private psyche may be an artificial monster of the most precious discovery. It is demonstrable that it had a historical origin and that this "artifact" may have a contemporary demise in this electronic age of discarnate togetherness. Until recently this private psyche seems to have been the means of repelling all investigations of its individual responses to environmental and technological change. Where this precarious and isolated entity did not occur, as in preliterate societies, the effects of technology on society have been studied with great concern. Resistance to innovation has been the norm in preliterate society, including the Oriental world, where awareness of the magical powers of technology to transform the world of man has been acute.

Apart from those shaped by the phonetic alphabet, the universal condition of man has been corporate and tribal and family-oriented. The Greek and Roman civis, the private individual equal before a code of written laws, cannot hold up to the new all-involving power of electric communication or change. For communication is change, and Christianity is concerned above all and at all times with the need for change in man. St. Paul states his theory of communication everywhere. In Romans 1.21-25, it is:

(21) Because that, when they knew God, they glorified Him not as God, neither were they thankful, but became vain in their imaginations, and their foolish heart was darkened.

(22) Professing themselves to be wise, they became fools,

(23) And changed the glory of the incorruptible God into an image made like to corruptible man, and four-footed beasts and creeping things.

(24) Wherefore God also gave them up to uncleanness through the lusts of their own hearts.

(25) Who changed the truth of God into a lie and worshipped and served the creature more than the Creator Who is blessed forever. Amen.

That is, as soon as men identified God with His creation they could also glorify their own handiwork as extensions of God. The initial merging of God and His creatures may have begun with art and technology. It certainly led to much technology and to the clouding of the mind. St. Paul has no more doubt than the Hebrew prophets about the transforming power of technology on the human powers of perception: "They became what they beheld." That Western literate man who rejoices in the unique possession of a private identity should at the same time initiate and innovate beyond all other men, and yet be unable to confront the effects of his own innovations upon his unique psyche — this sounds like a classical or pagan instance of fate and *hubris*.

∞

There is another matter related to the Western private psyche which the Church must face in the electric age. I refer to the role of the Greco-Roman tradition in the life of the Church. Like most of the questions of communication theory, this question I would prefer to see broached by theologians. It seems to me hugely presumptuous for an individual to attempt to evaluate the role of artifacts in society. When the wheel or the stirrup or printing transformed the lives of countless people, how can one person presume to add up the human and spiritual credits and debits for such a thing? When in *The Gutenberg Galaxy* I refrained from moral evaluation and merely recounted the dynamics of the book before and after Gutenberg, it was assumed that I had denigrated the printed word and that I rejoiced to see the enemies of the book closing in. As one who has spent his life in the joyful study and teaching of the printed word, I felt like a man who has been arrested for arson because he turned in a fire alarm, or like a passerby who hurries to tell a householder, "there are flames coming out of your attic," only to be rebuffed, "A very interesting observation, Mr. Busybody. Couldn't disagree with you more. We're quite comfy in here."

Since the theologians don't seem interested, I feel impelled to ask whether the Church has any inherent and inseparable bond with the Greco-Roman tradition of civilization.

Relating to the political character of Protestantism, on one hand, and its doctrinal character, on the other hand, the countries outside the "grand design" — that is, countries outside the Latin tradition of Spain, France, Italy — almost automatically become Protestant for political rather than doctrinal reasons. That is, any "backward" or tribal community automatically considers itself to be its own Pope in religious matters. Switzerland, Germany, Scotland, England, Scandinavia, countries peripheral to the central group in the "grand design" found it difficult to accept the bureaucratic homogeneity and specialism of the great central Latin core. These relatively tribal communities with their strongly paternalistic feeling for the family chief were not inclined to submit to the highly literate and centralist patterns of the Latin community in the grand design. Much less could an Oriental community be expected to have any feeling for the centralist bureaucracy of the Latin core group in the Church.

I have been prompted to meditate on these patterns by the recurrence of "Protestantism" in the contemporary Catholic Church. Today, when the entire Western world is moving inwards under profound electronic pressure, and when this same world is losing nearly all of its outer goal-orientation, there has been a recurrence of extremely decentralized habits of thought and feeling such as in the sixteenth century had been prompted by the innovation of the printed word. Whereas, at first, the effect of the cheap printed book had been to create the illusion of enormous self-sufficiency and private authority, the ultimate effect of the same book had been to homogenize human perception and sensibility, making possible centralism on an unprecedented scale. The Roman Church avoided as far as possible the individualist effect of the printed word and, by a centralized program of uniformity for education in devotion in liturgy, invested the book with a corporate clout from the first. Not surprisingly, the "backward" areas where literacy and bureaucracy held less sway, the peripheral regions outside the grand design of the Latin core, were the areas in which the book played a private and individualist role from the first.

I am suggesting that the book had a totally different meaning to a relatively tribal community like England or Scotland from the meaning it had in Spain, or France, or Italy. I am using the word "tribal" here in no evaluative sense but merely structurally, to refer to cultures where oral tradition and the extreme decentralism and diversity of audile, tactile communities obtain. Most of the traditional societies studied by anthropologists belong in this area but anthropologists themselves, being extremely literate, prefer to classify the societies without reference to their primary involvement in acoustic space and the auditory imagination. In fact, both "acoustic space" and the "auditory imagination" are merely paradoxical mysteries to most highly literate individuals since psychologists do not admit the existence of any kind of space except visual — uniform, connected, quantifiable — space. Since acoustic space has none of these characteristics and is constituted by a simultaneity of resonance from all directions at once, it is not visualizable at all. In fact, for the visual man, acoustic space is a form of ESP. It is the space of James Joyce's *Finnegans Wake* which is naturally very opaque to the visual imagination.

Paradoxically, then, the innovation of the printed book, with its extreme visual stress, had its greatest appeal in the backward acoustic countries of the sixteenth century. The same paradox appears today in the world of Vatican II, where acoustic man has reappeared in the midst of the great nineteenth-century bureaucracies that still dominate the political, educational, and religious spheres. Acoustic, or tribal, man responds like a deviant or "Protestant" when confronted with the central bureaucratic and legalistic hierarchies which are now our literate heritage. In a word, "Protestantism" once more appears as a political ploy rather than a doctrinal adhesion. The question, therefore, that needs to be decided in our time is whether the entire Greco-Roman inheritance which had been the early cultural matrix of the Church can now be seen in the electric age as a mere expendable husk. Is the Greco-Roman thing a mere political escarpment that can now be flooded with the seas of electric information which now engulf the entire planet? To what extent need the Church transmit the Greco-Roman framework of categories in psyche and society? Can all of these forms of visual experience now be bypassed by acoustic and discarnate man of the present electric world environment? Can the Church now move directly into the lives of all Africans and Orientals by merely submitting to the electronic pressure to abandon the visual and rational space that began with Plato?

Pedro Lain-Entralgo's *Therapy of the Word in Classical Antiquity* (Yale University Press, 1972) is a study of the pre-Platonic uses of the word in Greek society. It is a study of Greek culture when it was entirely shamanistic and magical and when the word was used for treating mind and body therapeutically. The word as a means of healing or of magical change is precisely what phonetic literacy rejected, and precisely what the TV generation now seeks to bring back into all aspects of language. From the moment of the rise of phonetic literacy the Greek world turned from ESP. Since then, the Greco-Roman world has ceased to provide man with any theory of communication or psychic change. Paradoxically, then, the Church became embodied from the first in the only culture which had developed a rigid position. The Church, which offers and demands constant change in the human heart, was invested with a visual culture that values permanence above all things. This Greco-Roman culture, now seemingly imposed upon the Church as the shell on the tortoise, itself allows no possibility of a theory of communication or change. It is the "hard shell" which is interposed between the Church and all of the other culture of the world with their soft, pliable, and changeable forms.

Some Further Comments on Liturgy and Media

Since writing the [above] article, which appeared in the January-February issue, two related matters have come up. While reading Margaret Atwood's *Survival*, I discovered the reasons why North Americans go outside to be alone and inside for company and social life. She points to the persistent theme of conflict between man and nature in North America and to the persistent presentation in Canadian and American literature of nature as hostile to man. This aspect of North American literature is also the theme of *The Bush Garden: Essays on the Canadian Imagination* by Northrop Frye (House of Anansi Press, Toronto, 1971, page 146):

> What the poet sees in Canada, therefore, is very different from what the politician or businessman sees, and different again from what his European contemporaries see. He may be a younger man than Yeats or Eliot, but he has to deal with a poetic and imaginative environment for which, to find any parallel in England, we should have to go back to a period earlier than Chaucer.

It is not so much that the environment of North America is different from that of other continents as the fact that the settlers in North America mounted a full-scale attack on nature as a thing to be subdued as quickly as possible. The settlers who came in the sixteenth century, and afterwards, were trappers and fur traders whose object was a quick raid on resources. The Conquistador imagination of the Renaissance men who first came here resembled the outlook of commando raiders with specialized objectives. Even the settlers who came after the fur traders found themselves at war with the fur traders. As Harold Innis pointed out in his studies of the fur trade in North America, the developers of that time were the land surveyors, among whom were Thomas Jefferson and George Washington. As land developers, they naturally wanted settlers. The fur traders (that is, the British) regarded settlers as a danger to their trapping lines and to the fur trade in general.

∞

The fact that the settlers had somewhat less specialized motives and objectives than the British set up a conflict of interests which "became" the revolutionary war of 1776. The settlers themselves, however, mounted a crash program for mining the continent, for "subduing" nature and "taming the wilderness." Today, of course, this has ended with the collapse of nature under the impact of technology. Today the developers are grabbing dollars out of the air by mounting anti-pollution programs. It is perhaps relevant that the discovery of North America had been a major disaster for European hopes for a short-cut to the East. North America blocked the passage to India and China which they sought. Some of the resulting frustration may well have been spent in an angry onslaught on the continent that had frustrated their hopes for a quick and easy passage to India.

If the North American, alone of all people on this planet, goes outside to be a lonely hunter in the style of Melville's *Moby-Dick*, there is much need for study of this strange subliminal posture of the North American psyche. Just how rich and pervasive is this rich and unstudied theme appears in *The Disney Version* by Richard Schickel (Simon & Schuster, New York, 1968). He tells us that Walt Disney "was the sort of man who possesses, and is possessed by, a dream that seems to be particularly and peculiarly of this land, of a time only recently passed . . ." Simply summarized, it is that "it takes only one good idea . . ." He goes on: "In the U.S. one need not complete the sentence, so clear is the implication: all you need is one winner to get started on the road to success."

The dream's natural place of nurture is the workshop in the attic or basement or the garage in "Gasoline Alley" or "Out Our Way" where a man can be alone with his tools — free of the clock and the cautionary wifely voice and all other inhibiting forces of family and society. (page 42)

Karl Menninger provides another approach to this pattern:

I live in the country. I have no other home. I am impressed by certain things about farmers. One of them is their destructiveness. One of them is their total lack of appreciation of the beautiful — in the main.

Menninger is working here within a larger frame of the American passion to "tame the land." He speculates about why North Americans "have never learned to love the land as it is, for itself."

Footnote on the magisterium in the electric age:
The conditions attending the exercises of the magisterium of the Church in the twentieth century are such as to present an analogue with the first decade of the Christian Church. There is, on the one hand, the immediacy of interrelationship among Christians and non-Christians alike in a world where information moves at the speed of light. The population of the world now co-exists in an extremely small space and in an instant of time. So far as the magisterium is concerned, it is as if the entire population of the world were present in a small room where perpetual dialogue was possible. So far as the traditions of the Church are concerned, the present situation puts all knowledge and authority on an oral and personal basis. The habit of written communiqués and doctoral promulgation, which is inevitable under slower conditions of inter-communication, becomes an embarrassing impediment. Again, whereas the Church has through the centuries striven for centralism and consensus at a distance from the faithful, the electrical situation ends all distance and, by the same token, ends the numerous bureaucratic means of centralism. The magisterium is now experienced simultaneously in the entire visible Church. A complete decentralism occurs which calls for new manifestations of teaching authority such as the Church has never before expressed or encountered.

Footnote on the decline of the confessional and of vocations:
The current liturgical practice of having the priest face the congregation rather than the altar is a complex question which is greatly complicated by architecture. To face the congregation in a small space, or in a round space, has a quite different effect from facing the congregation in a Gothic nave. The strong visual and perspective stress of the Gothic nave creates remoteness and detachment of a special kind. By contrast, the small space or the secular space of the Byzantine structure creates a much higher degree of multisensory involvement of the participants. In both cases, however, when the celebrant turns to the audience he is putting them on as his corporate dignity or mask, just as when he turns to the altar he is putting on the divine mask of supernatural power. A continuous confrontation of the audience by the celebrant reduces the occasion to the merely humanistic one. A Catholic priest, in this regard, possesses no more power or mystery than a Protestant padre. "Putting on" only the congregation as his corporate mask of dignity deprives the celebrant of any compelling power or charisma; and this fact is not lost on the young adults who, naturally, can think of no reason for seeking divine absolution nor for pursuing a merely banal vocation of a humanistic padre.

15

"Achieving Relevance":
Letters to Mole and Sheed

[Written to John W. Mole, O.M.I., on 29 January 1974 from Toronto]

Dear Fr. Mole:

Just a note that I have looked at *Communio et Progressio*[1] and found it futile. Does this mean that I should say so in public? Or write to the members of the [Pontifical] Communication Commission about it?

Have been paying a lot of attention to Kant, Hegel, and phenomenology of late, with full realization that Kant and Hegel simply flipped out of Hume's visual determinism into acoustic subjectivism. All of their followers are still under the illusion that the acoustic world is spiritual and unlike the outer visual world, whereas, in fact, the acoustic is just as material as the visual. However, to Western man the acoustic always seems a release into another more relevant dimension. At least this was a possible hide-out until nuclear physics moved in with its acoustic structures. The "structuralism" of the European phenomenologists is the audile-tactile world which I know

---

1 The Pastoral Instruction on the media, emphasizing its moral aspects, issued by the Pontifical Commission for Social Communication (of which McLuhan was made a member) to implement the decree of the Second Vatican Council on Communications (*Inter Mirifica*, 1963). On 24 December 1973, Father Mole had sent McLuhan Chapter VIII of a typescript of his critique of it, which later appeared in *Christian Communications*.

very well, since I use it at all times myself. The logical, rational world is visual, continuous, and connected, but when pushed to its limit, flips into the acoustic form, as with Hume and Kant. What I am coming to is the question of the magisterium:[2] the Eastern Church, being iconic and audile-tactile, could not tolerate the visual hierarchy of Rome with external, materialistic aspects, and today, as the Western Church also is invaded by the simultaneous electric thing with its multi-locational boundlessness, the whole question of Roman authority becomes crucial.

"Process" theology and the speculative theology of the descendants of Kant and Hegel is unconsciously in the grip of the merely acoustic dimension. This is the world of involvement par excellence. It is the anti-Greco-Roman form of the pre-Socratic world of *hoi barbaroi*. The Third World is the world of the barbarians, of course. I do not pretend to perceive a providential plan or pattern in these matters, but I cannot see any reason for withholding intelligibility from the acoustic domain created by electric simultaneity. Have you, yourself, discovered any evidence of understanding these matters in their unique and antithetic structuralist terms? I have yet to meet a philosopher who understood what had happened to Kant and Hegel in their flight into the acoustic during their revulsion from the visual determinism of Locke and Hume.

An understanding of these factors provides an immediate release from the opacity and tension that now exists in these areas. Such understanding also permits a realistic programming of environments by media in suchwise as to relieve many psychic miseries, e.g., the current disasters in our schools and communities as we try to subject the students to the old disciplines of literacy, without considering that these students have been transformed by their electric environment. The electric transformation causes us to resist and to reject the old visual culture, regardless of its value or relevance. These kinds of psychic oscillation resulting from large environmental change are no longer necessary, any more than the plague. Psychic diseases can now be treated for what they are, namely manifestations of the response to man-made technologies. Environmental noise and disturbance can be controlled as readily as the unhygienic conditions that prevailed until

---

2 *Magisterium* is the technical name for the teaching authority of the Roman Catholic Church, which includes papal encyclicals and documents issued by the Holy See.

recent times. The psychic effects of TV are no more necessary than the physical effects of polluted drinking water. As long as people persist in ignoring the subliminal and hidden effects of media on psyche and society, they will attribute these things to the "will of God."

Yours in Our Lord,
Marshall

[Written to Frank Sheed on 20 February 1970 from Toronto]

Dear Frank: [3]

Here's one to play on Sheed's own trumpet! A guy who turns in a fire alarm is not necessarily an arsonist. Marshall McLuhan has never said that the printed page has come to an end. McLuhan has said that the book is obsolescent. So is handwriting. But there is more handwriting done today than there was before Gutenberg. Obsolescence never meant the end of anything — it's just the beginning. Take the motor car as an example. There is an old saying in the business world: "If it works, it's obsolete." This is literally true, since until a process has penetrated the sensibilities of an entire community, it hasn't begun to do its job.

As a full-time professor of literature my days are spent interpreting the printed page and in devising new ways for increasing our powers of perceiving and penetrating its mysteries. *Through the Vanishing Point: Space in Poetry and Painting* (Harper & Row, 1968), which I did with the painter, Harley Parker, offers an entirely new bridge to the printed word by comparing and contrasting the spaces created by its art form and neighbour art forms. I have spent a good many years in studying the cultural effects of print and in proclaiming the alphabet in its printed form as the sole basis of civilization. The electro-technical forms do not foster civilization but tribal culture.

Literacy in Traditional Societies edited by Jack Goody (Cambridge University Press, 1968) makes a few timid steps in the direction of recognizing the effects of Western literacy on preliterate societies. It shows not the slightest awareness that the many non-phonetic forms of literacy have no civilizing effects whatever. Civilization is a technical event. There is no other alphabet that has the effect of upgrading the visual powers at the expense of all the other senses. It is the dominance of the visual faculty that creates civilized values. Eric Havelock in his *Preface to Plato* explains the origin of Greek individualist civilization and Plato's war on the tribal poets as an immediate consequence of the phonetic alphabet.

As for the electro-technical development, its effect on our sensibilities

---

3 Francis Joseph Sheed (1897–1981), who was born in Australia, married Maisie Ward in 1926 and together they established in England the firm of Sheed & Ward to publish English Catholic authors; the New York branch was founded in 1933.

and our human society has never aroused the slightest enthusiasm in Marshall McLuhan. I have never endorsed the events I have described, nor have I ever condemned any of the things I analysed. I am interested in understanding processes. Such are the opaquities and obliquities of "value" judgments that they have always stood in the way of human understanding. This applies as much to the revealed truth of the Catholic faith as to the artefacts of human ingenuity. The fact of the Church is quite independent of human concepts or preferences. As for media and the Church, it is obvious that there was not anybody at the Council of Trent who had any interest in the shaping power of the Gutenberg technology in creating private judgment on one hand, and of massive centralist bureaucracy on the other hand. There was nobody at Vatican I or II who showed any understanding of the electro-technical thing in reshaping the psyche and culture of mankind. The policies adopted at these Councils manifested the spirit of Don Quixote who donned the latest print technology as his armour and motive and rode off valiantly into the Middle Ages. Since Vatican I and II the Catholic bureaucracy has moved resolutely into the nineteenth century, supported by plain-clothed priests and nuns. If a few people could only stop asking whether this is "a good thing or a bad thing" and spend some time in studying what is really happening, there might be some possibility of achieving relevance.

Sincerely yours,
Marshall McLuhan

16

Liturgy and Media:
Third Conversation with Pierre Babin

Pierre Babin: Professor McLuhan, you are as aware as I am of the upheavals in Catholic liturgy preceding and especially after Vatican II. However, it doesn't seem to me that these changes, which have traumatized an important segment of the Church, have in any significant way facilitated the awakening and development of Christian life. Nevertheless, isn't liturgy at the heart of Christian life and the communication of faith?

Marshall McLuhan: You said yourself that Christianity based on liturgy was, in the first centuries of the Church, the institutional means of transmitting the faith. Today, personal prayer and liturgy (which are inseparable) are the only means of tuning in to the right wavelength, of listening to Christ, and of involving the whole person.

Earlier, in making my case against catechism, I used my own children as examples. Perhaps we also have to examine the shortcomings of liturgies old and new.

Babin: Can we find an explanation in the liturgical upheavals of the sixteenth century for what is going on today?

∞ *From* Autre homme, autre chrétien à l'âge électronique, *Lyon: Editions du Chalet, 1977. Translated by Wayne Constantineau.*

McLuhan: Of course. Medieval liturgy was mostly acoustic. Church architecture was, above all, dominated by acoustic concerns, and Latin was used almost exclusively. But in the sixteenth century Gutenberg gave such intense visual stress to the vernaculars that it underlies all of our psychic, political, and spiritual specialization and division.

This specialization is particularly noticeable in Protestantism. You might imagine that the demand for a vernacular liturgy arose spontaneously in the sixteenth century, but it isn't so. In fact, that demand was linked to the invention of print, an invention that accentuated people's need to push towards individualism and nationalism. Add to that the fact that printed texts gave rise to textual exegesis from the pulpit. And finally, the new accent on the visual favoured placing the celebrant face to face with the congregation: we needed to see him and he wanted to be seen. These practices were adopted by the Reform churches while Rome rejected them until the beginning of this century. Under Protestant reform, liturgy split into a variety of new forms, each group with its own point of view. With it the sects appeared.

Babin: In the meantime, what was happening to Catholic liturgy?

McLuhan: Catholic reform didn't take the same route. It made the printed book an instrument of uniformity, fixity, and centralization, in liturgy as well as in education. Holding to Latin helped in this task. The Church made Sunday Mass obligatory and turned it and the cyclical liturgical calendar into teaching tools. Religious architecture, like the way the servers and congregation were organized, certainly followed visual lines, but all of it aimed at uniformity.

Latin, which was not spoken by most people, clergy and laity alike, nevertheless played a very important role. It followed a long history of complex relations between speech and writing, between high culture and popular forms. Latin had — and still has — its roots in the popular ground, much like today's folk music. The interaction between the Latin Mass and the congregation wasn't just added on. Latin wasn't grafted on to the experience, even for an English congregation. There is, in fact, a lot of Latin in the English language. Also, the interaction between the two languages, Latin and English, created a powerful and dramatic tension, a tension that dominated both languages from way back.

Yeats, the Irish poet, calls this "the emotion of multitude," an emotion rooted in the "auditory imagination" that T. S. Eliot was so fond of. To understand Latin's impact on liturgy, we should replay Eliot's definition:

> What I call the "auditory imagination" is the feeling for syllable and rhythm, penetrating far below the conscious levels of thought and feeling, invigorating every word: sinking to the most primitive and forgotten, returning to the origin and bringing something back, seeking the beginning and the end. It works through meanings, certainly, or not without meanings in the ordinary sense, and fuses the old and obliterated, and the trite, the current, and the new and the surprising, the most ancient and the most civilized mentality.[1]

At this depth, an effective and mysterious form of communication is established, one that is just as real as the conventional meaning of words and phrases in literary language, especially when written and printed. In the name of tradition and by some sort of instinct, the Catholic reformation also conserved many elements of the same origin, for example liturgical vestments, objects, materials, and symbolic gestures that the Protestant reformers rejected as being tainted with magic and superstition.

Babin: For you, then, Catholic liturgy up to Vatican II unconsciously retained its oral flavour. But, what do you think of the current changes in liturgy and the introduction of the vernacular Mass?

McLuhan: Latin wasn't the victim of Vatican II; it was done in by introducing the microphone. A lot of people, the Church hierarchy included, have been lamenting the disappearance of Latin without understanding that it was the result of introducing a piece of technology that they accepted so enthusiastically. Latin is a very "cool" language, in which whispers and murmurs play an important role. A microphone, however, makes an indistinct mumble intolerable; it accentuates and intensifies the sounds of Latin to the point where it loses all of its power. But Latin wasn't the mike's only victim. It also made vehement preaching unbearable. For a public that finds itself immersed in a completely acoustic situation thanks to electric amplification, hi-fi speakers bring the preacher's voice from several directions

---

1 T. S. Eliot, *The Use of Poetry and the Use of Criticism* (London: Faber and Faber, 1933), page 118. See also McLuhan's discussion of this quote on pages 107 and 122 of this book.

at once. So the structure of our churches was obsolesced by multi-directional amplification. The multiple speakers simply bypassed the traditional distance between preacher and audience. The two were suddenly in immediate relation with each other, which compelled the priest to face the congregation.

These essential aspects of liturgical change were neither predicted nor programmed, and they remain unnoticed by the users of church resonance. I make no value judgments in this regard. I merely suggest that these results come from a typical visual Western mentality as it approaches technological innovation. As soon as a new means of communication arises, we feel driven to adopt it without considering either the aim or the consequences.

However, that's no longer the mentality of the electric and acoustic age. What seems inevitable from a visual and linear perspective presents itself to electric man as just one of a number of possible choices. Electric man starts with the desired effects and works backwards to the means of achieving them. The man from a visual culture, on the other hand, welcomes all the available media as a kind of necessity that lead in the direction of continuous organizational change, without ever considering the enormous cost. Today, however, in the problem of liturgical change, it is important to note that electric communication, which brings speaker and audience together, demands another type of church: the visual structure that emerged from Gutenberg isn't compatible with electric, acoustic structures.

Babin: Yet it seems to me that a vernacular language, living in liturgy, has been very well received by a majority of Catholics. Doesn't it make it easier to communicate faith than would a dead language?

McLuhan: I'm afraid you are stuck in the visual trappings of catechism. I should summarize, here, the article I wrote a few years ago on liturgy and the media in *The Critic* [see chapter 13 above]. A language is infinitely more than just a conventional means of communicating ideas. I am speaking here of a spoken language, of oral tradition. A language is the encoded form of the collective perceptions and wisdom of many people. And, poetry and song are the major means by which a language purifies and invigorates itself.

What seems to me to have been misunderstood is that every technological innovation changes the human environment and in so doing alters all our sense ratios: consequently, new language solutions have to come into play. Language is, as it were, the great organic and collective medium that assimilates and organizes the chaos of everyday experience. Language is the conscious organ of the auditory imagination where countless changes and adjustments take place, much like the way dreams in the night purge daily experience.

That was the role of the oral tradition in cultures before the advent of writing. After writing, what was left of the oral elements continued to play a similar role. But the mountains of print tend little by little to choke and silence this tradition: what is left of it, however, is still enough to inspire a living popular culture. Confining myself to a few English-language examples, let me mention Irish folklore, jazz — especially in the southern U.S. — and, finally, rock 'n' roll in the cities.

This, it seems to me, is the level at which the faith communicates, not so much by transmitting concepts or theories, but by inner transformation of people; not by expressing a *figure* but by participating in the *ground* of secondary effects that transform life.

For a vernacular, used liturgically, to be able to play this transforming role, it would have to be truly popular. However, this demand points to one of the most traumatic developments of recent liturgical reform: I mean the intrusion of bureaucratic process into Catholic communities. Of course, the Eucharistic liturgy is now offered in the vernacular, but it is in the hands of commissions whose contact with language has all the frigidity of the computer. Minus the oral dimension of popular idioms and rhythms, the vernacular risks becoming a vacant lot and a spiritual desert.

So we can understand why a group of well-meaning innovators hasn't a hope of getting participation, worship, or comfort in liturgical experiences that are far too tentative. In order to grasp the problem of adapting liturgy to popular experience, you have to be aware of the extraordinary stylistic work done, for example, in the world of rock. Rock 'n' roll isn't something added on to the city: it is the city translated into music. If liturgical translators have done a shabby job, it's probably because they haven't much feel for their own language. For, to translate well, you have to go well beyond written or printed language. What has to be expressed is the thing as a whole, the whole language that has been shaped in experience across time. If those responsible for the liturgy are alienated from this whole, the faithful will be deprived of, and confused in, their own spiritual gestures.

By taking these basic essentials into account — and only by doing so — everyday language can become something other than the cause of division and disintegration in the Church, as it has been for the Protestants since Gutenberg.

Babin: Nevertheless, don't you think that post-Vatican II liturgy rid itself of the superfluous ornaments which masked its essential sense?

McLuhan: You put me in mind of an odd remark by a professor of rhetoric who spoke of the vigour of words by comparing them to an arrow that could hit its target better because he had gotten rid of the feathers. However, if you think about it for a moment, an arrow without feathers will go nowhere; it will never hit the target. The feathers are essential.

Consider these cumbersome but necessary feathers as the corporate costumes and ornaments: certainly we can consider them as trappings, but can't we see that they are communal forms? Like politeness and protocol, corporate costumes and ornaments are essential elements of communication. Of course, pontifical ornaments, for example, as human clothing are ridiculous and comical. They are caricatures. But for people who are on the same wavelength, they conceal a deeper sense. This tuning in to the right frequency obviously takes on different forms in different cultures, and since these are changing almost daily it is quite difficult to tune in properly. I just think that one cannot tackle these questions lightly. Why does the Church have to get rid of traditional roles and costumes at precisely the moment when these corporate modes of expression are recognized as essential to human survival in the secular world, and especially by our young?

Babin: You are very demanding of the attempts to renew liturgy and you have mentioned especially the difficulties, or more precisely, the incompatibilities between Gutenberg's visual frame of reference and that of the acoustic framework of electric media. Nevertheless, don't you think that the new age opens up great possibilities for a renewed liturgy?

McLuhan: First of all, it is clear that electric media have made mass assemblies possible. So we have the Olympic games where millions of people can watch simultaneously. In the same way, wouldn't it be possible to have people participate in a common liturgy globally? We could all assist at the same Mass. Nevertheless, if we want the entire world to be present, vernaculars, far from helping, pose a major obstacle.

But this is a surface approach, similar to the one we criticized in talking about catechism: to be hypnotized by the content, as though it were the most important thing, is to stop at the *figure* without perceiving the *ground*, the real message.

Babin: Do not such assemblies, by their enormity and in a certain way by their superficiality, put into question a liturgical life that is at the same time personal and communal?

McLuhan: Let's remember for starters that our sense of individuality and of privacy appeared with Greco-Roman culture based on writing: it barely exists in oral cultures, in certain parts of Africa and the East, for example. But today everything's changing. The big increases in size and mobility have quite simply wiped out the kinds of human community that we have known. It's normal every day to meet lots of new people for the first and only time, while we rarely see our old friends. On the other hand, electric information brings us into very close contact with all the inhabitants of the planet. Like urban congestion, this new electric interlocking of each with all creates a population implosion. While electric media link us to each other in depth, practically eliminating space and time from our lives, these same media strip away what we had considered for centuries as our individuality and private identity.

When you are involved in a new way and in depth in the lives of a horde of other people, it is undoubtedly natural not to notice the loss of your own identity. Do private identity and individuality have permanent value, beyond social change? This is a subject for theologians to debate. What I have noticed is a definite loss of our sense of individuality, at least compared to how this individuality used to manifest itself in life and liturgy.

Babin: Does this most important phenomenon affect everyone or mostly our adolescents?

McLuhan: Everyone, but especially our youth. Precisely because they have been more immersed in this acoustic environment than anyone else. It is probably also why the new liturgy — the one that I have so many reservations about — works better in small communities where people are happy with each other. But don't forget that young people today reject pre-packaged goods. They want to be the producers, the creators. Won't the Church have to accept a broader variety of expression than just the one that separates Roman liturgy from Eastern liturgy? It could be one of the results of the decentralization imposed on it by electric culture.

Babin: Where does that leave Sunday Mass and the liturgical cycle?

McLuhan: You have to remember that electric speed allows us to compress the entire year into an hour or a day. Therefore, in terms of distribution in time, the annual cycle of feasts no longer functions in the way that it should. At the speed of light, it has no more attraction. We want everything to happen at once, all the richness, all the feasts, all the Scriptures together and instantly. It is the same thing as having Christ right here in person. Electricity tends to evoke the presence of Christ immediately via the ear.

Babin: So what kind of liturgy would you propose today?

McLuhan: Well, I personally have no ideal to propose, no ideal of what tomorrow's liturgy should be like. You see, I grew up with Protestant liturgy. I only became a Catholic after taking an interest in liturgy. I wasn't looking for glamorous churches and beautiful services. I have always considered that once people knew the Truth they could produce beautiful things, at least if they wanted to.

I'd simply like to make a point using terms borrowed from computers: they speak of hardware and of software. Hardware refers to the machine itself which is more or less fixed, while software is mutable. Writing in general, given its predetermined and unchanging form, is like hardware; while speech, which is supple and changeable, is closer to software. The visual is hardware, the acoustic is software. Liturgy in its creative and improvisational aspects is software, but once it is fixed by the voice of authority, fixed in writing, and made uniform by print, it becomes hardware. Rome insists that liturgy become as rigid as hardware, and as soon as possible. To me, that is exactly what cannot work in an electric world, especially with our adolescents.

The changes imposed by the cultural upheavals that we are going through deeply affect liturgy, but the hardware form that these realities will wear, if they ever wear them, will take a very long time to show up. Perhaps liturgy will retain some semblance of software.

PART
4

Tomorrow's Church

17

Catholic Humanism
and Modern Letters

For 2,000 years, wrote Theodore Haecker, Western man has been pre-eminent because it has been possible for him to understand all other men through his Catholic faith. That is a scheme for meditation, it is a simple matter of fact.

It puzzles the anthropology staff at the University of Toronto that Catholic students grasp the problems and character of primitive societies more readily than other students. I suspect they are baffled because they imagine that persons with a definite religious outlook should find it *more* rather than *less* difficult to understand pagan societies. I am sure that they suspect that there is some deep and disreputable bond between the primitive mind and the Catholic mind. But on the other hand the Catholic espousal of reason as the creative principle is bewildering to anthropologists. For if the Catholic is the champion of rational principles and individual reason how can he understand primitive man who is embedded in a world of magical irrationalities and collective consciousness?

One answer to this last problem in the anthropological mind can be given in a quip to the effect that we grasp the irrational and the primitive today because, however uncongenial it be, we live it. But we

∞ Originally delivered as part of the McAuley Lectures, St. Joseph College, West Hartford, Connecticut, 1954, pages 49-67.

Note: The footnotes in this essay are Marshall McLuhan's original notes.

should reflect that the anthropologists and sociologists of our day are committed to the irrational and the collective as an ideal. Reason for them is the destructive principle deriving from demonic matter. Reason is the individualist principle which in their view has separated men, making them vertical and distinct. We must, they say, recreate man in the crucible of emotion. Reason stands between us and the new millennial mankind. It must be abolished except as a tool of applied science.

At the outset of a talk on "Christian Humanism," Maritain observed:

> Every great period of civilization is dominated by a certain peculiar idea that man fashions of man. Our behaviour depends as much on this image as on our very nature — an image which appears with striking brilliance in the minds of some particularly representative thinkers, and which, more or less unconscious in the human Mass, is none the less strong enough to mold after its own pattern the social and political formations that are characteristic of a given cultural epoch.[1]

What these dominant conceptions were in classical antiquity, in the Middle Ages and the Renaissance, has been established by a host of historians. But it calls for a desperate courage to venture to say what that idea is for ourselves. As a teacher of literature I have frequently to explain the nature of metaphor. From one point of view, Maritain's observation, about every period being shaped by the very view which itself is shaping, can be translated this way: When we look at any situation through another situation we are using metaphor. This is an intensely intellectual process. And all language arises by this means. So that it is a commonplace of the poetic and critical discussion of the last one hundred years to note that human languages themselves are the greatest of all works of art beside which the works of Homer, Vergil, Dante, and Shakespeare are minor variations. The English — or any other — language is itself a massive organization of traditional experience providing a complex view of the world. Today our increasing knowledge of the languages of primitive cultures has made it easy to observe how language itself is the principal channel and view-maker of experience for men everywhere. This reverent attitude to the human world which has unexpectedly sprung up in

---

1 Jacques Maritain, *The Range of Reason*, page 185.

symbolist, existential, and positivist circles alike is not unrelated to numerous other attitudes and procedures which are common today to the scientist, the historian, and the sociologist.

Personally, I have no doubt whatever that the present age is a very great age, humanly speaking. But it is a great period dominated not so much by any idea of man as by a method of study. And that is why, paradoxically, its greatest achievements and practitioners in the arts and sciences can look both puny and superhuman at the same time. Having espoused a method rather than a view, modern man can do anything even when he chooses typically to see nothing. His fidelity to the processes of reason goes hand in hand with a deep fear of the consequences of reason. Reason, he suspects, is the diabolic principle.

Having taken up Maritain's principle that there is in every great period of civilization a dominant idea, let me illustrate it from the work of Etienne Gilson. *The Unity of Philosophical Experience* is acknowledged to be the first work of its kind ever written. Put that way, some wag might be reminded of the crushing observation made in a Parliamentary debate: "The honourable member has dazzled us with a speech with much that is new and true. But unfortunately that which is new in his speech is not true, and that which is true is not new." Gilson's book is both new and true. What it does is to elicit the image of truth from past errors and to confirm the unity of man's quest from the jarring discords of unremitting debate. But what I wish to point out is that Gilson's method is that of contemporary art and science (for contemporary poetry has healed the old breach between art and science). Gilson does not set out to produce a theory or view that will unify the philosophical disputes of the past. He reconstructs the disputes. He enables us to participate in them as though we were there. We see that they were real. The questions had to be put that way at that time. And being put that way there were no answers, only wrong answers possible. By repeating the process of participation several times we are liberated from both past and present. We don't arrive at a simple unifying concept but are put on the road to achieving a wisdom. And the road to this wisdom is by way of sympathetic reconstruction, involving the abeyance of personal prejudice and preconception.

This method of reconstruction as the way to an even fuller sympathy appeared first in the Romantic poets of the later eighteenth century, and it went with a conscious concern with the creative process in the arts. The poet, said Thomas Brown of Edinburgh, is different from other men in that his mind works backwards in association. This insight, common to that age, has been steadily applied and reigned in all the arts and sciences since that time. So that Whitehead could say of the nineteenth century that its distinction lay not so much in the arrival at any particular discovery as in the discovery of the technique of discovery itself.

Having illustrated this discovery in the work of Gilson, let me show how it had appeared at more popular levels. A basic problem for Catholic humanism is at stake in this question as we shall see. Edgar Allan Poe has recently been honoured by the critical attention of Allen Tate. (The recent conversion of Allen Tate, which was preceded by that of his gifted novelist wife, seems to me to have for America the same sort of significance that the conversion of Newman had for Oxford. Tate is the voice and mind of the south and of the great Ciceronian branch of the tradition which it incorporates.) Tate's criticism of Poe is tempered by his recognition that Poe's Cartesian mind had one window open to the vision of analogy, and it is precisely the recovery of analogical perception that marks Tate's conversion.

Poe is most celebrated in the English-speaking world for his *Tales of Mystery and Imagination*. And among these pieces of science fiction are found his detective stories. If Poe didn't invent the detective story, he certainly invented the sleuth. And his sleuth is an artist-aesthete, Dupin. For Poe, the artist, the detective, and the man of science were one and the same person. That is why his revelation of this matter in "The Poetic Principle" made him appear like Leonardo da Vinci to Baudelaire, Mallarmé, and Valéry. This aspect of Edgar Poe has long been hidden from the English world which prefers to have both its art and entertainment minus the rational and intelligible principle. The French have not been mistaken in regarding Poe as one of the great exploring minds. And Poe's discovery has important consequences for the Catholic humanist today.

To put the thing briefly, Poe saw that poetry should be written backward. One must begin with the effect that is to be achieved and then seek out the means for obtaining that effect and no other effect. Thus the same insight which enabled Poe to be the inventor of symbolist poetry also made him the inventor of detective fiction. For the sleuth works backwards from the effect of the event to reconstruct the circumstances which produced the particular event or murder. In this way the detective (like Gilson) does not produce a theory or a view of a case. He recreates it for your participation. He provides not a view but total communication. In the same way the symbolist poet makes of the poem not a vehicle for views, ideas, feelings, but a situation which involves the reader directly in the poetic process. That is why he will always say that the poem is not about anything; it is something. It doesn't say anything; it does something.[2]

Now, I suggest that the poetic process as revealed by Poe and the symbolists was the unexpected and unintentional means of establishing the basis of Catholic humanism. Moreover, I shall show that the widest possible extension of this discovery to the transformation of all common life and politics has provided the intellectual matrix of a new world society. This is not a matter which I wish to prove; it is rather an aspect of our common life which I think it is possible to understand today.

The popular appeal of the detective and adventure story is not accidental any more than the magical power of the movie is accidental. It has, however, been a common mistake to brush aside these matters as gross obsessions of the mass mind. I do not think that the Catholic humanist can lend his support to this Manichean terminology. Let him consider instead that the poetic process as it appears in the work of Poe, Baudelaire, and Eliot, and in writers of detective fiction, is also the manifest principle of historical reconstruction as used by Gilson. At first glance this might appear to some as a scandal. For them let me say that there is also the scandal of human cognition. As language itself is an infinitely greater work of art than the *Iliad* or the *Aeneid*, so is the creative act of ordinary human perception a greater thing and a more intricate process than any devised by philosophers or scientists. The poetic process is a reversal, a retracing of the stages of human cognition. It has been and will always be so; but with Edgar Poe and the symbolists this central fact was taken up to the level of conscious awareness. It then became the basis of modern science and technology. That is what Whitehead meant when he said that the great event of the nineteenth century was the discovery of the process of

---

2 Of course, the various nihilistic conceptions related to symbolist and surrealist poetics are gratuitous. Self-professed Jansenists like Jean-Paul Sartre (in *What Is Literature?*) and Wyndham Lewis (in *The Diabolical Principle* and *The Writer and the Absolute*) can be disturbed by the destructive intentions of magical poetics because their theology compels them to suppose that Satan is artistically inclined. The Catholic knows that the devil can never engage in the art process as such. He may well be able to use art as a vehicle for error.

discovery. Because the dream of ordinary perception seen as the poetic process is the prime analogue, the magic casement opening on the secrets of created being.

Confronted with a consciousness of so revolutionary a kind the Catholic alone is not tempted by this to vertiginous dreams of the superman. The Catholic has never understood the value of the mystery of ordinary human perception and consciousness. Nor is he likely to overestimate them today. He knows created Being has been marvelously preserved and recreated by the Incarnation, and that the human race in particular has been assumed into the life of the Divine Logos, which is Christ. But the secular world does not know these things and the new consciousness has filled it with wild dreams and terrible programs for the ruthless refashioning of human nature. The result would seem to be that we live as Yeats says in a time when the good lack all conviction and the bad are filled with a passionate intensity. But I'm not sure that this is the whole story.

Looking back a moment at the poetic process and the detective story, I suggested that Gilson has used the method of reconstruction in the history of philosophy as a new creative technique which permits a new kind of communication between the present and the past. The reader of Gilson is typically given not a view or theory of the past but an experience of it. But the past as experience is present. It is available once more as nutriment. Previous theories of the past really amounted to a way of disowning it or of explaining it away.

As for Maritain, he has turned his great powers to the contemplation and analysis of the poetic process directly. The impact of *Art and Scholasticism* was owing to its masterly explanation of the art process as revealed by the symbolist poets. Maritain showed that the mysteries of this process became more luminous in the light of Thomas, that art was intelligible because making is rational. Art is important because it is natural to man as *homo faber*, as rational.

I hope that you will agree with me that it is important for the future of Catholic humanism that we understand why Gilson and Maritain have made themselves felt outside the Catholic world. It seems to me because they have mastered the central cultural discoveries of their time. Thus they can communicate with the top levels of awareness in their age. This would seem to be a Catholic obligation. The role of the Catholic humanist is to cultivate a more than ordinary reverence for the past, for tradition, while exploring every present development for what it reveals about man which the past had not revealed. To be contemporary in this sense is no mere snobbism, not a matter of faddishness. It is an arduous but rewarding business.

Maritain's recent work on *Creative Intuition in Art* carries us even deeper into the problem of the poem as process. But he has now become aware of the creative process in art as a potential bond between East and West, past and present. And again in this work he reveals the extent of his debt to non-Catholic poets, artists, and critics. The Catholic humanist in these matters can freely appreciate the insights of man in all times and places without the slightest qualm about their doctrinal convictions. This is not so easy to do, for the secular mind suspects Manichean boobytraps in every act or statement. The secular mind by and large has always approached art and aesthetics as religion and magic. So it does today. Hence the violent quarrels and exclusive coteries of the art world. Art and poetry are regarded as private religions, secret escape hatches from the sunken submarine or the unguided missile of existence. The Catholic alone can laugh at these antics. He alone need not be deceived by such qualms or pretensions. And what the esoteric cultist proffers as magic he can accept as a single shaping of natural experience.

It has been noted how Machiavelli in the sixteenth century created the crisis in which we persist today by raising an age-old truth to a new level of awareness. Practical politics had always had a very shabby side. But Machiavelli made of these imperfections the basis of the art and grammar of power. Today we have graduated from Machiavelli's school, as can be seen in the popular amusement at those who take his views earnestly. For example, Dale Carnegie is an exact imitator of Machiavelli's principles and there is I suspect a general tendency to regard him as comic. Carnegie tells us that the universal craving to feel important cannot be exaggerated. The most wicked criminals proclaim their absolute innocence. How much more does the ordinary respectable person, therefore, regard himself as a paragon of virtue. On this discovery of the abyss of human vanity and self-deception, Carnegie, like Machiavelli, erects his system for obtaining power. Look for a man's weakness, his ruling passion. Then feed it with words, words, words. He knows you are a liar and a flatterer? No matter. The mere fact that you think it worthwhile to lie to him will feed his insatiable vanity.

The positive value in Machiavelli's discovery was that it showed how man's factive intelligence could be turned to artistic use in fashioning cities and states. Machiavelli did not discover that rulers and princes apply perfidy, falsehood, cruelty, and treachery as techniques of power manipulation. Previously in doing these things rulers had felt guilty. By formulating bad faith as a principle of power politics, Machiavelli raised it to a new level of instrumental availability. He enabled men to use this age-old instrument quite impersonally and with a clear conscience. The ultimate receipt for deceit, said Bismarck, is truth.

Today with the revelation of the poetic process which is involved in ordinary cognition we stand on a very different threshold from that wherein Machiavelli stood. His was a door into negation and human weakness. Ours is the door to the positive powers of the human spirit in its natural creativity. The door opens on to psychic powers comparable to the physical powers made available via nuclear fission and fusion. Through this door men have seen a possible path to the totalitarian remaking of human nature. Machiavelli showed us the way to a new circle of the Inferno. Knowledge of the creative process in art, science, and cognition shows us either to the earthly paradise or to complete madness. It is to be either the top of Mount Purgatory or the abyss.

The whole of nineteenth-century art and science is charged with the implications of the poetic process and its discovery. Our own century has seen that process put to work in the so-called mass media. Before Poe and Baudelaire the impressionism of Romantic art had taught the artist to pay minute attention to his perceptions, to their mode and inner effect. These experiences he practised to arrest and to fix in external landscapes, as we see in Keats, Tennyson, and Hopkins. Romantic impressionism unexpectedly opened the door to the creative process by developing new resources of introspection. Impressionism was the parent of symbolism. And impressionism and symbolism alike insisted on attention to process in preference to personal self-expression. Self-effacement and patient watchfulness preceded the discovery of the creative process. Poets and artists literally turned their own psyches into laboratories where they practised the most austere experiments in total disregard of their personal happiness. Gradually it dawned on Mallarmé that pure poetry was impossible — a poetry which would have as its theme the poetic process itself. Henceforth the subject and framework of a poem would be the retracing of a moment of perception. For some of the Romantic poets the doctrine of the aesthetic moment as a moment out of time — a moment of arrested consciousness — had seemed the key to all poetry. The pre-Raphaelites had pushed this doctrine as far as they could. But Mallarmé saw deeper and Joyce saw the rest. Joyce it was who saw that Aquinas had the final answer sought by Mallarmé. The rational notes of beauty, integrity, consonance, and *claritas* traced by St. Thomas were actual stages of apprehension in every moment of human awareness.

And so we arrive at the paradox of this most esoteric of all art doctrines, namely that the most poetic thing in the world is the most ordinary human consciousness. It seems to me that this is at once a very democratic and a profoundly Catholic basis for any humanism. It is a crucial matter for us to understand in the age of the so-called mass media. Mallarmé wrote his most difficult poem, *Un Coup de Des*, in newspaper format, He saw, like Joyce, that the basic forms of communication — whether speech, writing, print, press, telegraph, or photography — necessarily were fashioned in close accord with man's cognitive activity. And the more extensive the mass medium the closer it must approximate to our cognitive faculties.

He who would discuss humanism and literature today must know something about the history of media of human communication, because so rapidly have the media changed of late that print and letters have been dethroned by radio, TV, movies, and mechanized pictorial communication in general. I wrote a book, *The Mechanical Bride: Folklore of Industrial Man*, on the role of the literary humanist confronted by the hostile forces of non-literary communication. But when I wrote that book I had not become aware, for example, that printing (the mechanization of writing 400 years ago) had liquidated 2,000 years of manuscript culture. Printing was as savage a blow to a long-established culture as radio, movies, and TV have been to the culture based on the printed book. Today, therefore, when writing, speech, and gesture have all been mechanized, the literary humanist can get his bearings only by going back to pre-literate societies. If we are to defend a civilization built on the written and printed word against the present threat from TV, for example, we must know what we are defending; because at first glance TV, as a blend of sight and sound, looks like a superior form of communication to writing or print. TV is the mechanization of total human expression, speech, and gesture. In the first place, then, pre-literate societies based on a monopoly of the spoken word, are static, repetitive, unchanging. They are, as it is said, "time-bound." Such societies find it difficult to explore space or to extend their communications horizontally. Writing is a tremendous revolution in such a world. For writing is the translation of the vocal or audible into spatial form. Writing gives control over space. Writing produces at once the city. The power to shape space in writing brings the power to organize space architecturally. And when messages can be transported, then comes the road, and armies, and empires. The empires of Alexander and the Caesars were essentially built by paper routes. But today with instantaneous global communications the entire planet is, for purposes of inter-communication, a village rather than a vast imperial network. It is obvious that writing cannot have the same meaning or function for us that it had for earlier cultures.

Plato regarded the advent of writing as pernicious. In the *Phaedrus* he tells us that it would cause men to rely on their memories rather than their wits. Renaissance scholars greeted the arrival of print with maledictions. They were sure it meant the breakdown of international Latin and the rise of a vulgar and superficial race of shallow wits. With the assembly liners of moveable type clicking away day and night, they could foresee not a type of man that would rely on its memory of the written page but a new man who need remember nothing because he could always reach for a reference book. Faster presses, better roads, quicker collecting of information, and we move from the world of the book to that of the newspaper, the cheap daily book of the people. A cross-section of the world each day of the year. The crowding together of all the cultures of the world and all the age-old interests of man on every page. The telegraph, the power-press, and then photography. And with photography we meet the first form of communication (since the decline of Latin in the Western world) which hops across vernacular language barriers. Photography and movies are, like music, a menace to nationalistic passions. They appear also to be a threat to the book and the printed page. They foster habits inimical to concentration on the page.

One generalization, popularized in the writings of H. A. Innis in view of the history of forms of communication since writing, is that any change in the form or channels of communication, be it writing, roads, carts, ships, stone, papyrus, clay, or parchment, any change whatever has revolutionary social and political consequences. Related to this fact is another one, that any channel of communication has a distorting effect on habits of attention; it builds up a distinct form of culture. The printed page, for example, is extremely abstract as compared with the spoken word or with pictorial communication. The printed page created the solitary scholar and the split between literature and life which was practically unheard-of before printed books. The printed page fosters extreme individualism compared with manuscript societies. It destroys the plastic arts and the sense of the living past compared with oral cultures or with societies with pictorial writing like China. The printed page was the cultural matrix of our abstract technological world today, just as the printing press was the ancestor of assembly-line production.

For the Catholic, the revealed Word of God is not the Gutenberg Bible, not the King James Version. But the Protestant cannot but take a different view of the passing of the pre-eminence of the printed book, because Protestantism was born with printing and seems to be passing with it. There again, the Catholic alone has nothing to fear from the rapidity of the changes in the media of communication. But national cultures have much to fear. In fact, it is hard to see how any national culture as such can long stand up to the new media of communication. Not America but the globe itself is the melting pot of cultures. At the end of the present accelerated communication process are we to expect a new world citizen? Cosmic man? We have switched from the problem of production to the packaging of information. It is not markets we now invade but cultures and the minds of men. And this process is furthest advanced here in North America.

To get a better view of this process, let me take you back to that point in the nineteenth century where we saw Edgar Poe discover the poetic process — a discovery which included the new symbolist poetry (very high-brow) and the new detective thriller (very low-brow). I suggested that it was typical of the developments of our age that they included the most esoteric and the most popular matters because they were basically related to a new grasp of the nature of human cognition itself. Thus, symbolist poetry gave rise at once to modern pictorial advertising.

It is popular or unpopular to attack advertising. But it is unheard-of to take it seriously as a form of art. Personally I see it as a form of art. And like symbolist art it is created to produce an effect rather than to argue or discuss the merits of a product. The Baron Wrangel, the man in the Hathaway shirt — white shirt and black eye-patch: what did it mean? Out of the millions who bought Hathaway shirts, how many could say what the ad meant? It was a piece of magic: irrational, meaningless. But it had a definite effect. The advertiser proclaims to his clients that his pictorial and verbal magic is linked to the assembly line. No pictorial magic, no mass production. The primitive witch-doctor had spells which controlled the elements. The modern advertiser concocts spells which compel the customer. What the advertisers have discovered is simply that the new media of communication are themselves magical art forms. All art is in a sense magical in that it produces a change or metamorphosis in the spectator. It refashions his experience. In our slap-happy way we have released a great deal of this magic on ourselves today. We have been changing ourselves about at a great rate like Alley Oop. Some of us have been left hanging by our ears from the chandeliers.

What I wish to say a few words about at this point, however, is the movie in relation to the central fact of human cognition and the artistic process. Everybody has noticed the curious tendency today to elevate the poet and artist to the status of philosopher-kings. Of course, they are kings with few subjects, but the tendency remains. There is a dim intuition current that the poet and artist have in some way the key to the modern world. It is interesting that poets and artists have none of the objections to technical innovation that most men experience. In fact, since Leonardo da Vinci, poets and painters have been in the forefront of change and usually decades ahead of the physical sciences with their discoveries of new techniques for manipulating human experience. André Malraux notes, for example:

> The Italians regarded their art history from much the same stand-point as that from which the West today views the development of applied science . . . Giotto was revered as a precursor but (until the nineteenth century) no one would have dreamed of preferring his work to Leonardo's; it would have been like preferring a Sedan-chair to an aeroplane . . . the history of Italian art was the story of successive discoveries. . . . For Florence to repudiate her art, the spirit behind it had first to be called in question. Botticelli's works were burnt there (by Savonarola) for the same reasons as that for which modern Europe might decide to destroy her machinery.[3]

---

3   André Malraux, *Museum without Walls*, page 98.

Thus the Romantic poets were consciously in revolt against printed books as shackles on the human spirit. They turned to landscape and the pictorial presentation of experience long before the arrival of photography. And Poe's discovery about writing poems and stories backwards contained, years in advance, not only the secret of modern laboratory science but of the movie.

One reason for dwelling on this point is in order to suggest a deep relation between letters and non-literary forms of expression. For if such inter-relations have previously obtained, it may provide hope and comfort for those who wish to see literature maintained at present. The movie camera is a means of rolling up the daylight world on a spool. It does this by rapid still shots. The movie projector unrolls the spool and recreates the daylight world as a dark dream world. In reversing the process of perception even the mechanical camera and projector bring about a mysterious change in everyday experience. The movie reconstructs the external daylight world and in so doing provides an interior dream world. Hollywood means "sacred grove," and from this modern grove has issued a new pantheon of gods and goddesses to fashion and trouble the dreams of modern man.

Another way of seeing this mysterious medium for transforming experience is to consider it as the exact embodiment of Plato's Cave. The dreaming eye of the movie god casting his images on the dark screen corresponds to that image of human life offered to us by Plato in the *Republic*: existence is a kind of cave or cellar on the back wall of which we watch the shadows of real things from the outside world of reality.

In ordinary perception men perform the miracle of recreating within themselves — in their interior faculties — the exterior world. This miracle is the work of the *nous poietikos* or of the agent intellect — that is, the poetic or creative process. The exterior world in every instant of perception is interiorized and recreated in a new matter. Ourselves. And in this creative work that is perception and cognition, we experience immediately that dance of Being within our faculties which provides the incessant intuition of Being. I can only regard the movie as the mechanization and distortion of this cognitive miracle by which we recreate within ourselves the exterior world. But whereas cognition provides that dance of the intellect which is the analogical sense of Being, the mechanical medium has tended to provide merely a dream world which is a substitute for reality rather than a means of proving reality.

The camera, however, in the hands of a realist is capable of quite different effects, and I should like to offer some remarks of Cesare Zavattini, the famous Italian movie-artist, as suggesting a humanist rather than an aspirin approach to the film.

I

No doubt one's first and most superficial reaction to everyday reality is that it is tedious. Until we are able to overcome some moral and intellectual laziness, in fact, this reality will continue to appear uninteresting. One shouldn't be astonished that the cinema has always felt the natural, unavoidable necessity to insert a "story" in the reality to make it exciting and "spectacular." All the same, it is clear that such a method evades a direct approach to everyday reality, and suggests that it cannot be portrayed without the intervention of fantasy or artifice.

The most important characteristic, and the most important innovation, of which is called neo-realism, it seems to me, is to have realized that the necessity of the "story" was only an unconscious way of disguising a human defeat, and that the kind of imagination it involved was simply a technique of superimposing dead formulas over living social facts. Now it has been perceived that reality is hugely rich, that to be able to look directly at it is enough; and that the artist's task is not to make people moved or indignant at metaphorical situations, but to make them reflect (and, if you like, to be moved and indignant, too) on what they and others are doing, on the real things, exactly as they are.

For me, this has been a great victory. I would like to have achieved it many years earlier. But I made the discovery, an appeal to order. I saw at last what lay in front of me, and I understood that to have evaded reality had been to betray it.

Example: Before this, if one was thinking over the idea of a film on, say, a strike, one was immediately forced to invent a plot. And the strike itself became only the background to the film. Today, our attitude would be one of "revelation"; we would describe the strike itself, try to work out the largest possible number of human, moral, social, economic, poetic values from the bare documentary fact.

We have passed from an unconsciously rooted mistrust of reality, an illusory and equivocal evasion, to an unlimited trust in things, facts, and people. Such a position requires us, in effect, to excavate reality, to give it a power, a communication, a series of reflexes, which until recently we had never thought it had. It requires, too, a true and real interest in which is happening, a search for the most deeply hidden human values; which is why we feel that the cinema must recruit not only intelligent people, but, above all, "living" souls, the morally richest people.

II

The cinema's overwhelming desire to see, to analyse, its hunger for reality, is an act of concrete homage towards other people, towards what is happening and existing in the world. And, incidentally, it is what distinguishes "neo-realism" from the American cinema.

What effects on narrative, then, and on the portrayal of human character, has the neo-realist style produced?

To begin with, while the cinema used to make one situation produce another situation, and another, and another, again and again, and each scene was thought out and immediately related to the next (the natural result of a mistrust of reality), today, when we have thought out a scene, we feel the need to "remain" in it, because the single scene itself can contain so many echoes and reverberations, can even contain all the situations we may need. Today, in fact, we can quietly say: give us whatever "fact" you like, and we will disembowel it, make it something worth watching.

While the cinema used to portray life in its most visible and external moments — and a film was usually only a series of situations selected and linked together with varying success — today the neo-realist affirms that each one of these situations, rather than all the external moments, contains in itself enough material for a film.

Example: In most films, the adventures of two people looking for somewhere to live, for a house, would be shown externally in a few moments of action, but for us it could provide the scenario for a whole film and we would explore all its echoes, all its implications.

Of course, we are still a long way from a true analysis of human situations, and one can speak of analysis only in comparison with the dull synthesis of most current production. We are, rather, still in an "attitude" of analysis; but in this attitude there is a strong purpose, a desire for understanding, for belonging, for participating — for living together, in fact.

III

Substantially, then, the question today is, instead of turning imaginary situations into "reality" and trying to make them look "true," to make things as they are, almost by themselves, create their own special significance. Life is not what is invented in "stories"; life is another matter. To understand it involves a minute, unrelenting, and patient search.

Here I must bring in another point of view. I believe that the world goes on getting worse because we are not truly aware of reality. The most authentic position anyone can take up today is to engage himself in tracing the roots of this problem. The keenest necessity of our time is "social attention."

Attention, though, to what is there, directly; not through an apologue, however well conceived. A starving man, a humiliated man, must be shown by name and surname; no fable for a starving man, because that is something else, less effective and less moral. The true function of the cinema is not to tell fables, and to a true function we must recall it.

Of course, reality can be analysed by ways of fiction. Fictions can be expressive and natural; but neo-realism, if it wants to be worthwhile, must sustain the moral impulse that characterized its beginnings, in an analytical documentary way. No other medium of expression has the cinema's original and innate capacity for showing things, that we believe worth showing, as they happen day by day — in which we might call their "dailiness," their longest and truest duration. The cinema has everything in front of it, and no other medium has the same possibilities for getting it known quickly to the greatest number of people.

As the cinema's responsibility also comes from its enormous power, it should try to make every frame of film count, by which I mean that it should penetrate more and more into the manifestations and the essence of reality.

The cinema only affirms its moral responsibility when it approaches reality in this way.

The moral, like the artistic, problem lies in being able to observe reality, not to extract fictions from it.[4]

---

4   Cesare Zavattini, *Sight and Sound*, October–December 1953, pages 64-65.

That I think represents a point of view which can only be regarded as a major addition to Catholic humanism and letters. And as we trace the rise of successive communication channels or links, from writing to movies and TV, it is borne in on us that in order for their exterior artifice to be effective it must partake of the character of that interior artifice by which in ordinary perception we incarnate the exterior world. Because human perception is literally incarnation. So that each of us must *poet* the world or fashion it within us as our primary and constant mode of awareness. And the mechanical or mass media of communication must at least parrot the world in order to hold our attention.

The movie can teach us something more about perception and the poetic process. The characteristic dream world offered to the movie spectator occurs when we reverse the spool on which the camera has rolled up the carpet of the external world. So reversed, the carpet of the daylight world becomes the magic carpet of dreams, carrying us instantly anywhere. Similarly, it would seem that the poet differs from other men only in his conscious ability to arrest the intake of experience and to reverse the flow. By this means he is able to externalize in a work the actual process by which each of us in perception or cognition incarnates the external world of existence. But every word uttered by man requires a large measure of the poetic ability. Our words are analogies of the miracle by which we incarnate and utter the world.

I suggest that our faith in the Incarnation has an immediate relevance to our art, science, and philosophy. Since the Incarnation all men have been taken up into the poetry of God, the Divine Logos, the Word, His Son. But Christians alone know this. And knowing this, our own poetry, our own power of incarnating and uttering the world, becomes a precious foretaste of the Divine Incarnation and the Evangel. We can see how all things have literally been fulfilled in Christ, especially our powers of perception. And in Christ we can look more securely and steadfastly on natural knowledge which at one and the same time has become easier and also less important to us. In our time Charles Du Bos and Paul Claudel have been eloquent in claiming for the poetic process a serious analogy to the divine Incarnation of the Word. And Du Bos expresses this under the figure of Mary Magdalene: "At the feet of Christ pagan beauty has been perfected. There is no other more irrefutable and sublime justification beauty as well as for that creation which God freely grants to the free creative genius of man."

I would also draw to your attention the extraordinary example of James Joyce, who, so far as I can judge, was the first to establish his insights into the creative process on the views of Aquinas with regard to perception and cognition. I am not attempting to represent Joyce as a model Catholic. But there is the universal non-Catholic testimony about his genius and his art that they appear unthinkable apart from his immersion in the traditions of Catholic theology and philosophy, just as he chose in his work to immortalize the culture and traditions of Ireland as well. The recent words of Mr. Arland Ussher, a notable Protestant figure in Dublin today, will serve to bring into focus both the theme of the poetic process and central aspects of Catholic humanism and modern letters:

> It may be that no nation and no literature can skip any of the "dialectical" phases of its development. The oddity of James Joyce seems to me partly that of a prodigious birth out of time — an oddity favoured certainly, but not engendered, by the artistic climates of the twentieth century. Ireland, owing to her isolation from the European development (and also in part no doubt to foreign domination) had produced no important body of literature during the Middle Age — an age which in her case has continued almost to the present day. Joyce is Ireland's first great native writer — her Dante or her Chaucer; though expressing his age, as every writer should, it was also necessary for him to express, in his manner, those buried ages — to achieve a great collective Yeatsian "dreaming back." He took with immense seriousness his destiny of "forging the uncreated conscience of his race" — so that he had to be, by turns, a St. Augustine crying aloud his sins, a Scholastic glossing on Aquinas, the producer himself of a "Summa" or great synthesis, and finally Duns Scotus splitting hairs and mangling words. And all the time he was essentially a humorous sceptical Dublin observer — an Everyman among artists, with a schoolboy love of puns, puzzles and indelicacies — sometimes distorted out of nature by these processes, at other times assisted to an immortal symbolization.[5]

---

5   Arland Ussher, *Three Great Irishmen: Shaw, Yeats, Joyce* (New York: Devin-Adair, 1953), pages 127-28.

Actually the side of Joyce that Mr. Ussher is able to see and enjoy is, great as it is, a very small part. For it was Joyce who first abandoned vertical or horizontal symbolism for horizontal symbolism. He lived amidst the orgy of Swedenborgian, Gnostic, and neo-Platonic symbolism which still envelops us. And he never ceased to have fun with its pagan confusion. His early instructor in much of this cabalistic lore was the famous AE (George Russell) to whom Joyce makes formal thanks in *Finnegans Wake* in precise but laughable formula: "AE"IOU. Now for the Platonist as for the Gnostic, a symbol, or a poem, is simply a sign linking Heaven and Hell. Art and beauty point from this world to another world from which we have all fallen. In this ancient pagan view, so predominant today, man is a fallen angel. For many years Maritain has explained this pagan view of man as an angel driving a machine, his body. So that granted the pagan premise that man is simply a fallen angel, the ideal of modern industrial humanism is quite consistent. Let us doll up the fallen angel and let us put it in ever more powerful machines until the whole world looks like Marilyn Monroe in a Cadillac convertible. Powered by the magic of the camera eye and the means of duplicating its imagery universally, we have begun to approach the realization of this angelic dream.

In this angelic view the business of art has nothing to do with the analogy of cognition nor with our miraculous power to incarnate the external world. It is a means rather to lift us out of our human condition and to restore us to the divine world from which we fell at birth. In this view the artist becomes one with the Nietzschean superman, the transvaluer of values. Reality is not to be trusted or revered but to be remade by social engineers.

Joyce is the single poet voice in our century raised not merely against this view but in wild laughter at its arrogant confusion. Far from turning his back on it he invaded it and took it up into the analogical drama of his art. For only the artist of analogical vision can freely adopt actual existence to the exigencies of art. But the traditional errors of men become for the analogical artist precious matter for his structures even as Gilson has used historical error in philosophy to build a path to truth. So in Joyce, Jung and Freud and Descartes and many others are whirled through his pages as in a Marx Brothers review [revue]. But always among the elements of the show is that due proportion which is beauty. In *Stephen Hero* Joyce wrote: "For Stephen art was neither a copy nor an imitation of nature. The artistic process was a natural process . . . a veritably sublime process of one's own nature which had a right to examination and open discussion."[6]

That this sublime process is that of ordinary apprehension is made plain a little further on:

> What we symbolize in black the Chinaman may symbolize in yellow: each has his own tradition. Greek beauty laughs at Coptic beauty and the American Indian derides them both. It is almost impossible to reconcile all tradition whereas it is by no means impossible to find the justification of every form of beauty — by an examination of the mechanism of esthetic apprehension whether it be dressed in red, yellow, or black. We have no reason for thinking that the Chinaman has a different system of digestion from that which we have though our diets are quite dissimilar. The apprehensive faculty must by scrutinized in action.[7]

What Joyce wrote down in this wise fifty years ago is dawning on political scientists and social engineers today as a revolutionary discovery about man and society. But the truth will always be upsetting to erring men as it is thrilling to others. Perhaps the besetting Catholic danger is to live with the truth until one is not concerned to look at it. We know it so well that we "couldn't care less." What Joyce did was to bring the great developments of symbolist art into the focus of Thomist philosophy. He created a great new cultural window, metaphor or synthesis. Everything the Schoolmen had written was suddenly seen through the Chartres-like windows of St. Thomas. (Be it said in passing that this same symbolist art and speculation had also the effect of stirring the most ancient roots of Spanish and Latin culture. Symbolism made Seneca alive and lancing once more in the Latin world, giving us the astonishing poetic Renaissance of Spain and Latin America in the past eighty years.) It was Aquinas who enabled Joyce to surpass all the Pre-Raphaelites. It was the Thomist awareness of analogy derived from sense perception that gave Joyce the means of digesting all the ideas of all his contemporaries without relying on any of them as a prop or a frame of reference.

This is Joyce's way of discussing what I have earlier mentioned and

---

6   James Joyce, *Stephen Hero* (New York: New Directions, 1944), page 171.
7   *Ibid.*, page 212.

illustrated as Edgar Poe's discovery of the poetic process and Gilson's use of the technique of living reconstruction of the past:

> The modern spirit is vivisective. Vivisection is the most modern process one can conceive. The ancient method investigated law with the lantern of justice, morality with the lantern of revelation, art with the lantern of tradition. But all these lanterns have magical properties: they transform and disfigure. The modern method examines its territory by the light of day. . . . It examines the entire community in action and reconstructs the spectacle of redemption. If you were an esthetic philosopher you would take note of all my vagaries because here you have the spectacle of the esthetic instinct in action. The philosophic college should spare a detective for me.[8]

This may seem very specialized, very arty. Actually it spells out into the most practical political and social consequences for each one of us. What Joyce is saying is that for the first time in history many now have the means of observing the social process as the process of redemption. This he can do because the social process is the analogue of the process of sense perception and interior cognition. And the process of perception is that of incarnation.

∞

For anybody concerned with the subject of Catholic humanism in modern letters I should think that Joyce's insight, which was marvellously realized in his work, is the most inspiriting development that is possible to conceive. But we must ask, what happens when this insight occurs even in a fragmentary way to the secular minds of our age? The answer can be found in *The Foundations of Social Survival*, a recent book by John Lindberg, a Swedish nobleman associated with the United Nations. His proposal for social survival is that we adopt the Christian doctrine of brotherly love. He is not a Christian but he thinks Christianity might be made to work by non-Christians. In short, he proposes practical Christianity as a sort of Machiavellian strategy of culture and power. And his reasons are directly linked to the developments I have outlined in modern letters. Namely that in

---

8 *Ibid.*, page 186.

the modern world we have through the very perfection and instantaneity of our means of communication made it impossible to resolve the conflicting claims of the numerous societies and cultures which are now in close association. Neither can we hope to impose any one culture on all the others and reduce them to a single form. But, he argues, we now have the key to the creative process which brings all cultures into existence (namely the extension into social institutions of the central form and mystery of the human cognitive process). And it is this key which he proposes to deliver into the hands of a world government.

Speaking as a student of literature who has seen and experienced the undermining of formal literary study in our time by the new media of communication, I think it relevant to observe here that it is especially the job of the Catholic humanist to build bridges between the arts and society today. Because the Catholic humanist can see the Incarnation which informs all arts and traditions of mankind. More specifically, in our time Catholic letters have approached much nearer to this awareness than ever before. But so has the secular world. The study of the arts of expression and communication can today give the Catholic an integral sense of religion and culture previously unknown. But if we use this awareness only for contemplation our secular contemporaries are just as certainly going to use it for power over the minds of men. We are, then, confronted by this contrast, that with Machiavelli at the beginning of the great secular era which we call the Renaissance and the modern period in history and letters, a lie about man was made the basis of secular prediction and control. And today at the end of the Renaissance a great truth about man is being taken up as the instrument of the totalitarian transformation of man and society. That truth which is our freedom can, neglected by us, become the means of an enslavement of mind and spirit surpassing any tyranny of which history makes mention. It is, therefore, through training in the precise awareness of these developments as offered in modern letters and communication that we can observe the appointed field of trial for the Catholic humanist.

18

The Christian in the
Electronic Age

Editorial note: At one point, in the early 1970s, my father and I discussed possibly writing a book about the fate of the Church — the fate of religion in the West — under the pressures and influence of electric media. Vatican II had clearly been a response to the pressure exerted by television on the general population. TV had made us all inner-seekers and had obsolesced hardware institutions and centralized authority. It was transforming politics and culture and changing the face of religion. It was reviving charismatic experience in our midst and, halfway around the world, Islam.

The following chapter-outline was drawn up in a morning, and like many other notes and small essays, it took shape over a couple of weeks while religious controversy filled the newspapers. The next step would have been to open a folder for each chapter and begin amplifying the themes and making additional notes and references. The book project went no further, although readers may recognize themes familiar in later work. These include the left-brain / right-brain discoveries, which at the time were fresh and exciting, the "Law of Implementation," the effects of bypassing the body — making it obsolete — by all electric media (the discarnate world), literacy and propaganda, etc.

The Christian in the Electronic Age

Chapter 1 Crisis of Faith is Generation Gap

I.e., cleavage between left hemisphere elders and right hemisphere young who are holistic.

a) change of polarity of young/old

b) new type of religious teaching "charismatic"/holistic total involvement

c) problem of irrelevance: "trying to do the new job with old means" (*Take Today*, page 236)[1]

Chapter 2 Two Hemispheres of the Brain

Keys to understanding media. [For us, living] at speed of light, all experience becomes simultaneous or right hemisphere, whereas formerly all experience had been sequential and logical and left hemisphere.

---

1 Marshall McLuhan and Barrington Nevitt, *Take Today: The Executive as Drop Out* (New York: Harcourt Brace Jovanovitch, 1972; Toronto: Longman Canada, 1972). Had Vatican II, for example, fallen prey to the "Law of Implementation"? Page 236:

There is still a widely held assumption that the most advanced discoveries can be translated into action only by the older forms of organization. *The "Law of Implementation" is that the newest awareness must be processed by the established procedures.* In the commando conference, those who were to implement the decisions were present and helped to make the discoveries that became the action. The commando team did not "delegate" but acted as a uniform task force. Its dialogue became dramatized. There was no question that once they had begun to confer they would then fall back on the old command structure for implementation.

The preceding paragraph had set the underlying theme, of what speed-up does to human perception and association:

. . . during World War II, commando raids called for a new kind of aggregation of human resources. This in turn related to great speed-up in the movement of human personnel as well as great increase in the portability and firepower of weaponry. . . . Increased demands of knowledge go with decrease in the amounts of "hardware."

The liberal bishops at Vatican II acted as a kind of commando: "What was here suspended was the entire structure of military organization, which had been transferred to the commercial establishment at the end of the nineteenth century." Politically, the conservative bishops represented the institutional Church, encumbered with bureaucracy and real estate. Moreover,

The dynamics of both miniaturization and "etherialization" call for an inclusive awareness of total situations. Before a commando raid was mounted, the practice was for officers and men to confer as equals. The military staff-and-line pattern of command was effaced. What was here suspended was the entire structure of military organization, which had been transferred to the commercial establishment at the end of the nineteenth century. Instead of approaching the problem from any particular point of view, they swarmed over the problem as a group, using their total knowledge to encounter its many unexpected facets. This procedure was in direct contrast to General Staff plans prepared by experts to meet all conceivable eventualities. The "blueprints and specifications" were scrapped. As in an Operations Research séance, these men stormed the problem from all sides.

Chapter 3 Religious Universe of Young People
Zen Buddhism, etc. Newman, Grammar of Assent:
notional theology vs. experiential faith[2] — understanding
the role of Eastern religion in faith today.

Chapter 4 Approach to Faith
Under electronic conditions man tends to be discarnate
and liberated from natural law and finds his only ground
in supernatural law and experience.

Chapter 5 Jacques Ellul explains in *Propaganda* that indoctrination
can only occur in a phonetically literate population. The
attention span of electronically conditioned man is insuf-
ficient. Likewise his power of retention is diminished.

Chapter 6 What we need is for a strategy of culture to fuse the old
and obliterated, the trite and the current, the new, and
the surprising, the most ancient and the most civilized
mentality.[3] At the speed of light, Humpty Dumpty goes
back together again and holistic man reappears.

Chapter 7 Liturgy and Media
Body language automatically takes primacy under electronic conditions. Electric media are inner trips and tend
to favour depth involvement in meditational forms.

Chapter 8 The Church of Tomorrow
When time and space have been eliminated by electric
communication, the Church becomes one as never before.

Chapter 9 Let us do with less and less hardware. We can do more
and more with less and less (Bucky Fuller). Beware the
pitfalls and booby traps of hardware media.

---

2 Consider the rise of charismatic religion within the Roman Catholic Church and Pentecostal
denominations, etc.

3 See T. S. Eliot's discussion of "auditory imagination" in his essay, "Matthew Arnold," in *The Use of
Poetry and the Use of Criticism* (London: Faber and Faber, 1933), page 118. Also discussed in this
book, pages 107, 122, and 143.

19

Wyndham Lewis:

Lemuel in Lilliput

In England and America we want a new learned minority
as sharp as razors, as fond of discourse as a Greek, familiar
enough with the abstract to be able to handle the concrete. In short we want a new race of philosophers *instead*
of "hurried men," speed cranks, simpletons, or robots.
(Wyndham Lewis, *Time and Western Man*, page xii)

I, at the outset, unmask the will that is behind the
Time-philosophy, by displaying it in the heart of the
representative ferment produced by it — in the full,
instinctive indulgence and expansion of the artistic
impulse, and imposing its values upon the impression-
able material of life. (*Time and Western Man*, page xv)

Both in England and America Catholics represent a minority, but not
the minority Lewis is looking for. Both England and America are
provincial countries. That is they buy their intellectual clothing ready-
to-wear. And the Catholic minorities of England and America are
provincial even by English and American standards. English and
American Catholics yearn for respectability. They crave to be regarded

∞ *From* Studies in Honor of St. Thomas Aquinas: Key Thinkers and Modern
Thought, *Saint Louis University, 1944, vol. 2, pages 58-72.*
Note: The footnotes in this chapter are Marshall McLuhan's original notes.

as "hundred per centers." More than their non-Catholic brethren they seek the security of complete social conformity. This of course is sad but quite natural. It is a fact which any Catholic thinker or educator must face at the outset. Nor is it a fact which will be modified for many years to come. Anybody trying to present Lewis to a Catholic audience must think about this problem, because Lewis is the least provincial intelligence which has been in England since St. Thomas More. His concern for the order of Western civilization has led him to contemplate the contemporary situation minutely and in its entirety. The toil of detachment has left him with a deficiency of national sentiment pleasing to neither Englishmen, Frenchmen, nor Americans.[1] Lewis pleases nobody because he is like an intruder at a feast who quietly explains that dinner must be temporarily abandoned since the food has been poisoned and the guests must be detached from their dinners by a stomach pump.

Another reason why it is difficult to explain the relevance of Lewis to a Catholic audience is that he assumes that people who have grown up since 1918 are perfectly acquainted not only with such writers as Hegel, Marx, Darwin, Nietzsche, Sorel, Proudhom, Freud, Bergson, and Spengler, but also with such artists as Joyce, Stein, Proust, Eliot, Pound, Picasso, Rodin, and Benda. This is a heavy demand to make on anybody. But the time-lag in the Catholic reading public is such that although Catholics necessarily live in the world of Eliot, Stein, and Einstein, their emotional organization is done for them by Kipling, Galsworthy, Shaw, and Chesterton. For let us not suppose for one instant that Catholicity of mind is conferred by grace or that we are freed from "the world's slow stain" by immersing ourselves in the best sellers of yesteryear.

All question of the artistic value of Joyce and Picasso apart, the man

---

1 Confronting the conventions of present-day Shakespearean criticism for example:

That large class of able middle-class men, domiciled in the universities, of the type of the correct and snobbish family solicitor, usually ending life with a few irrelevant honours, is responsible as a rule for Shakespeare criticism. (*The Lion and the Fox*, London, 1927, page 240)

Again,

This episode of the little budding Coriolanus is, however, with the utmost consistency, typical of the play and Shakespeare's treatment of Coriolanus from beginning to end. It is an astonishingly close picture of a particularly cheerless and unattractive snob such as must have pullulated in the court of Elizabeth, and such as the English public school and university system has produced ever since. He is a fearless and efficient leader in war, with every opportunity, and the stimulus of self-interest, to be such — and nothing else. In every other respect he is a glum, vain and extremely peevish dog, always abusing a crowd of supers for not incessantly flattering him and furthering his interests and those of Volumnia . . . (*The Lion and the Fox*, page 241) whose sensibility and judgment cannot cope with them easily and naturally has not the equipment to consider the world he lives in. Certainly there can be no Catholic action at the educated level until this equipment is acquired and mastered — a fact which explains why the Catholic mind never has to be seriously considered by the non-Catholic mind in England and America today. This situation can be illustrated by an exception such as Maritain. Maritain is perfectly at home amidst modern art and letters. He has a contemporary sensibility. This in turn has energized and directed his philosophical activity, and given a precise, contemporary relevance to the *philosophia perennis*. He is therefore a force to be reckoned with by non-Catholic philosophers. He can mesh with the modern mind, such as it is. He can impinge. For the English-speaking Catholic who would do likewise but who knows not how to begin (and his formal education will not be of any assistance in this matter), let him pore upon the works of Wyndham Lewis, let him read by day and meditate by night.

I propose to consider here only three or four of the thirty-odd volumes of Wyndham Lewis. This means neglecting the fact that he is the only serious painter England has had in the past fifty years, and that he is one of the half-dozen great painters of Europe in the same period. Similarly, as the author of *Tarr*, *The Apes of God*, and *The Childermass*, he takes his place in the literature of prose satire as a classic. It was not in a moment of enthusiasm that the stringent Edgell Rickwood said: "If there could have been any doubt, after *The Childermass*, as to Lewis being the most forceful and resourceful prose-writer of his generation there can be none now."[2] Works of this scope and importance must be reserved for separate treatment, especially since they are little read in America. Instead, something will be said about another side of his work — the pamphleteering. This is the side from which both the novels and the painting of Lewis are most readily approached. The pamphlets are, in fact, a strategy of fortification worked out by the creative Lewis to protect and to promote creative effort.

Today, the artist lives in a world which has no place for art.[3] The dehumanization of life by means of centralized methods of "communication," and by the lethal abstractionizing of the machine controlled by abstract greed, has left only a hole-and-corner existence for the

---

2 *Scrutinies II*, collected by Edgell Rickwood, London, 1931. Pages 159-60.
3 Yet there was never an age when "art" was so much talked of and exploited. The deep concern for art has led me to explain and expose this situation. The revolutionary rich of *l'haut bohème* exploit

serious artist. No great artist ever fought so furiously to maintain a tiny milieu for art as Lewis has done. The life of free intelligence has never, in the Western world, encountered such anonymous and universal hostility before.[4] To read the "pamphlets" of Lewis is to become aware not only of the scope of the forces arrayed against reason and art, but it is to have anatomized before one's eyes every segment of the contemporary scene of glamorized commerce and advertising, and, above all, of the bogus science, philosophy, art, and literature which have been the main instrument in producing the universal stupefaction.

Lewis confronts modern society with the trained eye of a painter to whom the cut of every garment, every gesture, every contour is a richly expressive language. However, the modern man has long lost the use of his eyes. He only has ears and those for the Napoleonic thunder of Beethoven, the turgid and Dionysiac megalomania of Wagner, the erotic day-dreaming of Tchaikowski, or the tom-tom and African bottom-wagging of swing calling to rut. With Dr. Coué-like repetition

---

two symbols in their craving for the joys of irresponsible power — the freedom of the child and the freedom of the artist:

> By this particular luxurious Western society the *artist* and the *child* are the two figures most heavily imitated . . . . So, of course, both true art and true infancy are in imminent danger of extinction or, "worse than death, dishonour." . . . If, however, *one* artist, and a *single* child, are preserved intact and unpolluted owing to my words, I should consider my pains richly rewarded. . . . The rich have developed it because, as it is impossible to enjoy openly the privileges of riches in the present period of transition, to exercise power openly, and openly surround themselves with its problems and satisfactions; as it is necessary to pretend to be merely private citizens when in reality they are the rulers of the world — so they covet the privileges of the artist. . . . And the rich and powerful, if prevented from indulging their natural taste for pomp and display (which in a socialist epoch is impossible) — if prevented from being artists in action (all actions containing naturally a great aesthetic element) — will invariably seek to be "artists" in some other way. *"Action" today is starved of art.* That is why there are so many "artists" and so little good art at all. (*Ibid.*, pages 154-55)

4 How perfectly a machine society caters to the base and anti-vital aspects of human nature no one need be shown. Agrarian societies impose discipline and self-denial on the majority, protecting men from themselves. Lewis says:

> It is a belief . . . at the root of a great deal of behaviour today, that *freedom and irresponsibility are invariably commutative terms.* The first object of a person with a desire to be free, and yet possessing none of the means exterior to himself or herself (such as money, conspicuous ability, or power) to obtain freedom, is to avoid responsibility.
>
> Absence of responsibility, an automatic and stereotyped rhythm, is what most men desire for themselves . . . but consciousness and possession of the self is not compatible with a set rhythm. All the libertarian cries of a century ago were posed on unreal premises, and impulses that . . . cannot be sustained by the majority of men. Luxury and repose are what most men undeniably desire . . . when action is required of them they prefer that it should be "exciting" and sensational . . . that is the only way they can feel. Sensationalism and Sadism are twins. The only effort that is acceptable to many people is violent, excessive, and spasmodic action. "Simple" delights, as we call them, appear to be the privileged possession of the chosen ones of nature. (*The Art of Being Ruled*, page 142)

we hear on every hand: "This isn't a war, it's a revolution." "We live in an age of transition." "Things will be different after this war." "This won't be the last war." Whether spoken by the responsible or the moronic, these remarks, and countless others like them, have no meaning. They are spoken in a trance of inattention while the reason is in permanent abeyance. They are typical of men who no longer understand the world they have made and which, as robots, they operate day by day. Such is the situation into which Lewis shot his pamphlet breezily entitled *The Art of Being Ruled*.

> *The Art of Being Ruled* is not intended for the docile consumer of the crude anodynes presented to him today by Hollywood, the press, the radio, and the book-of-the-month clubs: "Most books have their *patients* rather than their *readers*, no doubt. But some degree of health is postulated in the reader of this book. Its pages are not intended to supply the figurative equivalent of Kruschen Salts nor an enema. Nor is it the intention of its author to open a clinic or a nursing-home, or an institute for the half-witted, nor yet a beauty-parlour. Understanding on that point with the reader at the start will be an advantage."[5]

In America, all serious writing is done for professionals by professionals. There is no serious reading public but only a writing public. Outside a few specialized journals the whole output of print in America is intended as aspirin. Potential writers and artists are thus compelled into the fox-hole of teaching. (Teaching is not a fox-hole as such, but only because there can be little serious teaching done amidst current conditions.) Thus nobody in America in the past thirty years has ever faced the problem of writing a serious book for a general public. Such writers as have stayed out of teaching have automatically appealed to a ready-made audience such as is constituted by the Marxian socialists. Lewis, however, sets out to create an audience for himself:

> A book of this description is not written for an audience that is already there, prepared to receive it, and whose minds it will fit like a glove.

---

5   *Ibid.*, page xi. "To build up a critical organism, composed of the most living material of observed fact, which could serve as an ally of new creative effort — something like an immense watch-dog trained to secure by its presence the fastness of the generally ill-protected theoretic man . . . that was the kind of thing I had in mind in starting to write my recent book, *The Art of Being Ruled*." (*Time and Western Man*, New York, 1928, page 119)

There must be a good deal of stretching of the receptacle it is to be expected. It must of necessity make its own audience; . . . I do not invent . . . a class of *esprits libres*, or "good Europeans," as Nietzsche did. I know none.[6]

A little later, Lewis faces the same problem:

It has been my object, from the start, to secure an audience of people not usually attentive to abstract discussion. . . . Where everything is question, and where all traditional values are repudiated, the everyday problems have become, necessarily, identical with the abstractions from which all concrete things in the first place come. And the everyday life is too much affected by the speculative activities that are renewing and transvaluing our world, for it to be able to survive in ignorance of those speculations. . . . Everything in our life today conspires to thrust most people into prescribed tracks, in what can be called a sort of *trance of action*. Hurrying, without any significant reason, from spot to spot at the maximum speed obtainable . . . how is the typical individual of this epoch to do some detached thinking for himself? All his life is disposed with a view to vanishing reflection. . . . His life thrusts new problems upon him in profusion and simultaneously withdraws all possibility of his getting the time to grasp them, it would seem.[7]

Later still Lewis has become almost resigned to the obtuseness of his audience as he analyses the exploitation of "youth" snobbery by big business:

If you rationalize something that in its essence should be irrational, you banish forever the Schoolgirl Complexion — no argument is possible on that head. If that complexion really matters to you, you will be enraged by this book.[8]

It is obvious that Lewis has fought earnestly to provide the general reader with the equipment he needs to live rationally in the world today. Let those who calmly address themselves to a tiny specialist audience, and who accuse Lewis of arrogant contempt for his readers,

---

6 *Ibid.*, page xii.
7 *Ibid.*, page vii.
8 *Doom of Youth*, London, 1932, page 8.

take note. Nor let it be supposed that specialists today understand either Lewis or the material with which he deals. There is no evidence for such a supposition. They, above all, need to read him.

The Art of Being Ruled is a study of the major dichotomy of modern life. There is the romanticized machine on one hand, the vulgarized spawn of speculative science committed to perennial and ever-accelerated revolution. On the other hand are the traditional political and human values:

> The cultural "all-round" personage . . . is the opposite of the narrow class-man, or, better, caste-man, the narrow *occupational* mannequin, the narrow integral self-effaced unit of the syndic. The bootmaker (for the theorist of syndicalism) must have only boot-making thoughts. No god-like *éclairé*, gentlemanly thoughts must interfere with his pure, sutorial one-sidedness — thoughts that in any case he would get all upside-down, never have any time to properly enjoy, and which would only make him absurd and diminish his utility . . .[9]
>
> Syndicalism, specialism, whether theoretic (as in Europe) or actual (as in America), is the degenerate child of decadent scholasticism. It is anti-vital, anti-human. Perversely harnessed to it are the accumulated theological energies of many centuries. The fanatics of revolution and applied or vulgarized science from Rousseau to Lenin are apostles of a distorted creed.[10]

As a result of these distortions it has come about that:

> In our society two virtues are badly contrasted, that of the *fighter* and *killer* (given such immense prestige by nineteenth-century darwinian science and philosophy) and that of the civilizer and maker. . . . We confuse these two characters that we violently contrast. The effort in this essay is to separate them a little. It is hoped that certain things that have flown a grey and neutral flag will be forced to declare themselves as Ozman or Ahriman, the dark or the light.[11]

Against the pseudo-impersonality and supposed "drift of events" Lewis asserts the prerogatives of human intelligence and control. He

---

9 *The Art of Being Ruled*, page 21.
10 *Ibid.*, page 13.
11 *Ibid.*, page 15.

unmasks the long-preserved anonymity of supposedly unwilled and irresistible forces in modern life. The atomization of consciousness,[12] the attack on the continuity of personal experience, whether by the medicine man of the laboratory or the dionysiac ecstasies of advertisement and high-finance, are alike shown to be the products of deliberate *will*. The worship of the dialectic of history or of the "dynamic aspect of reality" in Hegel, Marx, and Bergson has its natural corollary on the "practical" plane:

> *Dynamical*, as the most "hurried" of men is aware, means the bustle and rush of action, — of Big Business, Armaments, Atlantic "hops," Wall Street and Mussolini. A "dynamic personality" means, in journalism, an iron-jawed oil-king in an eight-cylinder car, ripping along a new motor-road, with a hundred-million-dollar deal in a new line of poison-gas bombs blazing in his super-brain, his eye aflame with the lust of battle — of those battles in which others fight and die.[13]

Such are the results of confusing the "fighter and killer" (whether in the speculative or the practical order) with the "civilizer and maker." For Lewis, therefore, there are two kinds of revolution:

---

12 Lewis has shown at length how the fabric of modern life is woven without a seam. "Romance," "advertisement," "sensationalism," Bergsonism, Behaviourism, Pragmatism, are all the same thing. The world in which Advertisement dwells is a one-day world. . . . The average man is invited to slice his life into a series of one-day lives, regulated by the clock of fashion. The human being is no longer the unit. (*Time and Western Man*, page 12)

Cf. pages 55 ff for the Stein attack on language which insures the continuity of experience. I heard Miss Stein give a lecture at Cambridge entitled: "I am I because my little dog know me." That is, the only proof of the continuity of our personality must repose on our fitting into an external habit machine. Miss Stein's subtle attack on language is part of the child-cult and the flight from responsibility. It is no accident that she was the star pupil of William James, the prince of pragmatists. Our schools of education in America have lapped Miss Stein on the behaviouristic track. Teachers are now taught to abandon the stodgy ways of maturity. They are taught to enter the child's world by ingenious disciplines, guaranteed to deracinate every trace of rational criticism and adulthood. (One way actually in use is to compel adult students to "imitate loaves of bread" for minutes at a time.) The world of the child is the world of pragmatism, romance, make-believe, action, wide-eyed wonder, docility, tutelage, managerial revolution, and vulgarized art and science. Lewis treats all these things as aspects of "The War on the Intellect," in *The Art of Being Ruled*, pages 392-409.

13 *Time and Western Man*, page xiii. Hugh Gordon Porteus in his useful *Wyndham Lewis* (London, 1932), cites a related passage concerning the procedure of Lewis:

. . . having laid bare the will concealed beneath the doctrine, we analyse it; . . . when that doctrine is seen to flow from a not very beautiful Will, by which it is pumped out by the gallon, the doctrine loses its importance automatically. Hence, if we have succeeded in some instances in discrediting the will, it is to be hoped indirectly that we may have damaged the doctrine. (pages 267-68)

. . . there is permanent revolution, and there is an impermanent, spurious, utilitarian variety. Much "revolutionary" matter today is a mushroom sort, not at all edible or meant for sustenance.[14]

It is this latter variety pumped out from the lab into the pages of *The Reader's Digest* which evokes the spurious reverence of the modern world. Man, the master of things, is about to enter the terrestrial paradise of gadgets. His heritage has matured through bloody revolution and awaits him:

> The Heir of all the Ages . . . stands by the death-bed — *penniless*. The immensely wealthy society, at its last gasp, lies gazing listlessly across the counterpane, staring at a Pom, which stares back at him. The evening comes, the day has been spent in idleness. The Heir of all the Ages retires to his garret at the neighboring inn. The bulletin is issued, No change.[15]

Equally fatuous with the "revolutionary simpleton" is the "reactionary idiot" of the Charles Maurras variety:

> We listen to him for a moment, and he unfolds his barren, childish scheme with the muddle-headed emphasis of a very ferocious sheep. He lodges in the garret next to us at the inn, and is in arrears with his rent. The servants (who are all the reddest of revolutionists, of course) hate him. The Reactionary, in the long run, does not add to the cheerfulness of the scene.[16]

Lewis, confronted with the phony respectability of revolution today, asks, *cui bono*:

> The "revolutionary" of yesterday would at present find himself in the tamest situation, surrounded by a benevolent welcome. . . . At the millionaire's table, in the millionaire's press, as in the cabman's

---

14 *The Art of Being Ruled*, page 14.

15 *Ibid.*, page 23. Lewis cites H. S. Maine on *Popular Government*:
[There are] reasons for thinking that the love for change which in our day is commonly supposed to be overpowering, and the capacity for it which is vulgarly assumed to be infinite, are . . . limited to a very narrow sphere of human action, that which we call politics. . . . A man cannot safely eat or drink or go down-stairs, or cross a street, unless he be guided or protected by habits which are the long result of time. (*The Art of Being Ruled*, page 133)

16 *Ibid.*, page 24.

shelter or the labour journal, he would find nothing but the most respectable and discouraging conformity the his eager beliefs. . . . Every one who has money enough is today a "revolutionary"; that and the dress suit are the first requisites of a gentleman.[17]

Before answering the question *cui bono*, Lewis exposes the "non-impersonality of science":

Science is often described as the religion of industrialism. It is said to have provided man with " a new world-soul." Its public function is actually . . . to conceal the human mind that manipulates it, or that manipulates, through it, other people. Fore in its "impersonality" and its "scientific attachment" it is an ideal cloak for the personal human will. Through it, that will can operate with a god-like inscrutability that no other expedient can give. It enables man to operate as though he were nature on other men. In the name of science people can almost without limit be bamboozled and managed.[18]

In passing it may be as well to say that Darwin's particular evolutionary doctrine was responsible for an "industrial" type of thought rather than an "agricultural." As it tended to reduce all intelligent organisms to things, men's thoughts and wishes to stones and sticks, it was easy for its followers to substitute motor-cars and aeroplanes for sticks and stones.[19]

Consider how helpless millions of American parents are to protect themselves or their children from the "scientific experiments" in education initiated by a few individuals such as John Dewey. The vast American political machine of American education is directed not by thousands of "scientific experimenters" but by three or four minds of the most dubious quality.[20]

---

17 *Ibid.*, pages 24-25. "Today everybody without any exception is revolutionary. Some know they are and some do not; that is the only difference. Some, indeed very many people, actually believe they are Tories . . . they stay locked in a close embrace with the dullest form of Revolution, convinced all the time that they are defending the great and hoary traditions of their race. . . . Revolution is first a technical process; only after that is it a political creed or a series of creeds, and of adjunct heresies." (*Time and Western Man*, page 121)

18 *The Art of Being Ruled*, page 41.

19 *Ibid.*, page 34.

20 The fact that the modern state is necessarily an educationalist state owing to the huge impassivity of the urban masses on the one hand and to the closely centralized control of all agencies of communication on the other, does not prevent the teacher from being as much a victim as the pupil.

Consider again how the press of the world imitates and promotes "scientific detachment" in its methods of "impersonal" news coverage. Yet nothing is more hysterically personal than "news" in its reflection of the human will. *Time, Life,* and *Fortune* put up an enormous front of detachment which upon slight examination proves to be violently emotional and interested. The hysterical voice of Winchell or the pompous melodrama of "The March of Time" program is a precise index to the "impersonality" of these agencies.

It is therefore, politically and humanly speaking, a matter of the utmost concern for us to know from what sources and by what means the rulers of the modern world would determine what they would do next. How do they determine the ends for which, as means, they employ the vast machines of government, education, and amusement? Lewis gives the answer that "art and science are the very material out of which the law is made. They are the suggestion; out of them are cut the beliefs by which men are governed."[21] That is to say, the rulers of the modern world are not detached or critical. They do not reflect. They do not consider ends. They are wholly immersed in the matter which they utilize without understanding of its character. That is why our rulers seem so harmless, such pleasant and charming *hommes moyen sensuels*:

> That all your troubles come from that charming neighbor of yours, whose bald head you see peaceably shining in the early morning Sunday sun while he waters his lawn, who is always ready with a cheery word on the weather, the holy days, the cricket score — that is what is intolerable.[22]

This sort of revolutionary simpleton, this beaming child of the *Zeitgeist* is precisely the sort of ruler the modern world cannot afford

---

Within ten years England would be at war with Scotland . . . if the propaganda and educational channels received orders to that end. . . . The organization of suggestion and the power of education are so perfect to-day that nothing, given a little time, is impossible. (*Ibid.*, page 112)

21 *Ibid.*, page 111. Anybody who has had the opportunity to observe the workings of a modern university need not be told how the "administrative policy of a great teaching body" (such is the ludicrous terminology) is a brainless submission to the currents of technological (not human) change. Catholic institutions provide no exceptions. It is notable that Catholic educators in America follow along at the end of the procession of secular education, but they never break ranks. A slightly querulous submission is put in place of radical insistence on principles. Experiment along Catholic lines is done by Protestants or not at all.

22 *Ibid.*, pages 97-98. The point is made again when Lewis is considering the abysmal disgust of modern science with the "imperfections of *homo sapiens*":

to have at the head of its enormous machinery. Lewis presents a massive documentation and analysis of the art and science and philosophy which manufacture the *Zeitgeist* — the *Zeitgeist* being the force which manipulates the puppets who "govern" us. It should be said at once that Lewis regards, and has shown at length, Mussolini and Hitler to be more perfect instruments of the antecedently prepared *Zeitgeist* than, say, Mr. Churchill or Mr. Roosevelt.

As a preparation for intelligent action, Lewis advocates self-extrication from the ideologic machine by an arduous course of detachment, — the scrutiny of the philosophy of the past four centuries as well as of the art and science which that philosophy has engendered. For success in this task very few are well equipped today.[23] It is a truism to say that the last century has been one of materialism, but this fact embraces philosophers as much as philanderers. The scientist and the stockbroker today are alike materialists in that they have no detachment, they make no effort to criticize the total situation in which they find themselves. So with the ordinary artist and politician — they are immersed in matter, in their *Zeitgeist*, and they call it "timelessness," or they appeal to the relativity notion of all human action as an excuse for sinking deeper into the brainlessness of matter.

Consider how the "ideologic machine" has gone to work with the phrase "managerial revolution." Again, consider how calmly people accept food which has no nourishment in it, and then pay extra for advertisements which tell them that some of the nourishment (vitamins) has been generously restored.

It is the tone of indignation or of pedagogic displeasure that is the fault with the attitude of science towards man. . . . But all these tones are adopted by a certain class of men who from no point of view have very much right to them. (*Ibid.*, page 138)

This class of men is not really detached from the ideologic machine:

They cannot much longer be neglected, or resisted, rather — for they are now a part of the great system of *What the Public Wants*. (*Ibid.*, page 140)

The rulers of modern society are increasingly identified with these technicians who control "scientifically" educational experiment and the Gallup Poll:

In reality they are another genus of puppets, a genus of homicidal puppets, sure enough. And they bear a strange resemblance to the misanthropic masters of the doctrine of *What the Public Wants*. (*Ibid.*, page 141)

23 "To understand how ideas succeed you must first consider what that 'success' implies, especially with reference to this particular age. You would have to ask yourself who these men are. . . . Then, behind that professional and immediate ring of supporters, the mass of people who blindly receive them on faith — as helpless, confronted with the imposing machinery of their popularization, as new-born children — they, too, would have to be studied, and their reactions registered. . . . It is only if you belong to that minority who care for ideas for their own sake . . . possessing a personal life that is not satisfied with the old-clothes shop, or its companion, the vast ready-made emporium, that this procedure will have any meaning for you." (*Time and Western Man*, pages 87-88)

The particular means by which Lewis has extricated himself from the ideologic machine of our epoch with its inevitable labelling process — "liberal," "socialist," "reactionary," "fascist," "individualist," "realist," "romantic," "extrovert," etc. — is that of the painter's eye.[24] There are, of course, other possible means; but his early, scholarly approach to the history of art (and for ten years before he became the leader of English art, Lewis had studied the history of art) had shown him how very unfriendly European life has been, at the best of times, to the production of good plastic art. In the course of a careful study of the vulgarization of European culture which occurred in Shakespeare and the Elizabethan drama, Lewis makes a basic statement of the invariable situation of the sincere artist in Western civilization. There is nothing shocking or queer about the passage I am about to quote. It represents the opinion of modern historians who have finally been able to confront the evidence of the art of other civilizations and other epochs:

> The flower of European civilization and the only portion of it that can hold its own for a moment against the productions of the East or of Asiatic or Egyptian antiquity — is to be found in the Italian renaissance. The schools of painting of northern Italy, from Giotto onward, contain scores of significant names; the rest of Europe only a handful in comparison. The power and perfection of the italian work has never been equalled elsewhere in Europe. But this great flourishing period of culture was still, as such things have always been in Europe, a kind of breathless dilettantism. With a pathetic haste, and in a worldly competitive rush, these few generations of men trod on the heels of each other's achievements. They brought to birth gigantic and disparate masterpieces, which had too little congruity with the life around them. Tintoretto would paint his huge canvases in two days, and these wall paintings are full of imposing architectures that did not exist, and were placed in surroundings that they dwarf, or that do not suit them. No sooner was some great task started than it was assailed, and the first man to whom it was given superseded, or he was presented with a baffling multitude of colleagues. St. Peter's, in Rome, engaged the attention from start to

---

24 "When these popular movements of thought, expressing themselves as highly infectious fashions, are described as *theories* it is not meant that they are a body of formulated social doctrine, of course, but rather an instinctive and unconscious process, which is only a theory, properly speaking, for the observer." (*The Art of Being Ruled*, page 146)

finish of such different personalities as Bramante, Michelangelo, Raphael, Cellini, Peruzzi, Sangallo, Fontana, Maderna, and Bernini. This haste . . . gave the sudden renaissance flowering the appearance of a theatrical entertainment. The society for which it was organized was not secure enough or deeply enough established to give it such an immemorial foundation as is required by the perfect productions of such a culture as that of China or Egypt. In the baroque of the Jesuit counter-revolution it lapsed without disguise into an immense theatrical display, hardly more solid than the scenery of a ballet or court entertainment. It rose frothing but stark into a false imperialistic opulence, whose charm was its grimacing untruth, in which the beauty of vulgarity was patented, and which we weakly parody today.

Always these bursts of dilettante culture in Europe grow feebler and shorter; they are cut short by wars; or a little shifting of the political centre, and they snuff out. The death or failure of a single individual is enough to give them a mortal blow wherever they occur. . . . Their little attempt at "civilization" is played against an alien background, with whose life, progressively diminishing in significance, they have no connexion.[25]

Modern anthropology is likewise an important means of detachment used by Lewis. The findings of modern anthropology are subtly infused into the best art of our time — in *The Waste Land*, in Picasso's *Guernica*, and in Stravinski's *Sacré du Printemps*. How significant an approach anthropology offers to the student of Shakespeare, Lewis illustrates in *The Lion and the Fox*, pages 139 ff. Today, we know almost as much about anthropology as the Church Fathers.

We are so accustomed to having the art of Western Europe discussed as though it were the inevitable fruit of our civilization, or as though it were an affair dwarfing the art of other places that this casual statement may seem perversely eccentric. In this we are provincials, both of time and place. Lewis is making a serious and considered statement based on a consensus of expert contemporary opinion. We must recall that it is only within the last fifty years that it has been possible to contemplate non-European art in any quantity or proportion.[26] That is

---

25 *The Lion and the Fox*, pages 43-45.

26 The paradoxical corollary of this fact is the pathological blindness of the modern world to anything but itself.

    It is naturally, for itself, the best that has ever been — it is for *it* that the earth has laboured for so

to say that in this, as in the matter of science and politics, it has been impossible for Europeans to be detached in their view of themselves until recently. Of course, medieval Europe had no illusions about itself since it was over-shadowed by the brilliant Moslem culture, as well as by its ever-present image of ancient Rome. It thus had detachment forced upon it.

Led initially, then, by his training as an artist, Lewis won detachment from the ideologic machine. But in his practical life as a serious artist he was buffeted and hindered in his work by participation in the World War and by the economic and political conditions which resulted from that "colossal episode in the Russian revolution." Sheer annoyance, at first, led him to study a hostile environment to see how he might the better accommodate his creative work to it. This led to some basic "discoveries." In a word, not only was modern society hostile to art, but to life and reason also.

Paradoxically, the machine has not stiffened but melted life. Mechanism has imposed universal fashions of primitivism. It has rendered all the conditions of experience so fluid and frothy that men now are swimming in another Flood:

> It is because our lives are so attached to and involved with the evolution of our machines that we have grown to see and feel everything in revolutionary terms. . . . We instinctively repose on the future rather than the past, though this may not yet be generally realized.[27]

This is the key not only to the modern cult of the child, but to the imitation of the dress, games, and manners of children among the well-to-do.

Again:

> Science makes us *strangers* to ourselves. Science destroys our personally useful self-love. It instils a principle of impersonality in the

---

long . . . . Finally, under these circumstances, it is able to do what no former society has been able to do. It is able to dispense with the disguises and graces of art and the painful tasks of culture, its traditional shell. That remoteness that art can throw over even the most scarified, pitted, oozing, and shining close-up of the insolently bared human soul is denied to us. (*The Art of Being Ruled*, pages 152-53)

27 *Ibid.*, page 11: "We shall see that it is the first genuine philosophy of slaves that has ever been formulated . . . it consists in an exploitation of the joys of slavery and submission" (page 145). "But the child is the only creature that in its own right, and under favourable conditions, can enjoy unchallenged, and without forfeiting something else that cancels the advantage, this divine irresponsibility, which is the most ideal and utopian type of *freedom*" (pages 147-48).

heart of our life that is anti-vital. In its present vulgarized condition science represents simply the principle of destruction: it is more deadly than a thousand plagues, and every day we perfect it, or our popular industrially applied version of it.[28]

Basically, then, a society which is hostile to art is hostile to life and to reason. With this fact in mind Lewis conducts an elaborate survey of the art, entertainment, science, and philosophy of the contemporary Western world to determine what is going on. Wherever one looks one finds the vulgarization of the first-rate into the shoddy and the sensual by a swarm of dilettante competitors who relay their degraded product to ever lower levels of drab sensuality.[29]

And now to answer the question, *cui bono*? Who are the beneficiaries of the modern world? Are they that tiny handful of people such as Lord Beaverbrook and Henry Luce who exercise absolute control over the thoughts and emotions of many millions of people? Confronted with the evidence of intimate correlation between the nursery politics of a Disney cartoon, the prose style of Gertrude Stein, the systematic attack on intelligence by Spengler, and the brainless primitivism of a Hemingway hero, the cult of dynamism in Nietzsche, Bergson, and Planck on the one hand and the glorification of impulse and the intestines by Gaugin, Freud, D. H. Lawrence, or Sherwood Anderson on the other — confronted with such evidence, the first objection which is inevitably put is this: Lewis posits a super-brain behind this facade; but no human intelligence could control so minutely such a vast complex of phenomena. Lewis, however, posits no such brain.

---

28 *Ibid.*, page 13.
29 Exposing the modern myth of Shakespeare's "impersonality" which has arisen in the atmosphere of pseudo-science Lewis writes:

> The artist pretends to be nature: neither men's wits nor senses are very sharp, and they are easily deceived. They say: "Why that is nature." In the same way the philosopher claimed to pursue and to capture *truth*, with complete detachment. . . . Art, being of less practical importance, or thought to be, than philosophy, is allowed to go on with its pretence, and even to enrich itself with some of the trappings of the other defunct superstition. . . . Therefore, if we place the virtue which we find in a great creative artist in this attribute of impersonality, not only our critical picture of him, but what we hope to effect by it, is liable to be upset. . . .

> Another reason of course for the adoption of this disguise of "impersonality" is to be traced to the natural contempt of men for their fellows. . . . it is natural for them not to have much faith, or to take much interest, in a thing avowedly the utterance of a *person*. It is, especially, contemporary disbelief in the efficacy or importance of individual character, that makes the disguise almost essential. . . .

> The "impersonal" fallacy, again, is closely connected with the implicit non-recognition of status for the creative artist. (*The Lion and the Fox*, pages 286-87)

Modern man, philosophically conditioned to sensation and its twin, action, is automatically manifesting the fruits of that philosophy in a multitude of ways. Fanatically wedded to matter, he is giving an enormous inductive demonstration of the fact that matter has an appetite not for form as *better* but for form as *other*. The constituted of created being guarantees modern man that in seeking sensation and thrills, *all* his acts will uniformly possess a character of accelerated imbecility:

> But the man-of-action (low-browed, steel-jawed, flint-eyed, stone-hearted), has been provided (whether in mockery or not is aside from what we wish to prove) with a philosophy. And it is some form of that *Time-for-Time's-sake* philosophy which we have already briefly considered. But this mechanical functional creature would implicitly possess such a philosophy in any case; since the dream-quality of pure-action must leave him virtually a child, plunged from one discontinuous, self-sufficing unit of experience to another; always living in the moment, in moods of undiluted sensationalism . . . it is never the frantic servant of this doctrine of *action* who ever does anything, at least of use to himself.
>
> The super-ism or whatever you like to call it . . . is only the most exaggerated, fanatical, and definitely religious form of the doctrine of *action*. Mussolini is, of course, the most eminent exponent of both. As a politician he is only concerned with the *usefulness* of things. . . . If you applied the conditions and standards required for the flowering of a Jack Dempsey to a Beethoven, say, you would be doing what is done in a more general and less defined sense at this moment, as a thousand different activities mystically coalesce in response to the religion of merging, or mesmeric engulfing. . . . The intellect works alone. But it is precisely this solitariness of thought, this prime condition for intellectual success, that is threatened by mystical mass-doctrine.[30]

The answer then to the question of *cui bono* is ultimately this. Everybody loses. Society has been made into a machine but not a pinball machine. There are no beneficiaries. The Dagwoods and the billionaire power-gluttons are equally rushing to the suicide to total immersion in the chaos of matter. However, they are not equally responsible. There is moral accountability in the profound cynicism

---

30 *Time and Western Man*, pages 20-21.

of the Hollywood tycoons and of the Hearsts and Henry Luces who toboggan us down to the lowest levels (and biggest profits) of *What the Public Wants*. But as the "public" becomes more deeply bored with "what it wants" it turns not in wrath but with envy towards its tormentors.[31] The exploited and the exploiter coalesce.

Thus it comes about that the attack on the family, for example, which develops first (in the eighteenth century) as an attack on reason and the concept of authority, is conducted very thoroughly on the economic front as well. There is an intimate correlation of events but no plan. The dynamic logic of a cheap labour market naturally leads to an attack on the family. The only way to break down this expensive institution (which prevents half the world — women — from being mechanically exploited) is to pitch women into the labour market to force down men's wages to the point where home-making, house-keeping, and child-rearing is a luxury reserved for a small class.[32] These elaborate activities when carried on by the flat-dweller put an inhuman strain on him. He learns quickly to adapt himself to these Procrustean conditions, and to lead an I-can-take-it existence of self-distortion and self-mutilation.[33]

The destruction of family life, in theory and in practice, the flight from adulthood, the obliteration of masculine and feminine have all gone ahead by means of a glorification of those things. Never was sex so much glorified, children and motherhood so idolized and advertised in theory as at this present hour when the arrangements for their interment have been completed. (Under socialism parenthood

---

31 A relevant statement occurs in "The Incredible President" by G. W. Martin in the current *Harper's* (April 1944):

> Mr. Roosevelt came to the presidency extremely well prepared. He had spent twenty-eight years associating with the Long Island set before being emancipated. Mr. Wilson thought that the rich were villains; Mr. Roosevelt knew that they were foolish and ignorant.

This is not a question of *either-or* but of *both-and*. *Corruptio optimi pessima*:

> But with all the resources of his fabulous wealth, the democratic magnate is able to drag the poor into depths of spiritual poverty undreamed of by any former proletariat or former ruling class. The rich have achieved this awful brotherhood with the poor by bleeding them of all character, spirituality, and mental independence. That accomplished, they join them spiritually or unspiritually in the servant's hall. (*The Art of Being Ruled*, page 201; see also pages 146-54)

32 G. K. Chesterton's famous remark that women refused to be dictated to so they went out and became stenographers is apposite. Only a few days ago Churchill enthusiastically attacked the family again by refusing men's wages to women school teachers. The point is that nobody in England would hire women teachers when men could be had for the same wage. This would mean that men could then insist on higher wages. It will be interesting to see what size of a family Mr. Churchill's post-war houses will allow for.

33 "*So there is no longer any* family, in one sense: there is now only a collection of children, differing in age but in nothing else. The last vestige of the *patria potestas* has been extirpated. (The *patria potestas*

is merely biological.) It is like the courses in "personality development" for "introverts" which are guaranteed to make everybody exactly alike. The same sort of paradox is seen in the fact that we have today a maximum insistence on regional and national differences in direct proportion to the disappearance of all differences between the proletarian masses of Tokyo, Berlin, Milan, Marseilles, Manchester, and Chicago. Regional and national differences today offer at best decadent material for a peep-show or travelogue: "They no longer represent either a living culture or political power."[34]

The explanation of this paradox is simple. The intensity of mass-control and exploitation is increased by the multiplication of superficial differences:

> Thus, if a man can be made to feel himself acutely (a) an American; (b) a young American; (c) a middle-west young American; (d) a "radical and enlightened" middle-west young American; (e) a college-educated etc. etc; (f) a college-educated dentist who is an etc. etc.; (g) a "college-educated" dentist of such-and-such a school of dentistry, etc. etc. — the more flexible each of these links is, the more powerful, naturally, is the chain. Or he can be locked into any of these compartments as though by magic by anyone understanding the wires.[35]

Again, no plan or plot or super-brain is needed for the full inter-meshing and exfoliation of all these things to proceed through innumerable changes, and ever-increasing violence and intensity, to their natural term — the "dialectic" of matter itself guides the brutal-ized mind into the labyrinth.

Thus the modern world proceeds through the dialectic of violence

---

is now that great organizing power that is the new, pervasive, all-powerful principle of our blind complex side.)" (*The Art of Being Ruled*, page 186)

The child obsession is naturally the result of the decay of the parent (pages 189, 285-87). Proudhon says quite clearly in the nineteenth century that family life must go because in a socialist or industrialist state it costs too much. The concept of "woman" is likewise too great a luxury:

> The "woman" — the delicate, perfumed, carefully arranged, stilted, painted, and coloured femi-nine shell is a thing which a training as a painter can only help you to appreciate. (pages 207-08)

It was simple to destroy this with the aid of the suffragette and her "uplifting sense of the glorious-ness of woman's industrial destiny" (page 206). Short skirts did this at one blow. Short hair and skirts are *short for work*, not play. *Doom of Youth* is an elaborately documented analysis of all aspects of "feminism" and of its twin — homosexuality. Just as sex has been obliterated by overemphasis and hyperbolic close-ups, so men and women have been sterilized into "pals" for one another by insistence on "feminine rights" in a "man's world."

34 *The Art of Being Ruled*, page 103.

35 *Ibid.*, page 115.

to the rescience and privation of matter itself. That is the goal or limit which is automatically set for "change" and "revolution." Beyond the century of the common man await centuries of ever more common men. Against this "limit" Lewis always poses the limit of human excellence. His gaze is always fixed on the great achievements of individuals, in philosophy and art, who define the upper human limits; and within those rational limits he indicates a good life which is characterized by "sweetness and light" — a tense equilibrium of our best interests and energies.

In view of his advocacy and illustration of reasonable disciplines at all levels of human affairs he is a conundrum to modern philosophers. He is not only extremely unpopular, but he is also quite incapable of being popularized. As Miss Rebecca West once said:

> There is no one who has greater acumen in detecting the kinds of contemporary thought that are not candid, that are mere *rationalizations of a desire to flee towards death*.[36]

Taken simply on the merits of his pamphlets alone he is the greatest political theorist and observer since Machiavelli. Even Machiavelli can be put beside him only in point of accuracy of analysis — certainly not in respect of excellence of envisioned goals. For Machiavelli, like Marx, was not a free intelligence. He was enmeshed, unconsciously, in a particular situation against which he took a sadistic revenge. Lewis seeks no revenge beyond recapturing men for rational activity. He has no illusion about ever being influential or comprehended:

> I know that at some future date I shall have my niche in the Bolshevist Pantheon, as a great enemy of the Middle-class Idea. My "bourgeois bohemians" in *Tarr* — and oh, my *Apes of God*! — will provide "selected passages" for the school-children of the future communist state . . . to show how repulsive unbridled individualism can be.[37]

---

36 Porteus, *op. cit.*, pages 277-78.
37 Porteus, *op. cit.*, page 241.

20

The God-Making Machines
of the Modern World

John Lindberg is a Swedish nobleman long associated with the League of Nations and now with the United Nations. Catholics will be interested in his history of theology underlying the politics of Plato's *Republic* and the Western art of ruling and being ruled since Plato. Himself a Manichean resigned to the ordinary necessity of rule by myth and lie, Lindberg argues in his concluding chapter that the new conditions of global inter-communication compel us to scrap the rationalist Manichean hypothesis in favour of a plunge into faith and the City of Love. His march towards this city of the future is headed by a banner quote from Bergson's *Two Sources of Morality and Religion*: "The essential function of the universe which is a machine for the making of gods."

The revolutionary situation which faces us would appear to have suggested to Lindberg that the man-made machine is the new universe for the making of gods. And whereas the machine of nature made whatever gods it chose, the machines of man have abolished Nature and enable us to make whatever gods we choose. Perhaps a better way of saying this would be to suggest that modern technology is so comprehensive that it has abolished Nature. The order of the demonic has yielded to the order of art.

∞ *McLuhan's review of* Foundations of Social Survival *by John Lindberg (Columbia University Press), published in* The Commonweal, *vol. 59, no. 24, 19 March 1954.*

Lindberg speaks as one who has spent his life inside the great god-making machines of the modern world. He speaks also from inside the great classical tradition of European rationalist culture and scholarship. He does not write as a Christian. But Lindberg does write as a pagan for whom the Christian doctrine is now, for the first time in history, a plausible and even indispensable hypothesis for survival.

As an analysis of the pagan theology underlying dominant political theory since Plato, Lindberg's testimony is of first importance. Most readers would find Fustel de Coulange's classic, *The Ancient City*, a valuable preface to Lindberg's book. Jane Harrison's *Themis* and Rachel Levy's *Gate of Horn* are likewise filled with detailed information about the pagan theory of the universe and the city as a machine for the making of gods. And Lindberg assumes to some extent a reader who is at home in pagan ritual and theology.

So far as these concern politics, he also provides a good deal of information himself. For example, most of the first chapters are taken up with a discussion of vertical and horizontal conditions of society. The golden age of primitive man is horizontal socially because there are no institutions. Men are related laterally by kinship but there are no hierarchies and no authority. Moreover the horizontal metaphor (which provides the sleeping giant Finn McCool of *Finnegans Wake*) indicates a state of collective consciousness. A state of homogeneity and non-differentiation which in pagan theory preceded the fall of man. Vertical man, self-conscious man, rational and civilized man is in this view the result of a spiritual fall. Lindberg agrees with Karl Marx that this fall resulted from the first attempt to transfer or exploit a food or property surplus for private purposes. Horizontal man, prehistoric man, in this view, was innocent of "mine" and "thine." He was without individual self-consciousness. Technological man or posthistoric man is rapidly approximating the same state. Instantaneity of global communication plus the abundance of mass-produced goods has created a situation of mental and social collectivism.

It is to tracing the social and political consequences of the "fall" that Lindberg devotes much of his book. Paradoxically, the fall brings about the rise of individual reason and the invention of the instruments of culture and civilization. Reason, the tool-making faculty, is the fruit of evil. And reason is the myth-making power which produces the ruler. The ruler rules by the myth or lie which intimidates men to the point of social obedience. It is important to grasp

Lindberg's ideas of myths and norms since they have characterized all civilization till now. But henceforth they must have new functions. Myths are for Lindberg the traditional religions imposed on men. They are products of reason. They are expedient lies. They are the means of curbing the monsters bred of men's passions. Norms or moral conventions, on the other hand, are merely a cinematic projection on the screen of the city of the passions and preferences of men. Myths are vertical affairs imposed by ruling authority on the ruled. Norms are horizontal developments spreading outwards in accordance with men's desires. Myths are static. The authoritarian myth-built city is local, brittle, easily susceptible of shock. If one myth falls, all will tend to fall. But the norm-structured society is open, elastic, malleable, receptive of change. Under current conditions of communication the static, myth-built cities of the Western world are doomed, says Lindberg.

The foundations of social survival are, however, to be found in a switch from reason to passion, from fear to love. And the possibility of the switchover resides in our capacity today to discover the creative dynamics of norm-making. Norm, the region of passion and flux, was no basis for any past city. But norm seen as a produce of an individual and collective creative activity may be a clue to a new social dynamics. If we can discover by observation of many societies past and present the principle of creativity in morals, we shall have the master-clue to all future government of huge inter-cultural associations of men.

It is the conviction that such a possibility is realizable today that prompts Lindberg to espouse the idea of Christian charity in an spirit of positivism. Not belief but necessity urges him to a Christian idea of society and government. It is the same conviction which leads him to abandon the Manichean principles of *realpolitik*.

One tires today of hearing of "important" books. This book provides many striking perspectives on the theological principles underlying the practice of classical politics and economics in the past. It suggests some startling possibilities for Catholics today. And it will perhaps amuse Lindberg to learn that his book is the best introduction written to date to Joyce's *Ulysses* and *Finnegans Wake*.

21

Confronting the Secular:
Letter to Clement McNaspy, S.J.

[Written to Clement McNaspy, S.J., a professor at Saint Louis University, from Assumption College, Windsor, Ontario, on 15 December 1945 or 15 January 1946]

Dear Mac:

Flu before and during Xmas together with a two-week visit in New York has put me 'way behind in many things. But it would be a wretched way to begin the year by omitting to ask your blessing and prayers and by not assuring you of mine.

I am conscious of a job to be done — one I can do, and, truly, I do not wish to take any step in it that is not consonant with the will of God. What an object lesson a Christian has to-day in seeing so much good produce so much ill. Not for a moment do I imagine that I can frame a course of action which will do good.

My increasing awareness has been of the ease with which Catholics can penetrate and dominate secular concerns — thanks to an emotional and spiritual economy denied to the confused secular mind. But this cannot be done by any Catholic group, nor by Catholic individuals trained in the vocabularies and attitudes which make our education the feeble simulacrum of the world which it is.

It seems obvious that we must confront the secular in its most confident manifestations, and, with its own terms and postulates, to shock it into awareness of its confusion, its illiteracy, and the terrifying drift of its logic. There is no need to mention Christianity. It is enough that it be known that the operator is a Christian. This job must be conducted on every front — every phase of the press, book-rackets, music, cinema, education, economics. Of course, points of reference must always be made. That is, the examples of real art and prudence must be seized, when available, as paradigms of future effort. In short, the methods of F. R. Leavis and Wyndham Lewis applied with all the energy and order denied them from faith and philosophy — these can serve to educate a huge public, both Catholic and non-Catholic, to resist that swift obliteration of the person which is going on. Hutchins and Adler have part of the solution.[1] But they are emotional illiterates. Dialectics and erudition are needed, but, without the sharp focusing of training in moral sensibility, futile.

How easy it would be to set up a school on these lines, utilizing the encyclopedic learning of our age. But whether this is desirable?

Affectionately in Christ,
Mac

---

1   Robert Maynard Hutchins (1899–1977) was President (1929–1945) and Chancellor (1945–1951) of the University of Chicago. An enthusiastic supporter of adult education, he promoted the famous "Great Books" program. With Mortimer J. Adler (b. 1902), then Professor of the Philosophy of Law there, he edited the fifty-four-volume series, *Great Books of the Western World*. This provided McLuhan with a subject to discuss in *The Mechanical Bride*: "The Great Books." With Cleanth Brooks, McLuhan visited Hutchins at the University of Chicago on 20 June 1946.

22

Tomorrow's Church:
Fourth Conversation with Pierre Babin

Pierre Babin: Professor McLuhan, could we go beyond the questions of faith and liturgy and examine the overall fundamental structures of the Church, seeking to foresee what could happen to them over the next few decades or for as long as electric communication dominates our culture?

We have talked about the communities that attract today's youth. They are springing up all over the world and in the Church, but what is happening to the local parish? Does the parish have a future?

Marshall McLuhan: I don't know. But I am quite interested in its history. In the twelfth century, before the new cities appeared, the old parishes which had functioned for centuries turned obsolete. They were based on a mainly rural population governed by a feudal system which grouped rich land owners and their serfs. Then came the horse collar and the cart and new towns suddenly began to appear. However, there were no parish priests for these new towns, and as a result a mobile clergy of itinerant beggars, Franciscans and Dominicans, began to fill the gap.

However, what has happened over the last few decades? We have acquired a new kind of mobility. In Canada, the old parishes depended

∞ *From* Autre homme, autre chrétien à l'âge électronique, *Lyon: Edtions du Chalet, 1977. Translated by Wayne Constantineau.*

on horse and buggy to bring in the neighbouring farmers. Then suddenly the car appeared, and yesterday's communities disappeared because people no longer came together long enough to get to know each other. What sort of parish did that create? Made up of individuals who didn't know each other? Little by little we became like strangers at an airport waiting for the same airplane. And once in the airplane, we tended not to talk to our fellow passengers. To separate us better, we were supplied with headsets which, instead, put us in touch with the rest of humanity.

But now even that mobility is challenged. For the past eight years, for the first time in my life, I've lived in a small community. In Wychwood Park [a neighbourhood in Toronto], there are fifty or so houses. It's like a little village where everyone knows everyone. You know who lives where, when they leave, and when they return. Taking big holiday trips no longer holds any appeal for me. And obviously, thanks to electronics, I can work anywhere.

However, what attracts me is not a location but my relationships. The parish, as a static, territorial form, seems to me to make no sense anymore. What I find important, for example, is meeting the same people every Sunday in the restaurant after the Mass, but outside of these brief moments no one in the parish knows anyone else.

Babin: What form could the electric parish take?

McLuhan: There again, I have no set answers. What I do know is that the car belongs to the hardware world and that it's now in the process of being eliminated, bypassed. In North America, the car has served as a bastion of privacy, while the house was the centre of social activity. But this arrangement has been disrupted by television. By invading the home, TV lets the outside world in. It has turned the family circle into a semi-circle.

Where is the centre of private life? And that of social life? We are facing huge changes in our way of living which will necessarily affect all parish and liturgical activities. What form these realities will assume is going to take quite a long time to sort out. But will there necessarily be a specific form? Might the parish in the electric age specifically remain a pliable and adaptable form — software — as I suggested liturgy might?

Babin: But, these new communities, won't they need a new type of pastor?

McLuhan: Obviously, the electric age has a profound effect on vocations. The old idea of a vocation assumed a fixed, objective goal, one that we could think about, that we could imagine. The new vocation is hard to visualize: it is above all an inner requirement. Not that long ago, we had the idea of a unique goal or calling in life. However, young people can no longer accept this. They refuse to apprentice themselves for a career designed to last a whole lifetime. They want to have more than one vocation. And our entire sense of time is changing.

Relationships in the human community are changing because our sense of time is changing. Medicine gives us the opportunity to live longer: well, this by itself is enough to alter our concept of careers and education. It is useless to train oneself for only one life and only one career. We now need to prepare for several careers. An engineer must be able, at some point, to become a doctor and vice versa.

In the old religious orders, it was common to change the activities of the brothers every few years. It was found necessary for their psychic health. They needed change. Today the lay world has to do the same: we already envision several careers in a lifetime. And old age is taking on entirely new meaning because when people retire they often have enough money and are ready to go back to work. This is something new, which transforms our sense of old age as well as our sense of work. When these kinds of reality change, all the related structures must evolve with them.

Babin: We were saying that adolescents no longer accept the truths of faith from the voice of authority: but the entire hierarchic structure of the Church is founded on this communication system. What does an electric or acoustic hierarchy look like?

McLuhan: Hierarchy, in fact, in political or any other form, is visual, and for an ear-man, seems legalistic, detached, and restrictive. A few decades ago, I used to always see the faithful with encyclicals like *Quadragesimo anno* in hand. Now, this is seldom seen. Furthermore, we no longer see the new documents. I have never seen *Humanae Vitae*. If I wanted to read it, I wouldn't know where to find it. They no longer displayed these things at the church door.

To come back to our comparison, the choice between two forms of authority makes me think of the difference between hardware and software. The written or printed paper is hardware; the spoken or recorded word is software. Pontifical documents were hardware, as stable and as solid as matter. The new form is software, as malleable as electric information. The hardware document remains outer and we reject it as such. I think today we have to say that it's the Pope's spoken word that counts, the word that he utters, not the encyclical. In the electric age, live speech comes back into its own: it no longer needs to be hardened into documents.

Babin: But nevertheless, magazines and TV give us an image of authority. And don't they render it visually?

McLuhan: In electronics, it's no contradiction to speak of acoustic imagery. A recent American author explained that TV has the power to use the eye as an ear, that not only is the TV image audile-tactile in its structure and texture, but also that TV can cover its subject from multiple angles, which the eye alone cannot do.

TV images are software. Think of our political structures. Hardware means fixed and well-defined party lines: they are now useless. Take for example Jimmy Carter: what counted was his image. Political and party lines lost their meaning. Apply this to authority in the Church: what a change lies in store for the entire hierarchy!

As we saw earlier about faith, Church authority will have to work via resonance and involvement, inviting the listeners to vibrate together in harmony. Look at sports programs on TV, the instant replay in slow motion. The play itself is too fast — in a sense it is hardware. The instant replay has considerably more power than the actual play because it allows you to participate more intensely, you get to see what actually happened. Slow motion replay is an even newer electric dimension; it really is a form of re-cognition which lets us "read" reality whenever ordinary cognition is too slow or too fragmentary.

All of this relates to how we distinguish between listening and hearing. Listening is the game in live action, hearing is the replay. For authority, it is a question of getting people to hear and not just to listen.

Babin: Do you think that this new type of hierarchy can unify the Church?

McLuhan: Unity grounds itself primarily in Christ' speech: "My sheep hear my voice." The true form of possible unity in the Church comes from the ability of all Christians to hear this speech.

Babin: Do you think that the electric revolution offers new perspectives to ecumenism?

McLuhan: Certainly, but you must look at it in more detail in order to avoid certain recent errors made because those in charge didn't understand what had really happened in the Church's upheavals.

In order to gain that understanding, let us use the same innering/outering probes that we have so far used. The Eastern churches, including the Slavic churches, have preserved along with their cultures the oral tradition and a tendency for inner-directed experience. That's why, on the whole, they separated from Rome and the West when Rome's outer-directed visual stress became intolerable. Rome with its insistence on hierarchic centralism soon became the enemy.

However, for the last several decades we have become more open to the Eastern churches: and they have softened their stance towards us. But it is exactly this kind of swapping that is dangerous. While we are rediscovering our inner-directed spirituality under electric influence, the Oriental world as a whole is marching towards Western values and its external trappings. Isn't the East about to lose its inner richness in order to put on what we ourselves are abandoning? Instead of borrowing from each other what we each lack, each keeping what is good, we risk completely exchanging sides and discovering that we are still opposed.

Babin: But what about the Protestants? In general are they not being submitted to the same cultural revolution as we?

McLuhan: In fact, Protestants are also being tested by the electric revolution, but in an entirely different way than Catholics. We said that the Reformation resulted from the coming of print, insofar as it emphasized visual culture and the tendency towards outering and division. Also, when we speak of religious inner-directedness among the Protestants, we are in fact speaking of an individualized point of view. With the printed book, each person could withhold his agreement on the meaning of the same word, opposing the other meanings.

It is striking to see to what extent they have used this "inwardness" to, first, separate themselves from Rome by saying: "To me, this Church, this authority is about outer trappings; it does not concern me"; then they used the same ploy to divide themselves from each other. Hence the appearance of sects like the Puritans.

Babin: Meanwhile, between the Catholic evolution and the Protestant evolution, doesn't the influence of electricity open up new possibilities for unity ?

McLuhan: That's where I was going with all of this. I began by reflecting on the introduction of Protestant elements into the Church after Vatican II. The Council probably made a mistake on the idea of religious inner-directedness. With electric media, we have returned to a certain notion of inwardness thanks to the cultural acoustic surround, but unity won't come alive on visual terms. The current ecumenical model has me baffled because it seems to stem from an obsolete visual milieu. We are still discussing things on a hardware level, with rigid formulas, and we forget the essential, the software, our inner-directed attention to Jesus Christ. Also, instead of unity, we risk even more fragmentation. The solution in no way consists of reintroducing Protestant elements inspired by the Gutenberg revolution into the Catholic Church. We should aim for another kind of unity.

Let's take the microphone as an example. It is in the process of reversing many of the visual characteristics of printed everyday language. When ordinary language is used at Mass, thanks to the mike the congregation and the speaker merge in a kind of acoustic bubble that encompasses everyone, a sphere with centres everywhere and margins nowhere. Without a microphone, the orator is located in a single spot; with the mike, he comes at you from everywhere at once. These are the real dimensions of acoustic oneness.

Recall in passing the questioning and protesting attitude that an acoustic man puts on when he comes face to face with the bureaucracy and the pontiffs, a gift to the Church by the alphabet and print.

Babin: What you are making us foresee, then, has nothing to do with a Church dismantled by electric media, as it has sometimes been described, but on the contrary, you are presenting us with a Church ready to open up to vast new prospects.

McLuhan: Without a doubt. Think of the following paradox. The Westernization of the Church, the fact that it was founded on a Greco-Roman base, therefore visually oriented, meant that from the outset ninety percent of the human race was excluded from the Church. Only a very small portion of people alive at the time had access to Christianity. Today, thanks to electric information, the speed of communication, satellites, Christianity is available to every human being. For the first time in history, the entire population of the planet can instantly and simultaneously have access to the Christian faith.

Of course, this fact poses formidable questions to the theologians and to the hierarchy. The entire Greco-Roman inheritance which is the Church's old cultural matrix — can it now be seen for what it is, as packaging to be discarded? Is the Greco-Roman enterprise simply a political bastion that we can let sink under the electric waves that now cover the planet? How much of the Greco-Roman mind-set does the Church really need to transmit to persons and societies? Can its forms of visual experience and expression be dropped for acoustic and electric man? Can the Church now be introduced directly into the lives of all Africans, of all Orientals, by abandoning itself without question to electric mentality?

Babin: Enormous questions! Are you yourself not frightened by such a prospect?

McLuhan: I have already told you, my formation is owing entirely to the left cerebral hemisphere, which is literary. All my values, of course, were nurtured by Greco-Roman civilization. You can easily guess, then, what I am feeling.

In a certain way, I also think that this could be the time of the Antichrist. When electricity allows for the simultaneity of all information for every human being, it is Lucifer's moment. He is the greatest electrical engineer.

Technically speaking, the age in which we live is certainly favourable to an Antichrist. Just think: each person can instantly be tuned to a "new Christ" and mistake him for the real Christ. At such times it becomes crucial to hear properly and to tune yourself in to the right frequency.

Appendix 1

Note on Thomas Nashe (see Introduction, page xii above):

The problem of understanding Thomas Nashe is the same problem as that of discovering the main educational traditions from Zeno, Isocrates, and Carneades through Cicero, Varro, Quintilian, Donatus, Priscian, Jerome, and Augustine. Once one has established the main traditions as they are formulated by St. Augustine, one knows how to tackle the Middle Ages. Medieval culture was to be grammatical and not rhetorical because St. Augustine, though himself a Ciceronian, determined the mode at once of science and theology as that of grammar. The Carolingian renaissance is a renaissance of grammar. The renaissance of the twelfth century is the renaissance of dialectics and is a period of strife between dialectics and grammar, with dialectics achieving complete ascendancy in all places save Italy. The Grand Renaissance which traditionally is associated with Petrarch is, in the first place, the reassertion of the claims of grammar against the goths and huns of learning at Paris. From the point of view of the medieval grammarian the dialectician was a barbarian. Thus it was Petrarch the grammarian glaring at the dialectical triumphs of the twelfth and thirteenth centuries who provided the modern journalist with his cliché, "the barbarism of the Middle Ages." The Grand renaissance was

∞ *From Marshall McLuhan's introduction to his Ph.D. thesis.*

in the matter of the revival of grammar, both as the method of science and of theology, not fully achieved until the sixteenth century. Erasmus' great work was to restore patristic theology — that is, grammatical theology. His significance in his own eyes, as well as in the eyes of his age, was that of the man who cast out the stream-lined grammars of the diaecticians of the schools and who restored the full discipline as understood by St. Jerome, the great pupil of the great Donatus. "Humanism" was thus for Colet, More, Erasmus, a deliberate return to the Fathers. But that which equally marks the modern Renaissance and lends to it a character which has been much misunderstood is its "science." The great alchemists, the Paracelsans from Raymond Lully to Cornelius Agrippa, were grammarians. From the time of the neo-Platonists and Augustine to Bonaventura and to Francis Bacon, the world was viewed as a book, the lost language of which was analogous to that of human speech. Thus the art of grammar provided not only the sixteenth-century approach to the Book of Life in scriptural exegesis but to the Book of Nature, as well.

Finally, the Ciceronian concept of rhetoric as the art of practical politics which Cicero had taken from Isocrates is accounted for. The Ciceronian concept of the orator won St. Augustine entirely. St. Augustine's ideal theologian is described in the words which Cicero uses of his ideal orator — *vir doctissimus et eloquentissimus*. The Ciceronian ideal of the orator as one versed in the encyclopedia of the sciences and as one exercising the science of civil prudence, the supreme science, was an ideal for a world of educated laymen. Throughout the centuries from Alcuin to Petrarch we shall trace how this great conception survived in the medieval passion for encyclopedias of the Seven Liberal Arts. Not until the return of an opulent commerce to Western Europe and the growth of an educated laity did the full Ciceronian concept of the secular orator or statesman emerge once more. Cicero dominates all the Renaissance handbooks on the education of princes and the nobility. It is the ideal of the practical life, the service of the state and the exercise of all one's faculties for the achievement of glory and success. When we have witnessed the extraordinary anti-Ciceronian movement which emerges in Machiavelli, Vives, Ramus, Montaigne, Muret, Lipsius, Descartes, and which gives us our post-Renaissance world, we shall have completed the survey of the revolutions in education and culture which carry us from Isocrates to Nashe. Thus, this study offers merely one more testimony that there is no one way of studying Western society or literature which doesn't consider, and constantly reconsider, the entire tradition from its Greek inception. "In the history of Western culture, every chapter begins with the Greeks" (Etienne Gilson, *God and Philosophy*, page 1).

Appendix 2

Editors' Note on Newman, Eliot, and Tradition (see Introduction, page xvi above)

Note: All Eliot quotes in the following are from his "Tradition and the Individual Talent," reprinted in *The Sacred Word: Essays on Poetry and Criticism* (London: Methuen, 1920; reprint, New York: Barnes and *of Christian Doctrine*, John Henry Cardinal Newman (New York: Doubleday/Image Books, 1960).

It is altogether remarkable how closely Newman's and Eliot's insights echo and resemble each other. Although working in fields considered utterly distinct, nevertheless the overlaps reveal the same principles at work, and reveal that both have roots in the same perception and use of tradition. Perhaps what seem on the surface to be discrete but contiguous realities are actually the continuous flow of the same thing. So it might be that Eliot's idea of how tradition and the individual conform to each other derives from Newman's of how Tradition and a true development interrelate; or it might be that they are each simply independent manifestations of a resurgence in our time of that ancient perception of the dynamic relation between the *figure* and its *ground*.

Through Newman and Eliot we can see more clearly how McLuhan, having immersed himself in the literary tradition and having already in large measure acquainted himself with the Tradition and the *translatio studii*, approached the matter of the Church. Eliot discussed "conformity" between the old and the new, "the really new," between the literary tradition and the individual talent. He was addressing the popular prejudice that insisted on novelty as a necessary route to individual expression in poetry and art generally. However, he meant "con-form" literally, not in the conventional, superficial sense of "surrender," but rather in the deeper, etymological sense of mutual shaping and forming. First, then, as to the matter of individuality and conformity: Eliot was struck by

> our tendency to insist, when we praise a poet, upon those aspects of his work in which he least resembles anyone else. In these aspects or parts of his work we pretend to find what is individual, what is the peculiar essence of the man. We dwell with satisfaction upon the poet's difference from his predecessors, especially his immediate predecessors; we endeavour to find something that can be isolated in order to be enjoyed. Whereas if we approach a poet without his prejudice we shall often find that not only the best, but the most individual parts of his work may be those in which the dead poets, his ancestors, assert their immortality most vigorously. And I do not mean the impressionable period of adolescence, but the period of full maturity.
>
> Yet if the only form of tradition, of handing down, consisted in following the ways of the immediate generation before us in a blind or timid adherence to its successes, "tradition" should positively be discouraged . . . Tradition is a matter of much wider significance. It cannot be inherited, and if you want it you must obtain it by great labour. (Eliot, pages 48-49)

His sense of tradition exactly parallels that of the ancient *translatio studii* (the tradition of learned commentary on scriptural texts) and that of the Church. Tradition supplies the *ground* in which any given text from whatever time is regarded and understood. Chronology is suspended. Similarly, for Newman, the truth or falsity of a doctrinal development appears in its con-forming, or mutual shaping, with the Tradition taken as a whole. "This process," he writes, whether it be longer or shorter in point of time, by which the aspects of an idea are brought into consistency and form, I call its development, being the germination and maturation of some truth or apparent truth on a large mental field. On the other hand this process will not be a development, unless the assemblage of aspects which constitute its ultimate shape really belongs to the idea from which they start. (*Essay*, page 61)

Eliot called this indispensable sense of the wholeness of literary tradition "the historical sense":

The historical sense involves a perception, not only of the pastness of the past, but of its presence; the historical sense compels a man to write not merely with his own generation in his bones, but with the feeling that the whole of the literature of Europe from Homer and within it the whole of the literature of his own country has a simultaneous existence and composes a simultaneous order. This historical sense, which is a sense of the timeless as well as of the temporal, and of the timeless and the temporal together, is what makes a writer traditional. (page 49)

In all, a succinct contemporary re-statement of an intensely grammatical perception. Mere chronology, on which logical sequence depends, is set aside. Newman states the same idea variously, for example as the present being anticipated by an earlier occurrence: "Another evidence, then, of the faithfulness of an ultimate development is its *definite anticipation* at an early period in the history of the idea to which it belongs" (Essay, page 200). This is another way of saying that the *ground*, or effects, come before the cause (the present matter). The interchange between the *figure* and its *ground* Newman calls a dynamic unity:

[D]evelopment is such a principle also. "And thus I was led on to a further consideration. I saw that the principle of development not only accounted for certain facts, but was in itself a remarkable philosophical phenomenon, giving character to the whole course of Christian thought. It was discernible from the first years of Catholic teaching up to the present day, and gave to that teaching a unity and individuality. It served as a sort of test, which the Anglican could not stand, that modern Rome was in truth ancient Antioch, Alexandria, and Constantinople, just as a mathematical curve has its own law and expression." Apol. P. 198, vid. Also Angl. Diff. Vol. i. Lect. xii.7. (*Essay*, page 312, note 1)

This intensely grammatical sense of dynamic interchange forms a smooth bridge between secular poetics and an aspect of the Church's approach to doctrine that has often formed a stumbling block for the literal-minded.

Finally, here is Eliot on the delicate matter of conformity. Read it, as McLuhan was able to do, with both sacred and secular worlds in mind:

> No poet, no artist of any art, has his complete meaning alone. His significance, his appreciation is the appreciation of his relation to the dead poets and artists. You cannot value him alone; you must set him, for contrast and comparison, among the dead. I mean this as a principle of aesthetic, not merely historical, criticism. The necessity that he shall conform, that he shall cohere, is not one-sided; what happens when a new work of art is created is something that happens simultaneously to all the works of art which preceded it. The existing monuments form an ideal order among themselves, which is modified by the introduction of the new (the really new) work of art among them. The existing order is complete before the new work arrives; for order to persist after the supervention of novelty, the whole existing order must be, if ever so slightly, altered; and so the relations, proportions, values of each work of art toward the whole are readjusted; and this is conformity between the old and the new. Whoever has approved this idea of order, of the form of European, of English literature, will not find it preposterous that the past should be altered by the present as much as the present is directed by the past. (Eliot, pages 49-50)

Newman approaches the matter from an angle only slightly different:

> A true development, then, may be described as one which is conservative of the course of antecedent developments being really those antecedents and something besides them: it is an addition which illustrates, not obscures, corroborates, not corrects, the body of

thought from which it proceeds; and this is its characteristic as contrasted with a corruption. (*Essay*, page 201)

The true development, then, invigorates not obsolesces elements of
the Tradition, just as the serious artist invigorates the tradition rather
than trying to go it one better or to discover novelty in the wrong place.
The process may look linear, but it is really a matter of present and
past moments together in dynamic interchange:

> The development then of an idea is not like an investigation worked
> out on paper, in which each successive advance is a pure evolution
> from a foregoing, but it is carried on through and by means of com-
> munities of men and their leaders and guides; and it employs their
> minds as its instruments, and depends upon them while it uses
> them. And so, as regards existing opinions, principles, measures, and
> institutions of the community which it has invaded; it develops by
> establishing relations between itself and them; it employs itself, in
> giving them a new meaning and direction, in creating what may be
> called a jurisdiction over them, in throwing off whatever in them it
> cannot assimilate. (*Essay*, pages 61-62)

Or, reverse perspective and examine the matter from the standpoint of
the individual—talent or idea or doctrine:

> In time [the idea] enters upon strange territory; points of contro-
> versy alter their bearing; parties rise and fall around it; dangers and
> hopes appear in new relations; and old principles reappear under
> new forms. It changes with them in order to remain the same. In a
> higher world it is otherwise, but here below to live is to change, and
> to be perfect is to have changed often. (*Essay*, page 63)

Newman wrote his *Essay* more than 70 years before Eliot his, but
whether the latter derived from the former is immaterial. McLuhan,
well aware of contemporary literary and theological matters and controversies while at Cambridge, knew both and found them
complementary. Both, after all, brought up to date the traditional
sense of tradition — large or small T. Either could serve the investi-
gator equally well in one field, or both.